THE DISINTEGRATING SELF

THE DISINTEGRATING SELF

Psychotherapy of Adult ADHD, Autistic Spectrum, and Somato-psychic Disorders

Phil Mollon

Routledge
Taylor & Francis Group

LONDON AND NEW YORK

First published 2015 by
Karnac Books Ltd.

Published 2018 by Routledge
2 Park Square, Milton Park, Abingdon, Oxon OX14 4RN
711 Third Avenue, New York, NY 10017, USA

Routledge is an imprint of the Taylor & Francis Group, an informa business

British Library Cataloguing in Publication Data

A C.I.P. for this book is available from the British Library

   ISBN 9781782202103 (pbk)

Edited, designed and produced by The Studio Publishing Services Ltd

www.publishingservicesuk.co.uk

e-mail: studio@publishingservicesuk.co.uk

CONTENTS

Phil Mollon, PhD, is a psychoanalyst, clinical psychologist, and energy psychotherapist. He is well-known as a writer and speaker on topics including shame, trauma, dissociation, self-psychology, and EMDR—and has pioneered the development of Psychoanalytic Energy Psychotherapy. With 40 years of clinical experience, in both the British National Health Service and private practice, he has explored many different approaches, always seeking better ways of helping those who are troubled with mental health problems. His work remains rooted in psychoanalysis, whilst also incorporating neurobiological, cognitive, and energetic perspectives. He can be contacted via his website: www.philmollon.co.uk

*With gratitude to Dr Harold Maxwell, who first encouraged me
to write books, and to Dr Arthur Couch, who taught
classical Freudian psychoanalysis.*

Notes to the reader

I hope the reader will be able to dip into any chapter and find something of interest. It is not necessary to start at the beginning and read diligently to the end. For this reason, there is some overlap and repetition among the chapters, although each has a particular theme and focus. Some quotes from Freud are repeated in different places, reflecting their importance.

I also hope the book may be accessible to some who personally struggle with ADHD, autistic spectrum traits, high sensitivity, or somato-psychic conditions.

My aim is to write in a way that does not require of the reader any particular technical knowledge, and, therefore, I have tried to explain all specialist concepts within the text.

A book that aims for scholarly integrity inevitably contains a large number of references and citations, especially when dealing with matters of scientific enquiry in neurobiology. These might, in places, impede the flow of reading, but I hope they are of benefit to those who wish to explore further. I have endeavoured at all times to make clear whether statements are based on research findings, clinical observations, theoretical postulates, or merely personal opinion.

Although my work is rooted in psychoanalysis, I have studied and explored widely in other fields, including neurobiology, CBT, and energy psychotherapy. The latter has been my particular interest for the past fifteen years or so (Mollon, 2008), and, thus, provides some energetic perspectives on the conditions described here. Whilst I find the original Freudian framework of the ego extremely helpful (more so than many modern derivatives), especially when combined with the "self psychology" of Heinz Kohut, I do not believe there is any one correct or best approach. We must find what is most helpful for the individual who seeks our help.

With the exception of "Peter" in Chapter Nine (who kindly gave permission to for this account of work with him to be presented here), all clinical illustrations are composites, inspired by experiences and observations with many different clients.

CHAPTER ONE

Why this book was written—and why ADHD and autistic spectrum conditions are of interest to a psychotherapist

This book has been germinating for many years. It expresses my understanding of a variety of psychotherapeutic clients whose experience is of disintegration, or the dread of disintegration. I hope it will be of interest and assistance to those psychotherapists who, like me, remain puzzled and curious about the problems our patients and clients present, and dissatisfied with the help offered by prevailing paradigms. It is perhaps an attempt at reparation for the lack of understanding I have no doubt shown, in times past, towards many clients when, in accord with prevailing assumptions and attitudes within the mental health professions, I may have placed too much faith in the *dynamics of the psyche alone*—as opposed to the *psyche in relation to the brain and body*.

I feel a certain urgency in what I hope to convey, since I suspect my state of ignorance might have been shared by many colleagues. Long clinical experience, within the National Health Service (NHS) and privately, tells me that attention deficit hyperactivity disorder (ADHD) and related conditions (including those on the autistic spectrum), particularly in adults, are not generally well understood or even recognised. It is a subject I feel is vitally important to psychotherapists, for the following reasons:

- many psychotherapists have clients/patients with ADHD or autistic spectrum conditions, without realising this is the case;
- ADHD and the autistic spectrum are vivid examples of the interplay of the neurobiological and the psychological—and of how both perspectives are needed for a more complete understanding, each informing the other (Solms & Turnbull, 2002);
- there is a neurobiological impairment—which then interacts with the family, school, and social environment to create the problems the adult later presents;
- multiple psychological traumas result from the interaction of temperament and environment;
- there are profound impacts on self-esteem, self-image, and confidence;
- people with ADHD and autistic spectrum traits have a vulnerability to panic, anxiety states, depression, and personality disorders.

Adults with ADHD, unless they have been diagnosed in childhood, do not understand what is wrong. Years of difficulty, perhaps helped only minimally by doctors, psychiatrists, psychotherapists, or other mental health professionals, may have left the person battered and wounded deeply in their self-esteem. In brief:

- they know they cannot manage many ordinary aspects of life;
- they know they tend to be disorganised, forgetful, late, and erratic;
- they know they get bored easily and find this aversive;
- they know they can be impulsive;
- they know they get into fights and arguments;
- they know they often experience life as tedious, painful, frustrating and unrewarding—and feel restless;
- they know they can feel depressed and anxious;
- *they do not know they have ADHD!*

Attention deficit hyperactivity disorder, along with the autistic spectrum problems that are often associated, are common among clients seeking psychotherapeutic help, but the therapists they are seeing (of whatever variety) usually do not know this either. Most psychotherapists, psychoanalysts, psychologists, psychiatrists, CBT practitioners, and counsellors appear to have little or no understanding of these conditions. The results are frustration and puzzlement for the therapist, and less than optimum help for the client.

Too often, it is assumed that ADHD affects mainly attention, or perhaps levels of activity (as, indeed, the name suggests). Even worse is the common misperception that a person does not have ADHD if he or she is able *sometimes* to concentrate and focus when something is of interest. The capacity for *hyperfocus* coexists with attentional impairments in ADHD. In fact, ADHD affects almost every area of psychological functioning, deeply compromising relationships, career, health, and general level of happiness and satisfaction in life.

Typical ADHD traits of hyperactivity, impulsivity, proneness to rage, difficulty in taking in information, seeming "not quite there", egocentricity, low self-esteem combined with grandiosity, hypersensitivity and general narcissistic vulnerability, addictive tendencies, or unusual rigidity of thought and attitudes, could create bewilderment in the therapist. The client might be viewed as odd, difficult to engage, or as suffering from a "borderline" or even an "antisocial" personality disorder. Indeed, ADHD is often a hidden core within the clinical picture seen as borderline personality disorder.

If a child with ADHD is seen in a family context, there is a common and understandable, but nevertheless misguided, tendency to view the problem as arising from inadequate boundary setting and structure. Thus, it is seen as reflecting family dynamics. In many years of clinical practice within the NHS, I have often found that young adults with ADHD, and their families, have been given a disservice through a failure to appreciate the nature and causes of ADHD, actually adding to the family's despair and feelings of guilt. When I have spoken to them of the myriad expressions of ADHD and how these are all related, and the effects of these on both the person with the condition and their family, there has been great relief and the exclamation, "At last, someone understands!"

People with ADHD and autistic spectrum (Asperger) traits can benefit from psychotherapy, but do so more slowly and with more difficulty than others. There is a neurobiological basis to these problems, which gives rise to a variety of manifest behaviours, attitudes, anxieties, emotional states, and modes of cognitive processing. This does not mean, however, that pharmacotherapy is the only feasible option. After all, mental states and processes and behaviours *always* have a neurobiological basis, but we still attempt to help people *psychologically*, which, in turn, will be expressed in neurobiological changes. The important point is to understand something of how the client's brain works, the advantages and disadvantages of their processing style, and the emotional states he or she struggles with. Without this understanding, neither client nor therapist is likely to arrive at a helpful perspective that can facilitate positive change.[1]

Impaired ego functions

Within the ADHD and associated autistic spectrums, people feel in continual danger of a state of *disintegration*. They have a particular need for the organising, stimulating, and regulating empathic responsiveness of other people. When this is absent, they experience their mental world as falling apart, unable to think, plan, or focus. One result is rage (perhaps turned on the self), and another is addictive searching for stimulation. Shame, potentially overwhelming, is a constant threat. Where autistic traits predominate, the result might be a turning away from others, seeking comfort and security in inanimate objects or repetitive activities. In understanding and addressing these deficits in self-regulation, the dread of disintegration, and the associated need for empathic responses from others, the perspective offered by Kohut (1971, 1977, 1981) provides much illumination (Mollon, 2001).

People with these traits have impaired ego functioning. The Freudian concept of the ego, as the management of the interface between inner needs and external reality, provides a simple but theoretically potent framework that can embrace many different therapeutic approaches. It is also particularly helpful in understanding and addressing ADHD and related conditions. The traditional psychoanalytic focus on the nature of the "instinctual drives", their fusion and defusion, aim-inhibition and sublimation, also turns out to be highly relevant. Similarly, a psychoanalytic recognition of the rejection of the oedipal position, expulsion of the potential superego, and foreclosure of the Lacanian "law of the father" is crucial to understanding certain aspects of ADHD.

Although, in certain respects, capable at times of a high level of relatedness to others, people with ADHD and autistic spectrum traits have impairments in their perception of others, tending to view other people egocentrically as "need satisfying objects" rather than as individuals in their own right—and as "coming alive" when needed and fading out of psychic view when the need is gone. Another way of expressing this is to say that others are viewed solely in terms of their (Kohutian) *selfobject* function of providing empathy and other regulatory responses to distress. This is not an absolute trait, however. It may vary greatly from person to person, and also according to the person's own level of regulatory well-being at any one time.

An understanding of the neurobiological basis of the impairments in ego function is important. Without this, the client might be viewed merely as operating at the level of primitive mechanisms of defence. With knowledge of the neurobiological basis of ADHD and autistic spectrum conditions, it becomes possible for the psychotherapist to be much more empathic and appropriately supportive, and to alleviate the client's chronically impaired self-esteem and pervasive feelings of shame. Acknowledging the positive features of these conditions, which may be adaptive in certain contexts, is also important in supporting self-esteem.

Selfobject disorders: dread of helpless disintegration

It is the main thesis of this book that ADHD and related autistic spectrum conditions reflect states of impaired self-regulation and of enhanced need for regulatory assistance from other people. In Kohutian terms (Kohut, 1971, 1977), these others are experienced as *selfobjects*, meaning that psychological functions of empathy, soothing, recognition, and encouragement that are *provided by the other person* (or "object", in traditional psychoanalytic terminology) *form part of the regulatory system of the self*. In his important work, Schore (1994, 2003, 2011) has explored in detail the neurobiological and interpersonal components of the selfobject functions.

This is rather similar to Winnicott's concept of the "environment mother" (Girard, 2010; Winnicott, 1955, 1960a). In the beginning, the infant's ego functioning is provided by the mother, in the state of complete dependence. It is only gradually that this environmental provision is internalised. When these functions fail, the infant is faced with the experience of "falling for ever", or "falling into pieces"

(Winnicott, 1965, pp. 57–58). However, ADHD and autistic spectrum conditions are not "environmental deficiency" states—they are not merely a response to failures of the "environment mother". There is a neurobiological substrate that creates unusual needs for environmental ego support—needs that are difficult for mother, father, and other family members to meet. These are disorders at the interface of neurobiology and environment—in short, they are (in Kohut's terms) *selfobject disorders*.

People with ADHD particularly experience difficulties with the establishment of the Freudian "reality principle" in dominance over the "pleasure principle". Freud noted that the infant's initial state of helplessness implies a state where he or she has not yet developed a "reality principle" and is completely dependent on the mother to supply this.

> It will rightly be objected that an organization which was a slave to the pleasure-principle and neglected the reality of the external world could not maintain itself alive for the shortest time, so that it could not have come into existence at all. The employment of a fiction like this is, however, justified when one considers that the infant – provided one includes with it the care it receives from its mother – does almost realize a psychical system of this kind. (Freud, 1911b, p. 219, n. 4)

This is a state in which the mother must introduce reality to the child *in small doses* (Winnicott, 1962, p. 74). Indeed, Winnicott's entire elaboration on the role of the environment mother is based around this brief allusion by Freud to the care the infant receives from the mother. What we find in conditions of ADHD and the autistic spectrum is an *abnormal rejection of reality*, even when introduced in Winnicottian "small doses". The ADHD/autistic spectrum "No!" prevails, and there is an insistence on the "pleasure principle", even though pleasure is often not attained. These traits are indeed linked with a condition called "pathological demand avoidance syndrome" —basically a stance of saying "No!" to everything, perhaps driven by an anxiety-based need to preserve a sense of control (Christie et al., 2012). In a more normal ego state, the impingement of reality induces adaptation, but in ADHD this just results in an ever louder "No!" and spiralling rage and disintegration terror. The spiral of intensifying rage and terror is exacerbated further by the child's expectation, through projection of his or her own need for control, that others will similarly wish to impose *their* need for control.

The person with ADHD tends to experience a lurking dread of chaos, with the ever-present threat of disintegration anxiety, and psychoeconomic dysregulation. On one side of the chasm is the state of feeling bombarded and overwhelmed by internal and external stimulation. On the other side is the equally intolerable state of boredom, of understimulation, leading to addictive pursuits of various kinds, including the active (but unconscious) eliciting of arguments and drama. Self-esteem is always compromised for people with ADHD, caught between the grandiosity of unmodified narcissism and the reality of impaired achievement and repeated experiences of relational and professional failure.

Those with autistic spectrum traits (often "comorbid" with ADHD) might find almost everything frightening, overstimulated by incoherent fragments of intense sensation. For them, the Markrams' (2010) "intense world theory" seems highly apt. They cannot, of course, easily tell a therapist that this is their experience. To be able to identify this, and find words to describe the experience, is itself a major achievement, one that requires much prior assistance from a psychotherapist. Many psychodynamic compromises and "defences" might arise from the struggles with an autistic spectrum temperament, but the fundamental condition is not itself a psychodynamic product, and this is important to understand.

Value of the Freudian framework

> Psychoanalysis is a comprehensive theory of personality. . . . In its most expanded version, metapsychology implies that each psychic phenomenon and its behavioral manifestation can, and must, be stated and understood in genetic, dynamic, structural, economic, topographic, and adaptive terms . . . This comprehensive view of man is the strength of classical psychoanalysis as a theory of personality. (Bellak et al., 1973, p. 5)

Various psychoanalytic perspectives—particularly the Freudian concept of the ego and its functions, combined with Kohut's elaboration of the support to the ego provided by the environmental self-objects—provide a powerful framework for understanding and working with people with ADHD and other conditions where self-regulation is impaired. Many valuable aspects of traditional psychoanalysis, including the work of ego psychologists such as Hartmann (1939) and Jacobson (1965), seem currently out of fashion. A text from over forty years ago—Bellak and colleagues' (1973) *Ego Functions in Schizophrenics, Neurotics, and Normals*—is a neglected gem, exploring the assessment and treatment of all kinds of impaired ego functioning, and has been a significant influence on the work described here. These authors explore the multiple and varied ways in which the ego attempts to mediate between inner needs and external reality—tasks in which the ego afflicted by ADHD repeatedly fails. The classical psychoanalytic contributions (Couch, 1995, 2002; Freud, 1940a), in my view, provide a depth and range of therapeutic possibilities that greatly exceed those offered by more modern, depleted derivatives of psychoanalysis, which focus merely on patterns of object relations, clarifications of psychodynamic conflict, or upon helping the client identify the preconscious contents of their mind.

Energy perspectives

Since I am an energy psychotherapist,[2] as well as psychoanalyst and psychologist, I like to look at ADHD also from the perspective of subtle energy (as described in relation to acupressure meridians, chakras, and other aspects of the human energy system) (Keown, 2014). ADHD clearly displays an imbalance of yin and yang energies. Yang is the outgoing "masculine" energy, while yin is the more inward drawing "feminine" energy. In the typical hyperactive person with ADHD, the lively yang energy is uncontained, unfocused, and undirected; it is like a firecracker jumping and flashing all over the place causing a great commotion. At the same time, in such a person, yin energies are apparent in the tendency constantly (and even greedily) to be looking for, and consuming, novel stimuli and seeking sensation. By contrast, the quieter states of the non-hyperactive but dreamy and distracted person with ADD shows too much yin, unbalanced with sufficient yang. Such people tend to be dysfunctionally passive. People on the autistic spectrum similarly tend to be too yin. In terms of neurotransmitters, dopamine has a yang effect, while serotonin has a yin effect. However, these states are not simple matters of too much of one and too little of the other, but more to do with the *balance* between yin and yang, the organisation and flow of the energies, and their concentration in different areas of the body and brain. In a manner analogous to that discussed in relation to the psychoanalytic libidinal and aggressive drives, there appears to be a defusion of yin and yang in ADHD and autistic spectrum states.

Ehlers–Danlos and other somato–psychic conditions: the disintegrating body self

Another condition that few psychotherapists (or doctors) know much about, and which seems to have some link with states of high sensitivity, is Ehlers–Danlos syndrome (EDS), or hypermobility (of joints and connective tissues). It is to do with an inadequacy of collagen in the body, which makes the bones, ligaments, skin, tissue, and organs less resilient. The body has to work hard to hold itself together with muscular tension. As the condition deteriorates, dislocation of joints may become more frequent, and walking and other movements become increasingly painful. Being alive in such a body creates inherent stress. There can be associated disturbances of (low) blood pressure, cardiac problems, and cognitive deficits. As a result, the person feels continually in danger of *physical and psychological disintegration*. Over the years in which I worked within the NHS, I have known a number of patients with this illness.[3] None was diagnosed until many years after they first presented symptoms. Their multiplicity of diverse symptoms had been investigated by different specialists, but, typically, no one connected the dots and realised these were all related. They showed the following characteristics: great emotional sensitivity; chronic fatigue; high levels of stress; conscientious and perfectionist; gut problems; pervasive pains. Whilst valuing psychotherapy, they did not get better by normal methods of addressing anxiety, stress, and lifestyle. They did, however, benefit from exploration and understanding of their EDS.

EDS is not the only physical health condition that doctors and mental health practitioners might miss as a result of focusing on the presenting psychological features. Another common illness—and this really does need to be emphasised—is Lyme disease, caught from infected ticks. If this is not treated quickly and aggressively soon after infection, it becomes chronic Lyme disease, manifesting in a range of physical and psychological problems. It can mimic ADHD (Marzillier, 2009; Young, 2012),[4] with cognitive deficits, memory and attentional problems, hyperactivity, racing thoughts, "brain fog", vivid night-mares and intrusive imagery, mood and affect dysregulation, anxiety and depression, and seeming personality disorder; it can also give rise to sensitivities similar to those found among people on the autistic spectrum. When a person presents with varied somatic complaints, along with anxiety or depression, it is all too easy for these to be dismissed as "psychological", or to do with "stress", or "hysteria", or as "medically unexplained symptoms". The problems might be "medically unexplained" for the very good reason that the proper diagnosis has not yet been found! With these examples in mind (and there are, no doubt, many others), I urge psychotherapists, psychia-trists, and medical doctors not to dismiss too easily the role of abnor-malities in the person's brain or body as significant contributors to the presenting clinical picture.

The disturbances described here are not "all in the mind"; they cannot be understood or helped by a purely psychological framework. The workings of the mind are determined in part by the substrate of a compromised brain or body. In working with ADHD, autistic spec-trum conditions, EDS, and other somato–psychic conditions, it is important to understand the dread of falling apart, of losing coher-ence, of being traumatically overstimulated, or, by contrast, of being in a state of highly aversive understimulation—in short, the myriad terrors and dysphorias of the *disintegrating self*.

CHAPTER TWO

Some features of ADHD

"ADHD is not a benign disorder. For those it afflicts, ADHD can cause devastating problems"

(Barkley, 2002)

ADHD can indeed have a devastating effect on many aspects of a person's life. Follow-up studies (Barkley et al., 2008) suggest those with ADHD are more likely to

- drop out of school (32–40%);
- rarely complete college (5–10%);
- have few or no friends (50–70%);
- engage in antisocial activities (40–50%);
- experience teenage pregnancy (40%);
- experience depression (20–30%);
- suffer from personality disorders (18–25%);
- use illicit drugs, drive fast, and have multiple car accidents.

ADHD is probably not a single discrete syndrome and is best not viewed as a categorical diagnosis. There could be a number of forms and spectra of ADHD, with much overlap and comorbidity with other conditions. It lies on a spectrum, blending into normality (Ratey & Johnson, 1998). Nevertheless, it is a useful construct that is helpful in understanding common constellations of impaired attention, organisation, and impulse/affect regulation.

Succinct definitions of ADHD

At the neurobiological level, ADHD is a range of atypical features in the circuitry affecting the frontal lobes.

At the psychological level, ADHD is a range of conditions of enhanced need for "selfobject" (Kohut, 1971, 1977) responsiveness from others, to assist in the management of arousal, mood, impulse, and the relationship with the external world.

The latter could also be described in terms of an enhanced need for external assistance in ego functioning (Bellak et al., 1973).

The connection between the two levels of definition is that the frontal lobes are the "management" of the brain—"what a conductor is to an orchestra, a general to an army, the chief executive officer to a corporation" (Goldberg, 2001, p. 2). In this way, the frontal lobes can be likened to the Freudian concept of the ego and its functions:

> Functions of the ego center around the relation to reality. In this sense, we speak of the ego as of a specific organ of adjustment. It controls the apparatus of motility and perception; it tests the properties of the present situation at hand, i.e., of "present reality", and antici- pates properties of future situations. The ego mediates between these properties and requirements, and the demands of the other psychic organizations. (Hartmann et al., 1946, p. 15)

It is because this "management" of the system is impaired that there are enhanced needs for external ego support. ADHD can impair almost all ego functions, and in severe cases the person is compro- mised in every area of functioning, including reality testing, and is incapable of managing independently.

Thus, within a Freudian psychoanalytic framework, we might say that ADHD reflects a "weak ego" and comprises a general and pervasive deficit in ego functions.

The latter definition raises the question of how ADHD might differ from psychosis, which also involves a pervasive deficit in ego functioning (Bellak et al., 1973) and also is associated with impaired frontal lobe functions (Weinberger et al., 1994). In fact, ADHD *can* be associated with psychosis (Donnev et al., 2011; Pine et al., 1993; Sambhi & Lepping, 2009), and Bellak and colleagues, whose work has focused on ego functions, actually suggested a separate diagnostic category of *ADD psychosis* (Bellak, 1985, 1994; Bellak et al., 1987). Marsh and Williams (2006) note that

> inattention is a core symptom of both schizophrenia and ADHD . . . and retrospective studies show that "preschizophrenia" children who later develop schizophrenia, and children at high risk for schizophrenia (i.e. have a relative with schizophrenia) sometimes manifest behaviors including inattention, impulsivity, reduced frustration tolerance, and diminished social competency that parallel ADHD presentation. (p. 652)

Thus, apart from the schizophrenic symptoms of delusions and hallucinations, severe ADHD and schizophrenia can have much in common and people with ADHD do sometimes develop schizophrenia.

DSM *criteria*

Here are the current *DSM-V* (American Psychiatric Association, 2013) criteria for ADHD, first for inattention and then for hyperactivity.

Inattention

- Often fails to give close attention to details or makes careless mistakes in schoolwork, work, or during other activities (e.g., overlooks or misses details, work is inaccurate).
- Often has difficulty sustaining attention in tasks or play activities (e.g., has difficulty remaining focused during lectures, conversations, or lengthy reading).
- Often does not seem to listen when spoken to directly (e.g., mind seems elsewhere, even in the absence of any obvious distraction).
- Often does not follow through on instructions and fails to finish schoolwork, chores, or duties in the workplace (e.g., starts tasks but quickly loses focus and is easily sidetracked).

- Often has difficulty organising tasks and activities (e.g., difficulty managing sequential tasks; difficulty keeping materials and belongings in order; messy, disorganised work; has poor time management; fails to meet deadlines).
- Often avoids or is reluctant to engage in tasks that require sustained mental effort (e.g., schoolwork or homework; for older adolescents and adults, preparing reports, completing forms, reviewing lengthy papers).
- Often loses things necessary for tasks or activities (e.g., school materials, pencils, books, tools, wallets, keys, paperwork, eye-glasses, and mobile telephones).
- Is often easily distracted by extraneous stimuli (e.g., for older adolescents and adults, might include unrelated thoughts).
- Is often forgetful in daily activities (e.g., doing chores, running errands; for older adolescents and adults, returning calls, paying bills, keeping appointments).

Hyperactive-impulsive symptoms

- Often fidgets with or taps hands or squirms in seat.
- Often leaves seat in situations when remaining seated is expected (e.g., leaves his or her place in the classroom, in the office or other workplace, or in other situations that require remaining in place).
- Often runs about or climbs in situations where it is inappropriate (in adolescents or adults, might be limited to feeling restless).
- Often unable to play or engage in leisure activities quietly.
- Is often "on the go" acting as if "driven by a motor" (e.g., is unable to be, or uncomfortable being, still for extended time, as in restaurants, meetings; might be experienced by others as being restless or difficult to keep up with).
- Often talks excessively.
- Often blurts out answers before questions have been completed (e.g., completes people's sentences; cannot wait for turn in conversation).
- Often has difficulty awaiting turn (e.g., while waiting in line).
- Often interrupts or intrudes on others (e.g., butts into conversations, games, or activities; might start using other people's things without asking or receiving permission; for adolescents and adults, might intrude into, or take over, what others are doing).

For individuals over seventeen, five symptoms from either or both lists are required to merit a diagnosis. These symptoms must occur in two or more settings. There must be clear indications that these interfere with functioning in social, academic, or work contexts.

To diagnose ADHD, the symptoms must not be better accounted for by another mental disorder, including schizophrenia. One change in the *DSM-V*, compared to the earlier version, is that ADHD may be diagnosed alongside autistic spectrum disorders. Both ADHD and autistic spectrum conditions are categorised as "neurodevelopmental disorders". Some symptoms must have been present before the age of twelve to meet *DSM-V* criteria.

There are three subtypes:

- combined presentation (showing both inattention and hyper-activity–impulsivity);
- predominantly inattentive presentation;
- predominantly hyperactive–impulsive presentation.

The previous *DSM* had a category of "ADHD not otherwise specified (NOS)" for those who showed some symptoms but did not meet the full criteria. In *DSM-V*, this has been changed to two categories of (a) other specified ADHD, and (b) unspecified ADHD.

It is worth noting that subtle changes to criteria have been made, compared to the previous *DSM-IV*, such as the age of onset (previously before age seven, but now age twelve), and only five symptoms required in those over seventeen (reflecting the tendency for ADHD to settle somewhat as the person matures). These changes illustrate how diagnostic criteria for mental and behavioural conditions are based partly on a system of categorisation to which the diagnostic community agrees to adhere, rather than upon discovery of the inherent nature of the condition.

Broader features beyond the DSM list

While the *DSM* addresses problems to do with hyperactivity, impulsivity, and attention, a wider consideration gives rise to an expanded list, such as the following.

- Impulsivity and risk taking—inability to interpolate thought between impulse and action.
- Lack of normal social inhibition (when emotions are aroused).
- Pervasive anxiety.
- Difficulties with concentrating and attending.
- Difficulties in both short-term and long-term memory, in accessing and using these.
- Difficulty in making decisions and choices, these tending to cause marked anxiety.
- Low tolerance of frustration.
- Proneness to rage and tantrums.
- States of being overwhelmed with emotion, of having no "emotional brakes", resulting in escalating storms of rage and other emotions.
- Self-harm, when rage is discharged on the self.
- Aggression against others, particularly within the family.
- Difficulties in forward planning, establishing goals, and pursuing these.
- Social difficulties—resentment of the demands made by others.
- States of feeling overwhelmed by the demands of daily life.
- Often over-stimulated and over-sensitised to their surroundings.
- Overly excitable and reactive.
- Cannot shift attention from one task to another—tends to perseverate rather than adapting to the needs of a new situation.
- Difficulties staying on track—wandering off and being easily distracted.
- Very low tolerance of boredom—some people with ADHD describe boredom as "terrifying".
- Childlike neediness—appearing immature and experiencing difficulty grappling with the demands of adult life; can appear very demanding.
- Egocentricity, due to a difficulty in decentring from one's own need, emotion, and perspective.
- Lack of clear identity and self-concept.
- Low self-esteem.
- Restlessness, dissatisfaction, and dysphoric mood.
- Mood swings, with extremes of mood and emotion.
- Poor sleep, often waking feeling despondent or angry.
- Violent feelings of hatred.

The nine symptoms that most strongly differentiate people with ADHD

Barkley and colleagues (2008) reviewed the problems presented by patients attending the Adult ADHD clinic of the University of Massachusetts Medical Center and, using factor analysis statistics, arrived at the following list of nine symptoms that most clearly differentiated this group (p. 182).

- Makes decisions impulsively.
- Difficulty stopping activities when should do so.
- Starts a project or task without reading or listening to directions carefully.
- Shows poor follow-through on promises or commitments to others.
- Has trouble doing things in the proper order or sequence.
- Drives with excessive speed.
- Prone to daydreaming when should concentrate.
- Has trouble planning ahead.
- Cannot persist if not interested.

Link with other mental health problems

ADHD as a hidden core within borderline personality disorder and mood instability

ADHD often appears to be a hidden core within other mental health presentations. For example, there is a strong link between ADHD and mood instability, and Asherson (2011) reports that mood instability may often be the main presenting feature of ADHD. He also noted marked overlap with other mental health conditions, including bipolar disorder and borderline personality disorder. Similarly, Kooij (2011) found that adults with ADHD show an increased risk for bipolar disorder of 6.2 times, and this is associated with a more severe disease course.

Much of the symptomatology of ADHD is similar to that of borderline personality disorder (or emotionally unstable personality disorder), such as emotional dysregulation, anger, impulsivity, interpersonal coercion, and so forth (Davids & Gastpar, 2005). Philipsen

(2006) argues that since similar therapeutic strategies are helpful for both ADHD and BPD, and since neuroimaging and pharmacological data show much overlap between the disorders, it may be that ADHD and BPD are not distinct disorders but, at least in a subgroup, are "two dimensions of one disorder" (p. 42).

A study of 120 female patients diagnosed and treated for BPD found ADHD in 70% of these (Philipsen, 2006), and a further study concluded that adults with severe borderline personality disorder frequently show a history of childhood ADHD symptomatology, and that persisting ADHD correlates with frequency of co-occurring Axis I and II disorders (Philipsen et al., 2008). Similarly, a study of 60 patients with ADHD found that Borderline symptoms were common in this group (Philipsen et al., 2009). Another study (Ferrer et al., 2010) found 38% of a sample of patients diagnosed with BPD had comorbid ADHD symptoms (thus rather less than the Philipsen study), and that this combined BPD–ADHD group were more impulsive and had higher rates of comorbid antisocial personality disorder, substance use disorder, and obsessive compulsive personality disorder; the group with BPD without ADHD showed more anxiety, depression, and avoidance. Van Dijk and colleagues (2011) found that in their sample, all adult patients with BPD had some ADHD symptoms in both adulthood and childhood, and (2012) that the trait of novelty seeking was strongly associated with the development of combined BPD and ADHD.

Chronic conflictual difficulties in relationships, characteristic of those associated with borderline personality disorder, are a frequent feature of the problems presented by adults with ADHD. Psychotherapist Gabor Maté (1999) describes a patient, Trevor, who had many brief sexual liaisons, never maintaining these for any length of time. Trevor confessed that he felt devastated if a woman began to withdraw from him, explaining: "I just hate being left . . . I can't even stand it when a woman wants to end a telephone conversation. I deliberately start prolonging things, bringing up new topics I'm not even interested in, just to keep her on the phone" (p. 258). Maté comments,

> Fear of intimacy is universal among ADD adults. It coexists with what superficially would seem to be its opposites—a desperate craving for affection and a dread of being rejected. The reflexive shrinking away from intimacy undermines the ability of the ADD adult to find what he would find most healing: mutually committed loving contact with

another human being. Trevor may be an extreme example of the relationship nomad, but the issues that trouble him are, to one degree or
another, present in every relationship in which either or both of the
partners have attention deficit disorder. (Maté, 1999, p. 259)

Multiple mental health comorbidities

Barkley and colleagues (2008) report that ADHD adults had significantly elevated scores on all dimensions of psychopathology of the
clinical questionnaire, the SCL-90-R. These included the dimensions
of: somatic symptoms, obsessive–compulsive, interpersonal sensitivity, depression, hostility, anxiety, phobic, paranoia, psychoticism.
Eighty per cent of ADHD groups showed at least one other disorder
and one third had at least three other disorders. A high comorbidity
is found with dysthymia, depression, ODD, conduct disorder, alcohol
and drug use (Barkley et al., 2008; Ohlmeier et al., 2008). Studies of
cluster B personality disorders found an increased prevalence of
ADHD in childhood of up to 65% in some studies (Kooij, 2011). A
meta-analysis and meta-regression analysis, summarising and
analysing twenty-nine studies on the prevalence of ADHD in popula-
tions of substance use disorder patients, found an overall prevalence
of 23.1% (Van der Glind, 2011).

Link with schizophrenia

Although not often emphasised, there is significant overlay between
ADHD and psychosis, including schizophrenia. Thus, Davenport and
colleagues (2010) state, "Schizophrenia and ADHD are associated
with similar deficits in working memory, attention, and inhibition.
Both disorders also involve abnormalities of white matter integrity,
possibly reflecting neural communication disruptions" (p. 193),
although they found more widespread white matter connectivity
disruptions in schizophrenia. Marsh and Williams (2006) survey a
considerable amount of research literature, suggesting a great deal of
"phenomenological similarities between ADHD and prodromal schizophrenia" (p. 653). For example, two studies found that around 30%
of children with schizophrenia had a previous diagnosis of ADHD
(Alaghband-Rad et al., 1995; Spencer & Campbell, 1994), while
Menkes and colleagues (1967) found 22% of a sample of children with
hyperactivity subsequently developed a psychosis, and Gomez and
colleagues (1987) found 19% of their sample of adults with psychosis

had a history of both adult and childhood ADHD and a further 15% of their sample had a history of childhood (but not adult) ADHD. Asarnow and Ben-Meir (1988) found that 30% of a sample of children with schizotypal personality disorder had a premorbid or comorbid diagnosis of ADHD, and McDaid and colleagues (1999) found a strong correlation between schizotypy traits (such as unusual experiences, cognitive disorganisation, and impulsive non-conformity) and ADHD traits. Schaeffer and Ross (2002) found that nearly half of a sample with childhood onset schizophrenia had been given a prior diagnosis of schizophrenia, and they speculated that treatment with stimulant medication may have contributed to the onset of psychosis.

Bellak and colleagues (1987) proposed that those people with a schizophrenia type of psychosis might respond best to dopamine antagonists (the typical schizophrenia medications), and adversely to dopamine agonists (stimulant medication), while those with an ADD type of psychosis might respond best to the stimulants. This is one reason why responses to stimulant medication should be carefully monitored, although Sambhi and Lepping (2009) reported on two adult cases that responded well to a combination of stimulant and antipsychotic medication. Barr (2001) compared attentional processes in both ADHD and schizophrenia, and concluded that the latter might involve predominantly left frontal hemispheric dysfunction, while ADHD might stem more from dysfunction in the right frontal hemisphere (based on observations that right hemisphere damage can produce symptoms similar to ADHD), but Hale and colleagues (2006, 2009, 2010) review evidence and present their own series of research studies that consistently suggest ADHD involves *increased* right hemisphere activity, *lowered* left hemispheric activity, and an *abnormal interhemispheric relationship*. Others present evidence of right hemispheric dysfunction in schizophrenia (Barnetta et al., 2005; Schweitzer, 1982). While somewhat confusing and apparently contradictory, these varied findings do indicate that distinguishing ADHD and some aspects of schizophrenia is not as simple as might first appear.

ADHD and Asperger's/autistic spectrum traits

There is a strong link between ADHD and Asperger's. Both ADHD and Asperger's (autistic spectrum) children may show the following features:

- have difficulties mixing with other children;
- show no real fear of danger;
- be prone to tantrums and become easily distressed;
- be either hyperactive or extremely slow or lethargic;
- avoid eye contact;
- be very intelligent and have a high IQ;
- be hard to diagnose when very young;
- show problems with communication and social interaction;
- have deficiencies in coordination and fine motor skills;
- act impulsively;
- have very poor handwriting;
- show symptoms of anxiety;
- appear not to listen, even when spoken to directly.

Adult ADHD

At one time it was assumed that ADHD was a disorder only in children. Recognition of the disorder in adults became more widespread in the 1990s. Now it is recognised that children with ADHD may grow up to be adults with ADHD, although the symptoms might subside somewhat or could change in form: for example, overt hyperactivity in the form of running about could evolve into mere restlessness in an adult. Barkley and colleagues found that just 11% had completely outgrown ADHD by adulthood, although a much higher proportion showed some diminishment in symptoms, and results also varied according to whether the results were based on reports by self or other. Kessler and colleagues (2010) found that half of those with childhood ADHD still met full *DSM-IV* criteria for adult ADHD, although there was a greater persistence of inattention symptoms than of hyperactivity, and that executive function impairments were consistently important predictors of adult ADHD. In an earlier study, Kessler and colleagues (2006) found an estimated prevalence of ADHD in the adult population to be 4.4% (5.4% in males and 3.2% in females). However, Merikangas and colleagues (2010) found a prevalence of 8.7% among adolescents in the USA, and was three times as prevalent among males compared to females.

Regarding the overall prevalence among children, meta-analyses suggest this is around 5% (Barkley et al., 2008; Polanczyk et al., 2007).

Heritability

Twin studies suggest that ADHD is highly heritable.

National Clinical Practice Guideline (NICE, 2008) suggests genetics are a factor in about 75% of cases.

Other factors can be involved, including: complications and infections during pregnancy, early psychosocial stress and trauma, excessive exposure to lead, trauma and head injuries, pesticides.

The helplessness of the person with ADHD

People with ADHD can, at times and in some cases, be somewhat intimidating, with their loud and demanding presence and potentially aggressive manner. They can, on occasion, come across as coercive or manipulative. The helplessness, and associated anxiety, that drives this might be less obvious.

The person with ADHD often feels "powered like a motor", compulsively driven, like an automobile revving far too high. They may feel driven into dysfunctional speech and action that they feel helpless to control. In the grip of a hyperactive brain state, they experience a proliferation of thoughts, anxieties, and impulses, with little capacity to exert control over these.

Goldberg (2001) describes a patient, Toby, a highly intelligent man with severe ADHD. His parents found him intolerable and their attempts at sanctions on his wilful behaviour led him to run away from home as a child, living on the streets, progressing to prostitution and drug addiction. Later, he overcame the addiction, but his behaviour was still characterised by constant restlessness and impulsiveness, having "a dozen competing plans and thoughts at any given time", and a volatile temper, alternating between charm and rage. Goldberg describes finding Toby's outbursts disturbing and frightening. However, he comments, "Increasingly I was getting the impression that Toby's outrageous behaviors had a life of their own, that Toby was engaged in them *in spite of himself*, and that he was in pain" (p. 177).

Social perceptions may be askew because of a failure to grasp the overall context, resulting in continual experiences of shame and embarrassment. Repeated experiences of social, educational, and occupational failure exert a corrosive effect on self-esteem. The adult with ADHD typically is aware that he or she cannot manage many ordinary aspects of life, that they are forgetful, disorganised, and erratic, can be impulsive, get into arguments, fail to make friends or lose friends, find life often tedious, unrewarding, and boring, and tend to be depressed and anxious. He or she knows there is something wrong—but has no concept for what it is. They do not know they have ADHD. This lack of both concept and knowledge further contributes to the sense of helplessness.

Anxiety, self-doubt, and procrastination

People with ADHD tend to be pervaded by self-doubt and lack of confidence, even if these coexist with apparent bravado or grandiosity. This is because, quite realistically, they cannot trust their own minds to function reliably (although adaptive compensatory strategies can be developed).

Tasks are often left undone, partly because of the impaired motivation in ADHD when an activity provides no immediate reward, and partly because they might simply be forgotten if not a priority in the person's mind. This can lead to further avoidance of the task because thinking about the failure to do it evokes anxiety and guilt. Moreover, the internal instruction to do the avoided activity (which might be as simple as posting a letter, sending an email, or completing a form, or might involve a more complex task, such as preparing tax returns) may evoke a rebellion, somewhat like an internal "pathological demand avoidance syndrome" (Christie et al., 2012). In this way, an entrenched procrastination may set in, maintained and fuelled by the anxiety and internal rebellion it evokes. The person could then complain of being "stuck".

The chaotic mind in ADHD

The ADHD mind lacks coherence and order, and so the person is continually haunted by the dread of chaos. Although the chaos is internal, it can also be mirrored by visible aspects of the person's life, such as the state of rooms in their home, particularly any areas that are viewed as "private", such as bedrooms and bathrooms. One man with ADHD told me of his home that he had left undecorated for years, with peeling wallpaper, bare floorboards, and a pile of broken glass in a corner of his bedroom. He literally *did not know where to start* on cleaning, tidying, and decorating, even if he could muster the motivation. On the other hand, some with autistic spectrum traits may prefer an exceptionally tidy environment as a compensation for their internal chaos. External untidiness may trigger considerable anxiety for such people because then it seems as if there is chaos *everywhere*.

The lack of order can extend to perceptual experience, which might be abnormal in certain ways, less coherent, and perhaps captured by a particular element or detail. For these people, perception seems to lack a normal gestalt. They may look at a figurative painting and see something quite different from most other people.

Mental chaos is also created by the way in which emotions and impulses may intrude without the person understanding them. His or her experience might be likened to being inhabited by another being.

Those with autistic spectrum traits might panic if patterns of life are not as expected, the disruption of expectation again resulting in a sense of chaos. The ensuing flooding of emotion may further escalate the sense of chaos, resulting in mounting rage and panic, culminating on occasion in a full "meltdown".

Proliferation of "beta elements"

According to Bion's (1962) psychoanalytic theory of thinking, the raw sensory and emotional data that he calls "beta elements" are unsuitable for thinking and "learning from experience", unless transformed by a process (whose precise nature is deliberately left unclear) that he terms "alpha function" to produce "alpha elements". This process is apparent in healthy dreaming, where the events of the day and their meaning are worked over and digested, elements of experience being broken down and recombined in novel ways. This is also the case in a good psychoanalytic session, where an increased awareness of inner emotional meaning is achieved. Any time that we allow experiences to acquire emotional meaning, suffering the potential pain of this and enabling thoughts to form in our mind, would be an illustration of "alpha functioning".

By contrast, the primitive mind, resisting painful emotional growth, might attempt to expel "beta elements" rather than transform them. In such a case, the mind is, as Bion puts it, operating like a muscle. The mental states of people with ADHD appear to involve a proliferation of beta elements, bits and pieces of fragmented thought that cannot actually be used for coherent thinking. The person with ADHD might feel persecuted by the beta element contents of the mind, and terrified by dreams of being hunted or pursued (Schredl & Sartorius, 2010).

Bion writes of failures of alpha function in certain psychotic states of mind and he refers to "the patient who cannot dream cannot go to sleep and cannot wake up" (1962, p. 7). These evocative words are strikingly apt in relation to many people with ADHD, who appear stuck in a beta element world, where they cannot properly wake up, or have restful sleep, and certainly not have mentally digestive healthy dream processes. Bion (1962) comments further on such a state:

> If there are only beta-elements, which cannot be made unconscious, there can be no repression, suppression, or learning. This creates the impression the patient is incapable of discrimination. He cannot be unaware of any single sensory stimulus: yet such hypersensitivity is not contact with reality. (p. 8)

Although writing about certain psychotic states, Bion's rather startling description here seems to capture a great deal about the typical state of mind that people with ADHD commonly struggle with. It is a state of persecution by the person's own mind—a psyche full of irritating beta elements that cannot be used but can only be expelled. Bion (1962) comments on the frustration such a state induces:

> If the patient cannot "think" with his thoughts, that is to say that he has thoughts but lacks the apparatus of "thinking" which enables him to use his thoughts . . . the first result is an intensification of frustration . . . (p. 84)

It is not surprising then, that in beta element states of mind, such as ADHD, the person is in a chronic state of rage.

Family interactions: the malignant escalation

Family dynamics where there is one or more children with ADHD can appear very disturbed and it can be tempting for mental health professional staff to assume that this is a cause, rather than an effect, of ADHD. In countless NHS consultations, I have encountered agitated and enraged people with ADHD and exhausted and frustrated parents and siblings reporting years of unhelpful responses from the mental health services.

Adults with ADHD might report that they were recipients of anger, criticism, or even violence as a child. The naïve observer might conclude that ADHD results from dysfunctional families. In reality, there is often a vicious spiral of interaction between the child and the family which gives rise to a malignant escalation of mutual distress and intense negative emotion.

The child with ADHD, who is prone to rage, seemingly "strong willed", who does not respond "normally" to typical sanctions and socialisation, presents a dilemma for the family. Traditional methods of shaping a child's behaviour—indeed, ones that might be recommended by doctors and other clinicians and educators—do not work! When thwarted, the child becomes even more enraged. Moreover, he or she seems to seek out confrontations, within the family, amongst peers, and at school.

Typical patterns include the following:

- The child is hyperactive, does not sleep, and wants everything he/she sees.
- The child's behaviour is experienced by others as highly aversive, resulting in estrangement from both peers and the family.
- The parents do not understand why the child is "naughty" and is criticised by teachers. They become chronically exhausted, frustrated, angry, and despairing—and guilty.
- Parental criticism and punishment evokes more rage in the child, whose self-esteem plummets relentlessly.
- Parental helplessness, and their attempts to adapt to and tolerate the child's temperament, are misperceived by others as the cause of the problem. When the family seeks help from child and adolescent mental health services, they feel further misunderstood, increasing their despair, and the plummeting self-esteem of both parents and child.

Frontal lobe dysfunction and the struggle to "wake the brain up"

It has long been suspected that ADHD has something to do with dysfunction in the frontal lobes that control attention, goal-directed behaviour, and inhibit inappropriate expression of impulse and affect (Benson, 1991). This is seen as an impairment of executive functioning, the brain's management of itself and its relationship with the external world (not dissimilar to the Freudian concept of ego functions) or, as Goldberg (2001) puts it, "the brain's command post" (p. 2). People with ADHD show some similarities to patients with frontal lobe damage, who can be disinhibited, prone to rage, and unable to pursue goals to a satisfactory conclusion. The famous case of Phineas Gage, a railway worker who suffered an accident in 1848, is often cited. Following a severe injury to his frontal lobes, Gage retained many of his cognitive capacities (although memory was somewhat impaired) but displayed marked changes in his personality. Kean (2014) reports,

> It was his personality that had changed, and not for the better. Although resolute in his plans before the accident, this Gage was capricious, almost ADD, and no sooner made a plan than dropped it for another scheme. Although deferential to people's wishes before, this Gage chafed at any restraint on his desires. Although a canny businessman before, this Gage lacked money sense . . . And although a courteous and reverent man before, this Gage was foul-mouthed . . . (p. 335)

However, ADHD should not be viewed simply as an example of frontal lobe damage. In most instances, it is best assumed that there is an abnormality affecting the functioning of the frontal lobes and their connection to other parts of the brain, but there is no actual structural damage to the frontal lobes. Moreover, the brain circuitry involved in ADHD is likely to vary among individuals and to involve a variety of brain regions in addition to the frontal lobes. Nevertheless, we can be fairly confident that, in any case of ADHD, the frontal lobes are involved.

Goldberg (2001) describes the frontal lobes as "the one part of the brain that makes you who you are and defines your identity, that encapsulates your drives, your ambitions, your personality, your essence . . ." (p. 1). He notes that the connection with the frontal lobes makes a high prevalence of ADHD unsurprising:

Once we link ADHD to frontal lobe dysfunction, its very high prevalence . . . should come as no surprise. As we already know, frontal
lobes are particularly vulnerable in a very broad range of disorders,
hence the very high rate of frontal lobe dysfunction. The diagnosis of
ADD or ADHD commonly refers to any condition characterized by
mild dysfunction of the frontal lobes and related pathways in the
absence of any other, comparably severe dysfunction. Given the high
rate of frontal lobe dysfunction due to a variety of causes, the prevalence of genuine ADHD should be expected to be very high. (p. 171)

A particularly distressing and frustrating feature of the experience for people with ADHD is that when they put effort into focusing
or attending, their frontal lobes may shut down even more (Amen,
2001a). Joel Lubar, a brain scan specialist from the University of
Tennessee, found that when ADD children and teenagers performed
a concentration task there was an increased amount of slow brain
wave activity in their frontal lobes, instead of the usual increase in fast
brain wave activity that was seen in the majority of the control group
(www.amenclinics.com). The result is that, for these unfortunate
people, "more is less" when it comes to concentration.

Although the hyperactive and hyper-emotive state of a person
with ADHD might suggest an over-aroused brain (which, in terms of
the flood of stress hormones, it is), the ADHD brain is actually under-
aroused, underpowered, or insufficiently awake. The reticular activating system is underperforming (Goldberg, 2001, p. 172). This is why
stimulant medication often has a positive effect on functioning: the
stimulated ADHD brain functions like a normal brain while the
medication is active.

People with ADHD tend to have excessive slow waves (delta, slow
theta, and sometimes excess alpha) in the frontal executive area, associated with difficulties controlling attention, behaviour, and emotions
(Chabot et al., 1995). These phenomena can be shown with QEEG
technology (quantitative electroencephalography). This may be
another aspect of the dreamy, not quite awake state.

Nigg (2006) has described ADHD as analogous to a state of sleep
deprivation. The person is not alert, and cannot draw upon cognitive
resources efficiently. Reaction times are slow, and attention is difficult
unless the person is strongly stimulated. He or she might speak or
behave impulsively.

It has been found that the basal ganglia are smaller in people with ADHD (Aylward & Reiss, 1996; Nakao et al., 2011; Qiu et al., 2009; Schrimser et al., 2002). There may also be insufficient dopamine in these areas (Reimherr et al., 1984). This makes the basal ganglia insufficiently powered to drive the frontal lobes (Amen, 2001a).

The destructive search for stimulation

Because the brain, and particularly the frontal lobes, are insufficiently aroused and are suffering a kind of highly aversive "boredom", people with ADHD are inclined to seek out interpersonal sources of stimulation, such as arguments, drama, picking fights, emotional scenes, and an oppositional stance. This is not a conscious search, and neither could it be described psychoanalytically as an expression of a "drive derivative". It is an unconscious, addictive, "brain-driven" attempt to boost adrenalin and stimulate the frontal lobes. Emotionally negative interactions, based around aggression and fear, along with negative thoughts, are, unfortunately, more stimulating to the brain than are emotionally positive experiences. It has been found that positive thoughts calm brain activity, neutral thoughts have no effect, but negative thoughts boost activation to limbic areas involved in depression and the prefrontal cortex, enhancing focus (George et al., 1995). Here we have some explanation of why negative thoughts and ruminations, as well as arguments and drama, can be addictive, and also why some people with ADHD become addicted to violent video games, fights, and extreme forms of pornography, as well as films featuring violence or horror.

The need for stimulation can also drive overeating, as well as well as addictions to drugs and alcohol. The person with ADHD can experience a sense of emptiness, a compelling "hunger" for something, as commonly noted in borderline personality disorder, which might, indeed, be organised around ADHD. Often it is assumed that such emptiness expresses a lack of relational connection, but really it might express something more concrete—an insufficiency of stimulation of the frontal lobes (and perhaps of other parts of the brain as well). Such cravings to eat (when not actually hungry) could be similar to the ADHD continual search for novelty, and also the intense search for knowledge that can also feature. It is as if the ADHD brain is continually seeking something, but it does not know what it is.

Impaired sense of self and fragmentation anxiety

A clinical observation is that people with ADHD often seem to have a fragile or uncertain sense of self. The question "who am I?" haunts them, rather as if stuck in a prolonged process of adolescence. Partly, this is probably because the formation of a self-concept is a high level brain function dependent upon the frontal lobes, which are known to be impaired in ADHD.

However, a consideration of some Lacanian ideas suggests additional factors might be involved. Lacan (1949) postulates that an original state of psychological fragmentation gives way to an illusory coherence when the infant identifies with an image (in the mirror, or via another person whom he or she sees). People with ADHD seem particularly captivated by external images, which are part of a broader range of external stimuli that catch the person's attention. A little boy might, for example, on seeing a particular outfit in a toyshop window, decide he is "Superman" (or some other television or film character) and charge around attempting to fly and rescue people. Of course, such imitation and play is phase-appropriately normal, but for the child, and later adult, with ADHD this easy, rapid, and fluid identification with external images may be particularly pronounced. It is like the opposite of projection—the person is invaded by images from outside. Some of these identifications might be with parents issuing prohibitions, giving rise to admonishments towards the self. Others might evoke disgust or horror: for example, the child sees a slug or a spider and feels they have become such a creature. Thus, while some identificatory images may be narcissistically gratifying (e.g., Superman), others are repellent, giving rise to continual inner conflict and aggression (Lacan, 1948) and attempts to break out of the imprisoning aspect of the image. Breaking free of the image then gives rise to further fragmentation and "disintegration anxiety", which Kohut (1977) described as the deepest anxiety a human being can experience. This, in turn, stimulates the search for further images with which to identify.

The more normal or healthy development of a self-concept is via the recognition of reality-based aspects of self, including situating the self within a family and cultural lineage and (in Lacanian terms) the "network of signifiers" (Mollon, 1993). Kohut's (1977) helpful framework for the actual structure of the healthy "Self" is the twin poles of

SOME FEATURES OF ADHD 31

enduring ambitions and ideals, linked to the person's real talents and skills. Such a structure requires work, both developmental and in the world, as well as a process of learning. This healthy organic development of the sense of self, as opposed to the identification with images, seems often impaired in people with ADHD.

Confabulation and "false memory"

It is well known that people with ADHD may have impairments in working memory, and in accessing recall of information (Brown, 2013a). However, the tendency to confabulate, to create incorrect "memories", is less commonly noted in the scientific literature on ADHD. Clinical and anecdotal impressions suggest that this may be a frequent feature of the ADHD spectrum. Sometimes, insightful patients have noticed and described this. For example, one young woman spoke of her awareness that sometimes she would "remember other people's memories"; she said that she might speak to a friend about something she believed she had experienced, and the friend might point out that actually it had been *her* experience. Such phenomena suggest source monitoring errors (incorrectly identifying the source of a mental representation), lax reality monitoring, and a general state of not being fully awake and alert, consistent with the semi-dreamlike state people with ADHD are often in (Lubar et al., 1995). Given such mental conditions, extensive confabulation seems a possibility in some instances, particularly since it is thought that frontal lobe impairments might be a factor in confabulation (Kapur & Coughlan, 1980). This could be exacerbated by use of "recreational" drugs that people with ADHD are often drawn to. Confabulation appears to occur, in part, as a means of filling in gaps where there are memory deficits. Creation of stories that gratify an emotional need seem possible (Fotopoulo et al., 2004). The person's subjective perception and experience of belief in his or her memories is not a guarantee of objective veracity (Mollon, 2002a).

The deficit in the frontal lobes and their reality monitoring functions means that people with ADHD appear often to be prisoners of the Lacanian "mirror stage", captivated by illusory images (of self, other, and the surrounding world) and the associated activity of what may be thought of as the *falsifying ego* (Lacan, 1949). This can lead to the maintenance of a particular image of the self and associated personal narrative, supported by confabulation.

Low levels of neurotransmitters: a "reward-deficit" condition

People with ADHD have lower than normal levels of neurotransmitters, including dopamine, serotonin, and norepinephrine (Flory et al., 2007; Prince, 2008). Some have emphasised low dopamine (e.g., Volkow et al., 2011), arguing that this results in a deficit in the person's capacity to experience reward and pleasure. According to this perspective, a person with ADHD simply finds life inherently less rewarding, providing less pleasure, than do people without this particular neurobiology. Dopamine is what motivates people to pursue distant goals, and it mediates reward. There is not enough of it. As a result, the person is less motivated generally, and is constantly in an addictive search for stimulation, whether through drugs, alcohol, aggressive interactions, risk taking, overeating, or sex. Certainly such a hypothesis fits the experience of many people with ADHD.

Volkow and colleagues (2011) measured dopamine availability in reward pathways using PET scans and correlated these with scores on the Multidimensional Personality Questionnaire, using a group of forty-five adults with ADHD and forty-one controls. The ADHD group had lower scores on the Achievement and Constraint (control of behaviour) scale and higher scores on the Negative Emotion scale— all correlating with lower dopamine.

However, the true picture might not be as simple as a general deficit in dopamine. Some have reported an *excess* of dopamine (Pliszka, 2005), and in animals elevated dopamine is associated with hyperactivity (Viggiano et al., 2003). It might be that there is *too little* dopamine in the frontal lobes, which would explain quite a lot of ADHD features to do with motivation, attention, and executive control, but *too much* dopamine in the ventromedial areas that are also associated with obsessive–compulsive disorder, substance abuse, and impulsive disorders, all of which are often comorbid with ADHD (Previc, 2009). Since dopamine motivates and keeps people pushing on with an activity, it seems that the elevated dopamine in ventromedial areas locks the person into obsessive, compulsive, and impulsive behaviours, and also drives the autistic spectrum traits, while the deficit in dopamine in the frontal areas results in dysfunction in executive control of impulse, attention, and emotion.

Effects of food colourings, additives, and pesticides

Food colourings and other additives have long been suspected of triggering or exacerbating ADHD, and many parents certainly have this impression. This hypothesis is still somewhat controversial, but Bateman and colleagues (2004) found, in a double blind study, that removal of food colourings and benzoate preservative led to a significant reduction in ADHD symptoms in young children, and, similarly, McCann and colleagues (2007) found clear evidence of a link between hyperactivity and children's ingestion of six food colourings and also the preservative sodium benzoate. As a result of concerns about such effects, the European Commission ruled that any food products containing the following six contentious colourings must display warning labels on their packaging by 2010: sunset yellow FCF (E110); quinoline yellow (E104); carmoisine (E122); allura red (E129); tartrazine (E102); and ponceau 4R (E124).

One young man presented with problems of losing his temper at work, jeopardising retention of his job. There was a strongly ADHD quality about him. I enquired whether there was any food or drink that he tended to crave, which can be a sign of that substance being a source of sensitivity. He revealed that he consumed very large amounts of diet cola. Knowing that a sweetener used in diet drinks is suspected by some of giving rise to neurotoxins (a controversy well summarised on Wikipedia), I suggested he try eliminating this from his diet. He returned to see me three weeks later, saying that his angry outbursts had completely stopped since he had eliminated diet cola. Few cases of ADHD resolve so easily, but enquiring about food and drink cravings and excessive intakes can sometimes be useful. However, firm evidence implicating this sweetener to ADHD is lacking. The Peninsula Cerebra Research Unit, a collaboration of universities and NHS organisations in the south west of England, undertook a systematic review of available research on this sweetener and ADHD and found no evidence that it is a factor: the report can be found in their "What's the evidence?" section (www.pencru.org/evidence/). The reality may be that there is great variation in individual responses to additives, colourings, preservatives, etc.

However, a 2010 study found that *pesticide* exposure is strongly associated with an increased risk of ADHD in children (Bouchard et al., 2010). Researchers analysed the levels of organophosphate residues in the urine of more than 100 children aged eight to fifteen years, and found that those with the highest levels also had the highest incidence of ADHD. Moreover, they found a 35% increase in the odds of developing ADHD with every tenfold increase in urinary concentration of the pesticide residues. The effect was seen even at the low end of exposure: children who had any detectable, above-average level of pesticide metabolite in their urine were twice as likely as those with undetectable levels to record symptoms of ADHD.

Other causes of ADHD: Lyme disease and other infections

Lyme disease is widespread yet rarely diagnosed: the British government agency, Public Health England, estimates a prevalence of 2,000–3,000 new cases per year in England and Wales. It is caught from infected ticks that can be carried by deer and other animals, including domestic pets. The ticks are found in vegetation, woodland, and other places where the host animals wander. If not treated with intensive antibiotics soon after infection, the condition becomes chronic and systemic, giving rise to a wide range of disabling physical and mental symptoms, the latter including anxiety, depression, personality changes, cognitive deficits, and attentional problems. Chronic Lyme disease can give rise to ADHD symptoms (Young, 2012). The presence of such symptoms in a person who has not always displayed them merits consideration of the possibility of Lyme disease.

ADHD symptoms can also be caused by other conditions, infections, and toxins that affect brain function, such as heavy metals (Kim et al., 2013; Sagiv et al., 2012), hypothyroidism (Negishia et al., 2005), iron deficiency (Cortese et al., 2012), and ear infections (Adesman, 1990; Antoine et al. 2013). The diversity of factors that can cause or contribute to ADHD indicates its position as a final common pathway of multiple saboteurs of coherent brain function.

Impaired executive functioning and impaired ego functions

Several theorists have given emphasis to a general impairment of executive functioning as a means of conceptualising ADHD, drawing upon the key role of the dysfunctional frontal lobes. These formulations are actually not dissimilar to Freud's early model of the emerging mind in his Project for a Scientific Psychology (1950a), where he described four essential functions for the ego: (1) distinguishing reality from hallucination; (2) delaying or inhibiting motor discharge; (3) making use of memory; (4) interposing thought between impulse and action in order best to solve a problem. Thought is "trial action", using small amounts of energy rather than full motor discharge. The key function of the rudimentary ego is inhibition of motor discharge until desire is aligned with reality and there is no danger of pain or injury. This also requires the function of attention to the external world. All of this is Freud's "secondary process", as opposed to the "primary process", which does not distinguish hallucination from reality and allows immediate flows of energy into discharge.

The role of inhibition

Thus, Barkley (1997; Barkley et al., 2008) similarly gives central importance to the capacity for inhibition, which he sees as comprising three aspects: inhibiting an initial potential response; stopping an ongoing response; protecting the period of delay (and the self-directed processes of thought within it). He sees the failure of inhibition as the primary way in which ADHD impairs executive functions. Because the person cannot inhibit immediate responses, he or she cannot activate and use their inner system of self-directed action to work towards a desired future goal, and cannot organise their actions sequentially within a temporal framework.

Barkley sees executive functioning and self-regulation as involving a shift of behaviour from control by the immediate environment to control by internally represented forms of information. He sees self-regulation as future orientated behaviour which is directed at the self, with the aim of changing subsequent behaviour from that which it would have been if it was a direct expression of the impulse. This requires a preference for larger long-term outcomes over smaller short-term outcomes, and a capacity to organise sequences of behaviour across time. The whole process of self-regulation requires a neuropsychological capacity to conjecture the future, recall the past, and detect patterns among chains of events and behaviours—essentially the function of working memory.

Internalisation of function

Barkley emphasises the processes of *privatisation* of behaviours. This refers to the way in which behaviours that were at one time, in both early child development and human evolution, entirely public means of managing others and the world, become internalised as a means of self-regulation. For example, verbal working memory is a form of self-directed private speech, while non-verbal memory is the "privatisation of sensory–motor activities (resensing to or behaving toward the self)" (Barkley et al., 2008, p. 174), and planning and creativity are the internalisation of human play. Barkley sees emotional self-regulation as arising out of the privatisation of speech and self-directed sensory–motor behaviour.

From a psychoanalytic perspective, we might view these processes of privatisation in terms of developmental internalisation of function in the context of the caring early relationship. These include functions such as: (a) the internalisation of morality and control via the super-ego, which

> continues to carry on the functions which have hitherto been performed by the people . . . in the external world: it observes the ego, gives it orders, judges it and threatens it with punishments, exactly like the parents whose place it has taken. (Freud, 1940, p. 205)

(b) the crucial ego function of "interpolating, between a demand made by an instinct and the action that satisfied it, the activity of thought" (Freud, 1940a, p. 199); (c) the gradual taking on of ego functions that were initially provided externally (Hartman et al., 1946); (d) the establishment of the "reality principle" in place of the more primary "pleasure principle" (Freud, 1911b); (e) the processes of "transmuting internalisation" described by Kohut (1971, 1977, 1981) through the empathic responsiveness of the child's "selfobjects".

Within Kohut's framework, the regulation of the child's arousal, mood, and self-esteem is dependent upon empathic responses of the carers, whose psychological presence *functions as part of the child's own system*, and hence, the fused term "selfobject". Gradually, and partly through the inevitable failings and imperfections of the parental responses, these functions are internalised ("transmuting internalisation"). In the case of people with ADHD, these processes of internalisation go awry. There is both an enhanced need for selfobject responsiveness and a rejection of external control. It is as if the Freudian "primary process" and "pleasure principle" are constitutionally too powerful, and the ego too weak, with the result that the "reality principle" and "secondary process" are swept away like sandcastles at the mercy of powerful flowing waves.

Congruently with a psychoanalytic perspective, another prominent neuropsychological theorist, Brown (2013a), emphasises that executive functions are

> developmental in the sense that they emerge incrementally over the course of development . . . many of these functions do not appear, except in very rudimentary ways, in young children . . . starting from primordial forms that emerge first in the rudimentary effortful control that develops in pre-schoolers; these functions progressively become more elaborated and refined throughout childhood and adolescence. (p. 29)

Brown (2013a) presents a broader framework of failures of executive functions impaired in ADHD. He proposes six clusters that might be considered "baskets of related cognitive functions which interact in a variety of dynamic ways" (p. 22):

- activation: "organizing tasks and materials, estimating time, prioritizing tasks, and getting started on work tasks" (p. 23);
- focus: "focusing, sustaining focus, and shifting focus to tasks" (p. 23);
- effort: "regulating alertness, sustaining effort, and processing speed" (p. 23);
- emotion; "managing frustration and modulating emotions" (p. 23);
- memory: "utilizing working memory and accessing recall" (p. 23);
- action: "monitoring and regulating self-action" (p. 24).

Brown (2013a) distinguishes his framework from that of Barkley on three points. First, Barkley presents his model as applying to those with hyperactivity and impulsiveness, but not to those with a primarily inattentive form of ADD, and more recently Barkley (2012) has presented a syndrome of "sluggish cognitive tempo" (STD), with features such as excessive daydreaming, being easily bored, brain fog, underactivity, difficulty staying alert, etc., which he argues should be distinguished from ADHD. Brown views all these symptoms as aspects of impaired executive functions. Second, while Barkley privileges the function of inhibition, Brown sees regulating action as just one of six functions that might be impaired. Third, Brown sees most executive functions as operating automatically without deliberation or conscious choice, whereas he portrays Barkley as viewing executive functions as more conscious effortful actions.

As noted above, executive functions can, in general, be considered equivalent to ego functions. Where the psychoanalytic perspectives differs from the purely neuropsychological frameworks of Barkley, Brown, and others (e.g., Douglas, 1999) who have proposed models of impaired executive functioning in ADHD, is in the viewing of the development of these functions in the context of the relationship with the carers, and the intimate interweaving of the interpersonal, the intrapsychic, and the neurobiological.

ADHD as neurobiological dysregulation

Hallowell and Ratey (1994) present a neurobiological dysregulation model, which can incorporate most of the disparate features of ADHD. They view the condition as an essentially genetic syndrome where the neurobiology has been rendered out of balance, resulting in impaired coordination of brain systems, including the capacity to pay attention. As a result,

> The world becomes a land without street signs, the individual a car in bad need of a tune up ... Where one individual needs an oil change, the next needs spark plugs replaced. Where one individual is withdrawn and overwhelmed by stimuli, the next is hyperactive and can't get enough stimuli. Where one is frequently anxious, the other is depressed. To compensate, each develops his or her own coping

strategies that developmentally add to, or subtract from, the brain's various subsystems. So Mr A becomes a stand-up comedian, and manic. Ms B becomes an architectural wizard with obsessive compulsive traits. Their offspring become a sculptor and a stunt pilot. None of them can balance their checkbook. And all of them wish they had more time in the day. (p. 280)

This is certainly a very apt and vivid account of the range of manifestations and difficulties experienced by people with ADHD. The brain is in need of a tune up!

Link with chronic fatigue and fibromyalgia

There appear to be links between ADHD and chronic fatigue (Young, 2013; Young & Redmond, 2007), and also fibromyalgia (Davis & Stephens, 2002; Krause et al., 1998; Reyero et al., 2011). One possibility is that ADHD, chronic fatigue, and fibromyalgia share a common route. It is noted that all of them can respond to stimulant medication.

Davis and Stephens (2002) state that the following symptoms occur in both ADHD and fibromyalgia. Low stress tolerance; concentration or memory problems; mood swings, depression, anxiety; poor organisational skills; low energy; difficulty relaxing; sleep disturbances; poor regulation of body temperature; skin rashes, itching; urinary frequency; reflux, gastritis, ulcers, constipation or diarrhoea; aches and pains; low or high blood pressure; yeast or fungal infections; allergies, asthma, bronchitis, sinusitis; sexual over-arousal or under-arousal; numbness and tingling (carpal tunnel symptoms, legs "going to sleep", etc.); heart-related symptoms (chest tightness, palpitations, etc.); poor coordination, other gross motor skills; poor handwriting, other fine motor skills; impulsive eating or spending.

These observations, which are congruent with my own impressions, are of interest because, as the authors state, patients presenting with fibromyalgia are not usually assessed for ADHD symptoms, and those presenting with ADHD are not usually assessed for fibromyalgia. Moreover, clinicians might often not "connect the dots" with these diverse symptoms.

One hypothesis is that ADHD, fibromyalgia, and chronic fatigue have a common root, perhaps an autonomic nervous system dysfunction, with a dysregulation between sympathetic and parasympathetic components.

Another possibility is that chronic fatigue and fibromyalgia are results of the long-term stress that is inherent in ADHD. People with ADHD are often very stressed, agitated, angry, and anxious, do not sleep well, and become exhausted. These are very obvious outward signs. Being around a person with ADHD is often very stressful for others, which perhaps reflects a combination of other people's resonance with the stress experience by the person with ADHD and also that person's continual attempt to "export" their stress in order to gain some relief.

However, there is a more hidden stress that occurs even with those who have the quieter forms of ADD. The brain is mistuned. Different brain systems do not harmonise, and the two hemispheres do not engage well to undertake complementary functions for any given task. People might describe feelings of stress and tiredness on attempting to read or concentrate. Reading might feel very effortful. There might be a sense of seeing the words but not grasping their meaning. Similar discomfort could be experienced on listening to spoken words, or in engaging with any cognitive or attentional task. This can make social occasions tiring, even if they are otherwise welcomed and sought after. Just as a mistuned engine will run very inefficiently, using up and wasting far more energy than it otherwise would, so a desynchronised brain will consume a great deal more energy than a more efficient brain. Although the relationship between energy use (in the form of glucose) and cognitive work appears far from simple (Clarke & Sokoloff, 1998; Van den Berg, 1986), the subjective experience of tiredness after mental work can be very compelling, and this is particularly so for those who have suffered traumatic brain injury (TBI) from a blow to the head (Belmont et al., 2009; Johansson & Rönnbäck, 2014):

> A typical characteristic of pathological mental fatigue after TBI is that the mental exhaustion becomes pronounced during sensory stimulation or when cognitive tasks are performed for extended periods without breaks. There is a drain of mental energy upon mental activity in situations in which there is an invasion of the senses with an overload of impressions, and in noisy and hectic environments. The person feels that their brain is overloaded after a tiny load. Another typical feature

is a disproportionally long recovery time needed to restore the mental energy levels after being mentally exhausted. . . . The fatigue can appear very rapidly and, when it does, it is not possible for the affected person to continue the ongoing activity. Common associated symptoms include: impaired memory and concentration capacity, slowness of thinking, irritability, tearfulness, sound and light sensitivity, sensitivity to stress, sleep problems, lack of initiative and headache. (Johansson & Rönnbäck, 2014, pp. 492–493)

Such symptoms are not dissimilar to those reported by people with ADHD, Asperger's/autistic spectrum traits, and chronic fatigue. Trying to do work with a brain that is not functioning well, whether through injury or ADHD, results in severe fatigue, although the reasons and mechanisms are not well understood.[5] It is of interest that the stimulant methylphenidate relieves the symptoms of both ADHD and fatigue resulting from traumatic brain injury (Johansson & Rönnbäck, 2014). Moreover, meditation has been found to improve fatigue in those with TBI (Johansson et al., 2012) and relieve symptoms of ADHD (Grosswald, 2013).

Benefits of ADHD: creativity

With so many disadvantages and abnormalities apparent in ADHD, it is important to acknowledge significant benefits, particularly when the condition is mild to moderate rather than severe.

ADHD can be associated with creativity (Carson, 2010; Cramond, 1994). It is not difficult to understand why this may be the case. A degree of distractibility and "mental scatter" makes stimuli, thoughts, and information available from many sources, particularly when combined with the ADHD search for novelty. Impulsivity, including impulsive directions of thought, along with a dismissal of convention, received knowledge, and protocols, can sometimes lead to novel solutions.

People with ADHD tend to be adventurous, and might be less restricted by social convention (although they can experience social anxiety). They are restless, tending to be always enquiring, questioning, searching, and reject authority, including the authority of "official knowledge". The same inclination that might lead some with ADHD to engage in fights, aggressive exploration, or military conquest, might lead others to engage in expansionist intellectual or artistic pursuits. Rock musicians seem likely to have ADHD traits.

The slow brain waves shown by people with ADHD may create a somewhat dream-like state of mind. Dreams are the ultimate in the creative process, breaking up and recombining elements from entirely disparate sources to form completely novel images and scenarios. To be in such a state of mind while awake is obviously likely to facilitate creativity.

Another quality of ADHD that can contribute to creative work is the capacity for hyperfocus. Although people with ADHD often experience difficulty attending and focusing, this characteristic can disappear entirely when they are engaged in a task that is inherently interesting and rewarding for them. At such times, the activity will seem more important than anything else and the difficulty is in stopping for rest or to attend to other pressing requirements. This hyperfocus allows for sustained work towards a goal.

The qualities that give rise to creativity in ADHD must be present to an optimum degree for this to occur. If there is too much random activity, grossly impulsive behaviour, intolerance of frustration, and rage, then the person will be unable to engage in any constructive task, or, indeed, manage any social intercourse.

An evolutionary perspective on ADHD, developed in a series of books by Thom Hartmann (e.g., Hartmann, 1993, 2003), is that ADHD characteristics might have been of adaptive value in early nomadic conditions, where being adept at searching, seeking, taking risks, and engaging in competition could have facilitated a *hunter* lifestyle. Such characteristics might have been of less value in later developing farmer communities, where a more ordered way of life, with sustained attention to a variety of tasks, was required.

"Indigo children"

Some who are diagnosed with ADHD may correspond to the "Indigo children" described originally by Lee Carroll and Jan Tober (Carroll & Tober, 1999, 2009; Dosick, 2009; Healy, 2013). These are children with a strong inner will and sense of their own authority, strongly rejecting of control by others. They are generally non-conforming, frustrated by, and rejecting of, rituals and rules that appear without reasonable justification, do not respond to sanctions based on inducing guilt, and can make their views and needs known quite forcefully. Thus, they can be experienced as "difficult" by parents, peers, and educators. They are highly intuitive and may have strong spiritual interests. The name "indigo" refers to the predominance of blue in their energetic aura, as perceived by some with clairvoyance. These children and adults respond best to respect for their individuality and nurturance of their particular talents and interests. They may also fit the description of "highly sensitive person", as outlined by Aron (1999, 2010). However, Carroll and Tober (1999) emphasise that not all Indigos have ADHD and not all with ADHD are Indigos.

The concept of Indigos is meaningful to me, at least in relation to a minority of people who present features of ADHD, and I also find that some people correspond to what I think of as "damaged Indigos". Being inherently very sensitive, in almost every way (emotionally, physically, psychically), and often perceived as "odd" by others, Indigos find being in the material world quite difficult. Not only are they easily hurt by the ordinary emotional rough and tumble of the narcissistic injuries of everyday life, but also they can easily be targets for mockery or bullying. They might attempt to survive by suppressing their Indigo nature. The result may be a persona that appears cold, cynical, or exploitative, fearful of emotional closeness and expressions of love. Turning to drugs and alcohol may frequently occur among this group. In time, and given appropriate signals and nurturance, the damaged Indigo may discover his or her true nature.

Controversies

As a concept and as a diagnosis, ADHD tends to be controversial (Saul, 2014). The arguments against it tend to be:

- It is a medicalisation of common and ordinary childhood traits, particularly among boys.
- It is a way of pathologising and medicating disruptive children who really need a better classroom environment with more opportunity to play.
- ADHD is really a heterogeneous collection of a range of problems that are better treated individually (Saul, 2014).

- The core of ADHD is essentially a combination of attentional problems combined with anxiety—all other presumed features follow from this or are comorbid (Fisher, 2013).
- ADHD is a condition endemic in the culture of the USA.
- It is a response to diminishing opportunities for preschool children to engage in self-generated social play in modern urban environments (Panksepp, 1998, 2007).
- It is a condition promoted by drug companies and associated psychiatrists and psychologists, resulting in over-diagnosis, for commercial gain.
- It is better understood as an interaction between biology and environment and culture (Hinshaw & Scheffler, 2014).
- ADHD is a "social construction". Societies determine the line between normal and abnormal behaviour. Authorities within society, such as doctors, teachers, and parents, determine where that line is. Thus Szasz (2001) asserts that ADHD was "invented and not discovered" (p. 212).

It is not difficult to see elements of truth in each of these criticisms. However, many of us still feel there is value in the concept of ADHD as capturing constellations of pervasive dysfunction of executive functioning and self-regulation. Of course, it may be that a better name could be found for this that more accurately reflects what is now understood of the condition, such as "pervasive brain dysregulation", a concept that would capture many different expressions of dysregulation.

These trends towards dismissal of ADHD as a valid diagnosis prompted Barkley and eighty-four other recognised experts in the field to issue a "consensus statement" (Barkley, 2002), which included the following:

We, the undersigned consortium of international scientists, are deeply concerned about the periodic inaccurate portrayal of attention deficit hyperactivity disorder (ADHD) in media reports. This is a disorder with which we are all very familiar and toward which many of us have dedicated scientific studies if not entire careers. We fear that inaccurate stories rendering ADHD as myth, fraud, or benign condition may cause thousands of sufferers not to seek treatment for their disorder. It also leaves the public with a general sense that this disorder is not valid or real or consists of a rather trivial affliction. . . . To publish stories that ADHD is a fictitious disorder or merely a conflict between today's Huckleberry Finns and their caregivers is tantamount to declaring the earth flat, the laws of gravity debatable, and the periodic table in chemistry a fraud. (pp. 89–90)

However, Timimi and thirty-three co-endorsers (2004) issued a rebuttal to this statement:

Why did a group of eminent psychiatrists and psychologists produce a consensus statement that seeks to forestall debate on the merits of the widespread diagnosis and drug treatment of attention deficit hyperactivity disorder (ADHD) (Barkley, 2002)? If the evidence is already that good then no statement is needed. However, the reality is that claims about ADHD being a genuine medical disorder and psychotropics being genuine correctives have been shaken by criticism. Not only is it completely counter to the spirit and practice of science to cease questioning the validity of ADHD as proposed by the consensus statement, there is an ethical and moral responsibility to do so. (p. 59)

Of course, a balanced perspective would see merit in both positions. Severe ADHD is a very serious condition with devastating consequences for the person's life. On the other hand, it is a complex and somewhat varied constellation, with contributions from biology, family environment, and culture. Moreover, those afflicted with ADHD deserve more than just medication.

Summary and conclusions

ADHD consists of a spectrum of difficulties affecting multiple areas of functioning. The deficits are not restricted to the domains of attention and levels of activity, but disrupt all areas of self-regulation, management of affect, goal-directed activity, and relationships with others. These difficulties can all be conceptualised within the Freudian framework of impaired ego functions and enhanced needs for regulatory assistance from others—the *selfobject* functions described and theorised by Kohut. ADHD can be comorbid with many mental (and physical) health conditions and may be a hidden core in borderline personality disorder. Abnormal functioning of the frontal lobes appears to be a key feature, but many factors can contribute to this.

CHAPTER THREE

Experiencing ADHD

A DHD is often a hidden constellation, based around certain neurobiological features, which underpins many mental health presentations including some personality disorders, particularly borderline personality disorder. Without an understanding of this core, clients presenting with emotional and psychological problems can easily be misperceived and wrongly formulated, thereby compounding the person's false perception of self. The person with an ADHD spectrum brain will display a bewildering combination of "dis-order" and unusual talent. Indications of learning difficulties, attentional problems, and slowness of processing (like an overloaded computer) may be interwoven with creativity, intuition, and, in some cases, a high level of intelligence that might strike many as somewhat eccentric. In addition, emotional responses and mood states of those with ADHD are different from those of the general population.

The following are three common features of the ADHD experience:

- a core sense of chaos and disorganisation;
- a proneness to states of high anxiety or rage when subject to stress;
- a lack of feeling that life is inherently rewarding.

A further frequent aspect is an almost automatic or instinctive dislike of, and rebellion against, authority and expected social rules.

The person with an ADHD temperament will tend to feel a chronic awareness of "difference" from others, along with a sense of being in some way defective. He or she may observe with astonishment the way that others often seem to be organised, arriving to work and other appointments on time, are able to focus on required tasks, and maintain clothes and a personal environment that are relatively neat and tidy. For the one with ADHD, these simple tasks of life can seem quite beyond his or her capabilities.

The ADHD temperament is deficient in the capacity for affect regulation, so that high anxiety and anger are common. In these states, the person has impaired capacity for rational and coherent thought, speech, and behaviour.

Another component of the ADHD temperament is a default mood of depression. Being alive lacks inherent reward. People without ADHD may be naturally cheerful and positive. Not so those with ADHD; for them, life tends to be tedious, boring, and unrewarding. A chronic mood state, expressed in words such as "what's the point?", might pervade the experience of life, generating a bewildered fascination with the organic good humour of others. This basic lack of pleasure will fuel a restless search for stimulation, whether in the form of drugs or sex, new information, or intense emotional experiences in relationships. It will generate a continual background sense of emptiness and lack of meaning, at times deepening into states of despair. "Getting going" on activities and projects tends to be difficult for the person with ADHD, so that procrastination may be marked. On the other hand, once started on an activity, it might be difficult to stop.

The ADHD temperament means the person will experience life as difficult, frustrating, and unfulfilling. Relationships with others, beginning with parents and siblings, followed by school and peer relationships, will have tended to be fraught. Often, the ADHD person will feel different, an outsider , and might indeed be viewed by others as somewhat odd or eccentric, although perhaps creative in artistic or other ways. Aggressive or abrasive encounters with others might have been the norm.

As a child, the person with ADHD might have experienced a more pronounced need for the continual presence of carers in order to provide stimulation and organisation. Fears of abandonment would coexist uneasily with aggression towards carers, other family members, and peers—a conflict of emotions expressed aptly by the famous book on borderline personality disorder, *I Hate You—Don't Leave Me* (Kreisman & Straus, 1989). Later, the need for these selfobject functions (as Kohut, 1971, 1977, described them), where the empathically attentive carer brings coherence to the child's mind, could lead to a resort to the more pathological selfobject substitutes of drugs or alcohol. The person with ADHD is continually searching for a missing piece of psychic structure, an absent realm of brain function.

Storms of rage may have punctuated the person's life, provoked by frustration and humiliations in relation to others. Commonly, other people would react with counter-aggression to the angry onslaughts generated by the ADHD temperament, but these would often lead to an escalating state of arousal, so that any capacity to inhibit or regulate expressions of rage is swept aside in the volcanic wave of exploding fury. I have known several cases of men with severe ADHD who are afraid to go out because of the danger of getting into rage and potential violence with strangers, such as people in shops, on buses, or in other cars.

Social interactions can be stressful and challenging for people with ADHD. The difficulty in maintaining focus and concentration means that the person might easily become distracted during conversation, completely losing track of what has been said. Rather than risk the embarrassment of having to ask for repetition of what has just been said, the person might anxiously try to make a guess as to what has been missed, sometimes resulting in misunderstanding. Trying to listen when not really interested in what is being said can be extremely aversive for the person with ADHD. In addition, the impulsiveness inherent in the ADHD temperament can result in blurting out comments, or cutting across the other person's speech, in ways that might appear rude. A person with severe ADHD may be quite unable to think before speaking, or inhibit or modulate what comes out of their mouth.

The legacy of repeated negative and unrewarding experiences with others will lead to an accumulation of injuries to self-esteem, culminating in a pervasive sense of being defective. This may be countered by defensive efforts to claim superiority over others or by extreme endeavours to achieve success in certain realms where talent is apparent.

This combination of low self-esteem, restless search for reward, and the continual irritation of an inherent mental chaos, can indeed, in some cases, generate high levels of creative accomplishment. Certain artists, writers, musicians, or creative scientists may show this constellation. For many people with ADHD, making music, writing, or other creative activity is soothing, reducing the oppressive psychic chaos, bringing order and coherence to the brain, as well as rewarding stimulation and focus. Some with ADHD might develop obsessional traits, demanding strict and consistent order, in an attempt to counter the underlying chaos.

If presenting to a psychotherapist or a mental health service, such a person might appear to be suffering from an anxiety disorder, or depression. Further exploration of the patterns of that person's life could lead to an impression of borderline (or even antisocial) personality disorder, or perhaps to a bipolar II disorder. All such diagnostic hypotheses could be valid (in so far as any psychiatric diagnosis is valid), but they miss the more hidden core of ADHD. Very rarely is this hidden core easily recognised, unless the clinician has a particular awareness and sensitivity for this.

Whatever the initial symptom presentation of the person with ADHD, the therapist will find that resolution of problems is slower and is a more complex process than with clients without this temperament. As one symptom is addressed, other problems will come into view. The pattern of the person's life will appear to have a chaotic quality. A sense of confusion and frustration might begin to pervade the clinician's experience when with the client.

At times there might be a vacant, "empty headed" quality to the client's presentation and state of mind during therapy. He or she might not know what to say and might feel oppressed by this inner absence. The emptiness, or absence, can be experienced as highly aversive, triggering repetitive discourse designed to create stimulation. Outside the consulting room, this "absent" state might drive the person to various familiar addictive pursuits, such as eating, shopping, television, the Internet, computer games, etc. At other times, the presentation in the consulting room might be one of pressure of speech and high emotion.

The therapist's experience might be one of confusion—or even exhaustion. The latter is particularly likely if, not appreciating the essentially ADHD nature of the presentation, the therapist attempts diligently to follow every detail of the client's discourse.

One of the most significant features of ADHD, from the psycho-therapist's point of view, is that the client will not seem to improve in the way normally expected. This is likely to be most apparent when short-term therapies are used as treatment for particular presenting problems, such as anxiety or depression. Initially, progress might appear to be made, but a continual stream of further problems may be presented. Although the person with ADHD may be intelligent, areas of marked immaturity of thought and egocentricity may be discerned with further enquiry.

A further feature of the therapist's experience of the person with ADHD is that emotions may be expressed strongly, but these might have an oddly shallow quality, reflecting their lack of connection to deep structures of the psyche.

If psychotherapy is conducted with a person with ADHD, without an awareness and understanding of this underlying neurobiological condition, the work is likely to become mired in misunderstanding. Distorted impressions of the person's environment and childhood situation may arise. A person with ADHD might have difficulty in giving a balanced account of a situation, including childhood events, taking account of other people's points of view and experience. This is because his or her perspective is so dominant, and it can be difficult to decentre from this. As a result, the person might present a version of events that fail to reveal fully his or her part in them, perhaps giving the impression of extreme forms of behaviour by parents or other family members, which might actually have been, in part, responses to the child's abnormal temperament. The adult with ADHD, with low self-esteem, will often have a fear of being blamed and might fear that if the therapist does not accept the narrative of parental blame, then a counter-narrative of patient blame will prevail. The more balanced truth, of course, is that no one is to blame. A complex and spiralling interaction of neurobiological temperament and family and school environment will have taken place.

If the ADHD perspective is explained to clients who have this con-dition, two kinds of response seem characteristic. One is an indignant and hostile dismissal of such a diagnostic "label". The other, perhaps more common response, when the nature of ADHD is explained care-fully and empathically, is one of great interest and relief. One young woman I saw for a consultation seemed more and more astonished as we explored her ADHD and childhood experiences, eventually asking, "How come you have understood all this about me in half an hour when all the other people I have seen did not understand me?" Similar reactions of surprise and relief may arise when speaking with the parents of people with ADHD, who might be in a chronic state of despair about their family situation. As I spoke to a mother about the family experiences with their, now adult, son with ADHD, she remarked, with the relief of feeling finally understood, "It is as if you have been observing our family from the beginning." These reactions occur because the phenomena of ADHD, and its interaction with the environment, all make sense in a coherent and holistic way once the condition is understood, but do not make sense at all when the core constellation is not grasped. Without the ADHD concept, the problem might easily (but mistakenly) be viewed as one of inadequate parental discipline and boundaries, or of some kind of inherent "antisocial personality disorder" in the child. This is why an understanding of ADHD is important: it is a core construct, around which many presenting features can be organised meaningfully. Unfortunately, it is often missed.

One young man reported considerable benefit from a single consultation regarding his ADHD. He had been aware that he had been described as having this condition from an early age, but his understanding of what it meant was limited. After a more detailed exploration and discussion of the neurobiology of ADHD and its core features, with an empathic recognition of his chronic struggles with his temperament, he was able to explain to his family how they could help him de-escalate his rages by not responding with counter-aggression. They were able to do so and he felt much calmer. He was also able to make more use of simple strategies, such as removing himself from a situation that was provoking his anger, prior to its escalation to a "no return" threshold of rage.

When understood correctly, both client and parents are relieved of a burden of guilt and shame, recognising that no one is to blame, that all have been struggling with a challenging neurobiology, which, nevertheless, has benefits. There can then be a focus on finding ways of working with the "gifts" of ADHD, recognising its creative potential, rather than trying to fit into modes of work for which this temperament is not suited. In addition, strategies can be developed for managing affect, compensating for the attentional deficit, and discharging excess energy in the nervous system.

Case example[6]

John sought a consultation with me because a friend suggested his longstanding difficulties with attention and regulation of his emotions might be to do with ADHD. Having lost a series of jobs as a result of arguments with colleagues or the public, as well as jeopardising his relationship with his girlfriend through his angry outbursts, John recognised he had a problem. Moreover, he was embarrassed by his inability to take in information when given instruction by managers or other senior colleagues. He found that even though he intended to pay attention to instructions, his mind would appear to shut down or veer off into irrelevant daydreams. Often, he would lose attention even half way through the other person's sentence. In order to take in information, he needed to sit quietly on his own, with the material in front of him. In fact, John found life inherently extremely frustrating and irritating, so much so that he was often on the edge of "losing it". Friends and family became fearful of his temper. Once enraged, John could not stop. He would rant and rave, shouting and swearing, and sometimes even hurling and smashing objects. When he was younger, at school, John would often get into physical fights. Sometimes he was bullied by his peers, who enjoyed provoking his rage.

John had always felt different and somehow defective. He knew that others seemed to find life less stressful than he did, and seemed to manage to get on with the ordinary tasks of life, such as getting up in the morning and getting to work on time, attending to bills and other paperwork, keeping his belongings in reasonable order, and remembering important matters that required his attention. For him, all these were problematic, leading him to feel secretly defective.

John often felt anxious. He could also feel confused in new situations. Although he was a moderately competent driver, there were times when he encountered unfamiliar situations on the road where he was overwhelmed with visual information and for a few seconds would be uncertain how he should proceed. He found pubs and nightclubs overstimulating, with too much noise, lights, and proximity to others. Frequently, his mind would be racing, as if seeking sources of anxiety, sometimes bordering on panic. At other times, his mind would seem to be shut down, as if unable to think. The frustration of this could be unbearable, generating states of rage that might seem to emerge "out of the blue", with sudden impulses to smash up his belongings or lash out verbally at those close to him.

John spoke of the people in his life who caused him annoyance, complaining that his parents were always criticising him, had been punitive when he was young, and that his girlfriend would nag him. He spoke of managers at work who had behaved, in his view, unreasonably. It seemed difficult for John to perceive his own role in his difficulties, although at times he could, and this vague sense of his own responsibility had contributed to his decision to seek help. As he talked of his childhood tensions with his parents and their attempted punishments and sanctions, I asked if he had been described as an "impossible child". John acknowledged that such a description had indeed been used and he also admitted to a childhood pattern of rages and tantrums when thwarted. I asked if he had experienced difficulty sleeping as a child and he revealed that his mother had said he "never slept" and that he had been "on the go" all the time. He also told me of his problems at school, where teachers would perceive him as naughty, always disobedient and disruptive, shouting inappropriately in class and getting into fights.

Although John had heard of the concept of ADHD, and had some idea that it applied to him, he did not understand what it meant. I explained to him that ADHD is a brain state condition, which is expressed in various forms of: (a) attentional disorder, (b) hyperactivity or restlessness, (c) difficulty in regulating emotions and impulses, and (d) a deficit in the experience of reward. I explained further that many of these problems stem from an underfunctioning frontal lobe, which is concerned with planning, forward thinking, staying focused, and regulating emotions and impulses. The additional point I emphasised was that a deficit in dopamine or other neurotransmitters might mean he tended to lack the experience of pleasure, might find life unrewarding, might search for stimulation, and could tend to be depressed. John found this account to be revelatory, bringing a new perspective of understanding to his experience of life. He began to see that both he and his family had struggled with the challenge of his ADHD, but these problems were not anybody's fault. His impulsiveness, restless search for stimulation and horror of boredom, and difficulties in focusing, were all due to a brain state, rather than a defect in his character. Moreover, I pointed out the inherent frustrations of this condition—that brain scan studies had shown that the more a person with ADHD tries to focus, the more the frontal lobes, paradoxically, shut down. Yet another point that he felt highly relevant was the observation that people with ADHD will often have storms of rage, which rapidly subside once expressed, so that the shell-shocked others may be bewildered that the person is now "acting as if nothing had happened". He said this was exactly what members of his family had said—that they could not understand how he could be in a state of violent rage one moment and then seemingly acting as "normal" a few minutes later, while his own perspective was to wonder what they were making a fuss about.

As we continued to explore these various aspects of ADHD and how they have affected the course of his life, John's perception of both self and his family began to change. He could now see that it was inevitable that he would have experienced difficulties as a result of his neurobiological temperament and that his problematic behaviours and experiences were driven by brain states. The process of self-acceptance always has profound and extensive consequences and, in John's case, these extended out through his relationships with friends and family. He was able to discuss the diagnostic concept of ADHD with those close to him, enabling both him and them to take a different perspective. Just as he felt less ashamed and guilty about his ADHD, so his family and girlfriend felt more accepting of their own responses when stressed by John's behaviour. This began a more benign cycle, countering the "vicious circle" of rage and counter-rage, guilt and shame that all had been caught up in.

John needed time to come to terms with some of his episodes of losing control and engaging in extreme behaviours, such as self-harm. For example, on one occasion, he had been so enraged and alarmed by his girlfriend's dismissive response during a period when he feared she was being unfaithful that he resorted to slashing at his arm with a kitchen knife. His state of mind at the time had been one of rage and panic, his mounting brain arousal impairing his capacity to think rationally. It had been literally an *impulsive* act, since at that moment he had few resources to inhibit impulses. John felt shame about this and other similar events.

Another recurrent part of John's experience was of finding his mind wandering in a dreamlike manner, which could then cause him anxiety at work. He would suddenly become aware that his mind was wandering far from the task in hand, imagining a variety of unlikely scenarios, sometimes of a wishful nature, sometimes of feared events, and sometimes simply bizarre. This sudden awareness would cause him to feel anxious that he might have missed some important information or communication, and that his dreamlike state might be apparent to others. He would then find that the more he tried to focus and pay attention to his work, the more unfocused his mind would be (a common problem for people with ADHD is that effortful attempts to focus lead, paradoxically, to a greater decrease in activity of the frontal lobes that regulate attention and focus). He would then feel self-conscious, flustered, and confused.

John experienced chronic struggles with his nervous system reactivity. He would easily and rapidly become physiologically and neurobiologically aroused. For example, in a social or work situation, he might make some error in speaking or in performing a task in front of others, then have the automatic thought "they will think I am an idiot", which would then instantly trigger embarrassing physiological responses such as blushing and sweating. These responses would then cause him further embarrassment and anxiety, resulting in yet more blushing and sweating, and so his panic and embarrassment would spiral. Although most people will experience some degree of physiological arousal of this kind from time to time, with ADHD these responses can be more marked.

John found that he was extremely aversive to boredom. Work that was routine and repetitive would cause him to feel extremely agitated and restless, unless it was so routine and undemanding that he could drift off into daydreams. We came to understand that sometimes John would pick arguments with work colleagues, or family members, in order to provide his brain with stimulation. This was not a consciously motivated behaviour, but was a non-conscious "brain state driven" search for stimulation, the under-stimulated and under-aroused ADHD brain seeking compensatory regulation from the interpersonal environment. This pattern was extremely irritating to other people. Once John was able to understand what was driving this, he was able sometimes to inhibit his impulse to engage in his argumentative behaviour.

Although John could be overwhelmed by noisy environments, or by other forms of sensory stimulation, his dread of boredom and restless search for stimulation for his under-aroused brain (frontal lobes) meant that he was drawn to experimenting with altering his brain state through drugs. Over the years, he had tried many different drugs and had found that amphetamine seemed to calm him and improve his cognitive functioning. This effect is common with people with ADD or ADHD, resulting from the stimulation of the frontal lobe and general "waking up" of the brain produced by amphetamine.

A positive aspect of the search for stimulation and novelty-seeking behaviour was that John would often be drawn toward exploring new aspects of life and information. In every way, if something new caught John's attention, he would want to explore it, whether it was a book, an idea, a shop, an item of technology, a path or a road. This meant that he could potentially draw upon a range of experiences and sources of knowledge to inform and enrich his work in a creative field.

Because of his tendency to be in a somewhat "dreamy" brain state (slow brain waves), John could more easily than most people access intuitive, clairvoyant, or other non-ordinary sources of knowledge and awareness. He had tended to be dismissive of these and some-what embarrassed to acknowledge them, and, on occasion, had felt confused and overwhelmed by accurate perceptions of other people's motives, thoughts, and emotions that were incongruent with the overt discourse. Once John understood that these were part of the ADHD constellation, he could more easily accommodate and integrate these "extra-sensory" forms of knowledge (Brottman, 2011).

Summary and conclusions

People with an ADHD temperament experience life as difficult, stress-ful, frustrating, and unrewarding. They have difficulty regulating their impulses, moods, and emotions. High levels of anxiety pervade their experience. Shame and low self-esteem result from the inability to manage tasks that others find easy. A psychoeducational compo-nent to therapeutic work, explaining to the client the nature of ADHD and its effects, can be helpful in alleviating shame and self-blame, as well as in facilitating more constructive ways of managing the diffi-culties and building on the creativity that this temperament can offer.

CHAPTER FOUR

Some helpful and less helpful ways of viewing people with ADHD and autistic spectrum conditions

Whilst my clinical perceptions are profoundly rooted in psychoanalysis, and it seems to me that Freudian psychoanalytic perspectives can be extremely helpful in understanding and working with ADHD, I fear that some kinds of (non-Freudian) psychoanalytic stance can, potentially and in certain circumstances, be detrimental (Mollon, 2011, 2014b). When confronted by typical ADHD phenomena, it is easy to see expressions of destructiveness and primitive defences, such as splitting, projection, denial, and rejection of reality, as well as manic, omnipotent, and narcissistic defences. However, if these are addressed without an empathic understanding of ADHD, such interpretative interventions can be experienced as shaming and persecutory and further undermining of self-esteem.

These points can be illustrated through consideration of my (composite) patient, Andrew.

Andrew is a man in his twenties, referred via his GP, and apparently with the encouragement of his parents. He talks quickly, speaking of a variety of frustrations in his life. In the first session, he tells me of feeling unappreciated by his boss (he works in IT), of financial worries, of problems with his girlfriend, and of criticism by his mother and father. He alludes to harsh treatment from his parents during his childhood and of feeling that all he has heard from them is criticism—"whatever I do it is never good enough". It is difficult to find a clear focus for his distress, other than a general sense of frustration, agitation, anger, and depression and other negative emotions, and of feeling disappointed in others. Andrew does not locate his difficulties in himself, but in his environment. There is always someone else to blame. When I point out this pattern, he engages in further rapid talk of why this is the case. He says it is his mother's fault—she did not understand him when he was young, and did not help him discipline himself and learn to pursue goals. Apparently, this is why he has not so far progressed in his career. He complains that his parents were often violent towards him. Moreover, he says he was bullied and brutalised at school, by both teachers and other children. It seems he was always getting into fights as a result of being "picked on" by his peers.

It is an NHS setting. Andrew tells me that his parents, with whom he currently lives after falling out with his girlfriend, would like to join us for his next meeting with me (our second meeting). Since Andrew thinks this is important, I agree. On the basis of his account, I expect to encounter somewhat intimidating, possibly even thuggish, characters who might aim to spend the time bamboozling Andrew and me with their point of view. To my surprise, I find two rather mild and gentle, softly spoken, middle-aged and clearly middle-class parents. They are polite, both to me and to Andrew, allowing him to express his point of view, while also keen to describe their own experience. It emerges that they feel dominated and controlled by Andrew. Apparently, he has always been prone to rages and tantrums. He expects them to take care of many aspects of his daily life, such as getting him up in the morning, feeding him, helping him organise his daily schedule. They describe how he creates damage in the home, sometimes as a result of smashing objects or punching walls in rage, and sometimes as a result of his clumsiness. On several occasions he has hit each of his parents. They are clearly intimidated by him and fearful of his tantrums. As a result of the relentless stress created by Andrew's behaviour, they have at times contemplated divorce.

During the subsequent therapy sessions, Andrew continues with his "centrifugal" discourse, like a spinning vortex continually expelling his objects of irritation. His distress and dissatisfaction is always someone else's fault. It remains difficult to focus on any particular matter or to find an opening in his constant stream of words. He is often engaged in some complex grievance against a person or institution that he believes has treated him unfairly. If his self-aggrandising perception is challenged, he becomes agitated, resulting in an intensified stream of angry words. He complains about family, his girlfriend, his neighbours, his boss and co-workers, and the government. Soon he starts to complain about me. I am not helping him— he needs medication, he needs advice, he needs some other form of therapy, etc.

Sometimes Andrew's excited and distracted states have a quality of mania, perhaps partly functioning to avoid more depressive states of mind. For example, on one occasion he spoke in a lively manner of his aggressive interactions with colleagues at work, only mentioning almost in passing at the end of the session that a friend had died a few days previously in a road traffic accident.

Primitive defences

The psychoanalyst within me notes Andrew's impulsivity and his impaired affect control. He appears to act and speak without pausing to think. His discourse is not communicative but has the quality of a stream of Bion's (1962) "beta elements", discharging tension but not for use in the service of thinking or of resolving problems. Primitive rage surges through his experience and perception of his life and the world and equally primitive defences are pervasive. He splits and projects with ferocious energy and uses manic defences. At one moment, this person is to blame, at another moment, this other person is the culprit—but most of the time it is never his fault. There are periods when, by contrast, everything is his fault, and his discourse is a sadomasochistic rampage against himself. I can see much of Andrew that corresponds diagnostically to the description of a borderline personality disorder. If I follow these forms of psychoanalytic understanding, focused on his primitive defences, narcissism, and destructiveness, I would be led to make interpretations that he might experience as criticism, further undermining his fragile self-esteem.

Helpless struggle with uncontained affect,
and lack of a sense of agency

The clinician within me, with a more empathic understanding of ADHD, sees Andrew somewhat differently. I see his desperate helpless struggles with his unregulated affect—the surges of emotion that overwhelm him. I recognise his inner passivity and lack of real sense of agency as the torrent of words and emotions pour through him and out of him. It is as if he is not the active agent of his own thoughts, emotions, and behaviours, but merely a passive and helpless onlooker of these events. He is both hyper-alert, highly sensitive to negative or critical responses from others, and, at the same time, drifting through his life with only partial awareness of the effect on others of his behaviour and emotional states. It is very difficult for him to decentre from his own immediate experience and appreciate the other person's experience and point of view. He is a *prisoner of his own perspective*. His brain is constantly searching for something (he feels something is missing but he does not know what), so that he feels restless, both agitated and bored, yet overwhelmed with the complexity of the everyday tasks of life. He is in a constant state of dysregulation, an id in search of an ego, desperately wanting the environment of other people to supply the missing stimulation, organisation, and direction. There is a quality of continual "unpleasure" in Andrew's experience: more than just an *absence* of pleasure, for him life and the world are pervasively aversive and irritating. This chronic low mood and deficit in pleasure makes life miserable and rewards are elusive. Andrew seeks stimulation, pleasure, and even pain is felt to be better than the dull grinding irritation and absence of desire that pervades his everyday life.

Blaming others

It is a natural (albeit infantile) tendency for people to attribute their internal state to external circumstances, to assume that the inner emotional state is a response to something external, and, thus, to "blame" that external factor or person. People with ADHD do this even more so than others. Not only does this add to the sense of passivity, it also contributes further to the acrimony of interactions with others. Thus, Andrew tends frequently to be angry with other people. He is always blaming someone for something. His perceptions and accounts of his interactions and experiences with others are honestly held, yet much of the time contain distortions, to a much greater extent than the ordinary way in which any person's perception will be in part subjective and idiosyncratic. Andrew always tends to see other people, whether these be family members, his girlfriend, or his co-workers, as the active agent and cause of his discomfort. Moreover, he *thinks with his emotions*—again, even more so than other people do. If his emotions are of anger, then he takes this emotion as the primary reality and confabulates reasons to justify this: for example, by accusing an other person of displaying characteristics or behaviour that merit his anger. However, Andrew does not really experience himself as an agent of his own thoughts. For him, thoughts and emotions are mental events that just "happen" in his mind and, thus, he feels a passive victim of these, too. They are almost always, to use Bion's (1962) phrase, "thoughts without a thinker". Sometimes these events, the *internal weather*, become *storms of affect*. Once Andrew has become angry, it is very difficult for him to become calm, and once a certain threshold of anger has been breached, it is near impossible for him to refrain from discharging his affect in some kind of aggressive act, which would almost certainly involve shouting, but might also escalate to hitting someone or smashing objects. On more than one occasion, Andrew has engaged in violent demolition of furniture flat packs he was trying to assemble, captivated by the illusion that the objects were deliberately and actively intending to humiliate him by their frustration of his efforts (to put them together without reading the instructions). He then felt himself to be a victim of the turbulent storm he had just experienced. Andrew cannot tell me any of this. It is not repressed unconscious content, but aspects of his functioning that are simply beyond his capacity to grasp. He cannot easily decentre, reflect, and use thinking as a means of exploring possibilities and logical processes of reasoning, or as a form of "trial action".

Because Andrew experiences himself as a passive victim of his own emotions, he attributes these to other people. Thus, he feels his anger is because another person is "annoying". When he is driven (by his inner rage) to acts of violence, such as attacking objects, occasionally himself, or (rarely) his girlfriend, he can say, with subjectively experienced truth, "You made me do it!"

Inaccurate perceptions and memories

Andrew's account (as narrated both to himself and others) of events and circumstances in the world is inaccurate, albeit honestly believed by him. Initially, this was not apparent to me, since I had access only to his version. However, when I had the meeting with his parents, they gave their shared version of events that contained striking differences from Andrew's. For example, Andrew spoke of an instance in which his father had criticised him and tried to throw him out of the house in the middle of the night. Without context, this appeared as an instance of a rejecting and brutal father, relating with anger and a lack of care for his son's safety and welfare. His parents explained that Andrew was in the habit of leaving the house with the door unlocked and/or ground floor windows open. He had done this several times, causing much anxiety for the parents since there had been a number of burglaries in the area recently. When his father tried to discuss it with him, Andrew reacted defensively, accusing his parents of only caring about material possessions; the argument escalated and Andrew then thumped a door in his rage, causing damage. In response, his father had said Andrew's behaviour was intolerable and that if he was going to continue in this manner he should leave. Thus, it became apparent that Andrew had left out important aspects of the context of the incident he described, and that his own perception and understanding was seriously skewed as a result. Over time, I also became aware of instances in which Andrew would refer to something he believed I had said in a previous session, but his apparent quotation would bear little resemblance to anything I believed I had actually said, or to anything I could imagine ever saying. Gradually, it would become clearer that Andrew had taken something I had said in one context, with a particular intended meaning, and had given it an entirely different internal context and meaning. The original message had been scrambled. For example, on one occasion he referred to my having said he should report his mother to social services. My inner reaction was that I had said no such thing! It turned out he was alluding, in a distorted way, to comments I had made relating to his mother's stated worry during his childhood that social services would take him into care because he was so out of control.

Broadly, there are three reasons for Andrew's impaired perception and memory of events. First, his inattention, or *scattered attention*, means the original information is not taken in accurately and coherently. Second, his internal representations of events are incoherent and disorganised. Third (and this is a very important and damaging step), he fills in the gaps and imposes a confabulated version and meaning, one that is more favourable to his own self-image. This is analogous to the way in which a dementing person, who is suffering memory impairment, may cover the cognitive lacunae with spurious but superficially plausible accounts of events, circumstances, and motivations, in order to present to self and others a coherent and continuous narrative of their life and experience.

Memory is always somewhat unreliable, open to influence by a variety of factors, as highlighted in the debates concerning "recovered memory" and "false memory" some years ago (Mollon, 2001), and inaccuracies arising from deficits in "source monitoring" (knowing the source of an idea) can play a significant role. However, these influences upon experienced memory can be particularly strong among those with ADD/ADHD. One young woman, whose ADD was combined with a particularly honest introspection, told me of how disconcerting it was for her to realise that not only is her memory of events in her life unreliable, but she sometimes experiences *other people's memories*. She explained that, in conversation with a friend, she might refer to some event or experience in her own life, but then be told by her friend that the experience in question was not hers but her friend's experience and memory. Prior to this being pointed out, she would, at the time, have believed it to have been her own experience. Similar processes of distortion, or "misfiling" of experience, appeared to occur in relation to things she read in books or saw in films. The quality of subjective certainty regarding an experienced memory is no indication of its actual veracity. People with ADHD can feel, and appear, very certain of the truth of their perception or memory, but this may be seriously distorted through omissions of context and detail, the scrambled information then being reworked to create a (spurious) narrative that is favourable to the person's self-image or public image. Again, this is not a simple matter of aspects of memories being "repressed" or otherwise avoided. The subtle deficits in attention and information processing render memory particularly unreliable for the person with ADHD—but he or she does not consciously know this.

Disintegration anxiety

Although Andrew gives the appearance of being excessively angry, argumentative, and demanding, he is, like most people with ADHD, very anxious much of the time. His anxiety is not always obvious, particularly since he tries to conceal it from others. Moreover, it is such a constant feature of his experience that he scarcely recognises it is there, like a continuous background noise. Eventually, he does disclose that very many ordinary situations make him anxious, even just walking down the road. More or less every situation where Andrew has to interact with others causes him anxiety, and when he is not interacting with others he worries about the many everyday tasks he has to accomplish. Continual anxiety had been a daily feature of his schooldays and now this was replicated in his life at work. The anxiety seems to be a response to the sense of continual fragmentation of experience that is inherent in ADHD and links to Kohut's often stated observation that *disintegration anxiety*, the threat of fragmentation, is the deepest anxiety man can experience. Andrew's defensive alternative to anxiety is to switch off, to be lost in daydreams, or in a sensation-based autistic state.

Selfobject deficits and narcissistic rage

Andrew can appear intensely demanding and controlling, requiring continual attention from the significant people in his life, especially his mother and his girlfriend. This need can be seen in terms of Kohut's (1971, 1977, 1981) concept of "selfobject", the functions of empathy, soothing, and regulation provided by the mother and other significant others that are needed to maintain a coherent state of self. While these selfobject functions are important for every human being, Andrew's need is particularly intense and urgent because of the inherently fragmented state of his inner experience. The outwardly apparent attentional disorder mirrors an internal scattering of experience, a fragmentation that leaves him constantly on the edge of chaos. It is this that gives rise to his chronic background anxiety that frequently threatens to escalate into storms of panic and rage, particularly when the selfobject soothing is not there or is threatened with withdrawal, and the rage further fuels his sense of chaos and disintegration and the desperation of his search for an external source of soothing and regulation. Like others with ADHD, Andrew can be viewed as suffering from a *selfobject deficit condition*, and his *narcissistic rage* (Kohut, 1977) and his demanding and controlling behaviours are driven by disintegration anxiety and the threat of disintegration anxiety.

Andrew's anxiety also drives his need for certainty and order. Disrupted expectations threaten to throw his subjective world into chaos. Against this threat he becomes more rigid and intolerant of change, and less able to accept others as having their own separate nature and "centre of initiative". The more anxious he is, the more egocentric he appears, since his own survival as a coherent self is at stake. Threats of abandonment, and fears of abandonment, evoke rage, not just because of the fear of loss of a significant other, but, more crucially, because of the loss of the structure- and cohesion-supporting psychological selfobject functions provided by the other. When escalating anxiety is in the ascendant, Andrew appears particularly self-centred, narcissistic, and volatile.

Relentless bombardment with words

My experience of being with Andrew in the consulting room is sometimes oppressive. His stream of words of complaint is relentless, like a continual bombardment by some kind of acoustic weapon of torture. Everything is wrong for him. Any attempt to challenge his point of view, or his reasoning, or his inferences, seems to provoke him to intensify his onslaught. The content of his discourse does not engage me. It all blends into a homogenised soup of dreary and dull fury. I find that Andrew responds best if I can tune into the emotion behind his agitation, such as his anxiety at feeling out of control, or the way he feels exploited (by his girlfriend or at work), or hurt by a lack of appreciation of his good intentions, or not heard, or in some way *invalidated*. If I manage to find a few succinct words that empathically capture his distress, he becomes calm, thus indicating his struggles with a selfobject deficit condition that is soothed by empathy. I find it is important not to interrupt Andrew too soon, to allow him time to discharge his immediate tension through talking, and for him to indicate his main concerns at that moment. If I speak too soon, he feels I am cutting him off and invalidating him and, at such times, he feels

I have become another "enemy" whom he has to control and ward off at the same time as needing my help. Andrew clearly appears to value, and benefit from, my non-judgemental attention to him as I empathise with his struggles. When he feels I understand him and accept him, it is easier for him to hear my careful comments that might be at odds with his own perceptions, such as when I draw attention to how his behaviour might be experienced by others.

Calming interventions

In addition to seeming calmed and supported by my empathic listening and gentle enquiry into details of his experience, Andrew benefits from various tasks and interventions in the field of "energy psychology", designed to balance left and right hemispheric functioning, calm his brain, body, and energy system, and target particular emotional experiences for desensitisation. Such exercises may involve holding particular postures briefly, breathing procedures, stimulating acupressure and chakra points, and use of imagery. These are gentle and non-distressing. Like most people who are agitated and disorganised, Andrew benefits from the modified collarbone breathing exercise (Appendix III). Discussion and clarification of his goals and life tasks, and drawing up priorities of these, are a further crucial part of the required work, countering Andrew's tendency to be lost in the immediate overwhelming complexity of events, circumstances, and demands.

Thus, the three broad areas of helpful interventions with Andrew are:

- empathic listening and other provisions of selfobject functions that help calm, soothe, and organise his experience, give words to his emotions and states of mind, and enable him more easily to be in touch with painful or depressive experiences and affects when these are potentially present;
- ego-supportive clarification of life tasks, managing his inner needs, desires, ambitions, goals, morals, and ideals against the demands, limitations, and possibilities of the external world. This work also includes helping Andrew consider ways in which his perceptions and recollections of events and situations might be impaired;

- use of energy psychology methods to balance, calm, and desensitise his mind–brain–body system.

My work with Andrew is informed particularly by Kohut's psychoanalytic self psychology, with the emphasis upon understanding the role of deficit, rather than by other psychoanalytic approaches (in the British Kleinian tradition) that emphasise inherent conflict and destructiveness. I see him, and others with ADHD, as suffering from a selfobject deficit condition, with multiple ramifications, interactions, and feedback loops that elicit adverse responses from his interpersonal environment. Depending on one's bias, it is possible to view him as suffering from a neuro-biologically based brain disorder, or a chronic traumatic stress and anxiety condition derived from adverse experiences within his family, school, and other interpersonal environments. Of course, it is both these, as they mutually reinforce each other.

The Freudian perspective: Freud's Project

Freud's original perspective—beginning with in his *Project* (1950a [1895]) and elaborated through his subsequent writings—provides a helpful framework. His *Project* contains many of the basics of his later theorising, and explores in detail the fundamentals of how a human biological entity develops the capacity for constructive engagement with external reality. For this, there must develop an ability to distinguish reality-perception from hallucination, to delay or inhibit discharge in motor action, to make use of memory, and to engage in a process of thought in order to arrive at solutions to the problems encountered in satisfying inner needs and avoiding pain (or "unpleasure"). The unimpeded flow of energy (which he calls Q) follows the *primary process*, resulting in hallucination or the experience of "unpleasure". An organisation of neurons develop which is called the "ego", whose fundamental function is to inhibit motor discharge until there is a correct alignment of desire with reality and there is no danger of unpleasure—this is called the *secondary process*. This process of inhibition of discharge is closely linked to the development of thought, the use of small amounts of Q as a form of trial action. The capacity for attention to perception is also a crucial component of this process, since it is this that enables the ego to discover what perceptions coincide with the fulfilment of a wish or satisfaction of a need:

> The education and development of this original ego takes place in a repetitive state of craving, in expectation. It (the ego) learns first that it must not cathect the motor images, so that discharge results, until certain conditions have been fulfilled from the direction of the perception. It learns further that it must not cathect the wishful idea beyond a certain amount since otherwise it would deceive itself in a hallucinatory manner. If, however, it respects these two barriers and directs its attention to the new perceptions, it has a prospect of attaining the satisfaction it is seeking. (1950a[1895], p. 369)

The functioning of this ego depends upon a group of "nuclear neurones" retaining a degree of constant cathexis—that is, retaining a quantity of Q. In modern brain models, we might think of this as consisting of higher parts of the brain being sufficiently activated or aroused.

Like others with ADHD, Andrew's brain tends towards the primary process. He will act without thinking and then experience pain and rage when his actions result in frustration or "unpleasure". His responses to his inner needs and stimulations from outside often bypass processes of thought. He does not easily delay immediate satisfaction for the sake of later reward or avoidance of pain. His attentional processes are impaired, so that his grasp of the details and overall context of external reality is filled with lacunae. Often, his brain state is somewhat akin to that of a dream, and he might sometimes be confused about reality and about whether he has carried out an action or has simply thought of doing so. It is as if his brain is not fully awake.

In his final account, *An Outline of Psycho-Analysis* (1940a), Freud formulated the analytic task in a way that lends itself to a wide range of activities, depending upon the needs of the person. The ego needs support, in its struggle with the inner instinctual demands and drives, the requirements of the inner morals and values, as it endeavours to engage with the reality of the external world:

> The ego is weakened by the internal conflict and we must go to its help. The position is like that in a civil war which has to be decided by the assistance of an ally from outside. The analytic physician and

the patient's weakened ego, basing themselves on the real external world, have to band themselves together into a party against the enemies, the instinctual demands of the id and conscientious demands of the super-ego. We form a pact with each other. The sick ego promises us the most complete candour – promises to put at our disposal all the material which its self-perception yields it; we assure the patient of the strictest discretion and place at his service our experience in interpreting material that has been influenced by the unconscious. Our knowledge is to make up for his ignorance and to give his ego back its mastery over the lost provinces of his mental life. This pact constitutes the analytic situation. (1940a, p. 173)

Andrew has needed a lot of help in supporting his efforts to interpose thought between impulse and action, in assessing more fully the information available to his perception, and in general strengthening the role of the *secondary process* in his mind and brain. He did try stimulant medication, prescribed by his psychiatrist, and this did have a positive effect. The stimulating effect helped his brain to "wake up" and strengthened his ego; in terms of Freud's project, this could be seen as increasing the "cathexis in the ego-nucleus".[7] Unfortunately, Andrew did not like some of the unwanted effects of the stimulant medication, such as his worsening state of irritation as it wore off at the end of the day, and so, after discussion with his psychiatrist, he decided to discontinue this.

Autistic spectrum aspects

Like many people with ADHD, Andrew also displays autistic spectrum features (Fein et al., 2005; Reiersen et al., 2007; Rommelse et al., 2010; Roy et al., 2013; St Pourcain et al., 2011; Tani et al., 2006; van der Meer et al., 2012). These tend to blend into the ADHD traits, but can, to some extent, be disentangled. Andrew is very intolerant of change in routines, particularly if they are unexpected. He can appear perturbed by a change in his appointment time at the NHS clinic, or by a change of room, or by anything that strikes him as different or unusual in my appearance. At home, he has always apparently displayed a tendency to explode in a tantrum if any of his belongings were moved or if the visual appearance of his room changed. In the workplace, he is disturbed by extraneous sounds, and the conversations and body movements of his colleagues. His capacity for empathy with others is limited—in fact, other people frequently puzzle him, and he often does not understand jokes. When given instructions, requests, or advice at work, he has a tendency to take the meaning overly literally and precisely. For example, a new colleague asked Andrew if he could show him around the office building. Andrew obliged, by walking with the new colleague around the building, pointing to different features of its physical structure, but without engaging in any of the friendly and informative conversation and enquiry that would normally be expected in such an interaction.

From a certain psychoanalytic perspective, Andrew could be viewed as displaying fantasies of omnipotent control, attempting to impose complete order over the world. It could appear that unconsciously he views his significant environment, of both people and the material world, as extensions of his own body. His fantasy of projective identification with others and with the physical environment is catastrophically disrupted when the world does not respond as expected or in accord with his will. He is intolerant of the existence of others as separate and independent centres of initiative. Thus, Andrew could be seen as stuck in a Kleinian paranoid-schizoid level of development dominated by omnipotent phantasies of projective identification and other primitive defences.

The threat of disintegration anxiety and the deficit in selfobject functions

From a more empathic perspective, I see Andrew struggling with high levels of anxiety, as if he feels always on the edge of chaos and disintegration. His efforts to ward off "disintegration anxiety" lead him to try to maintain some order in his subjective world by rendering his environment predictable and unchanging. His deficit in processing social information means he cannot make use of normal selfobject functions (of empathic soothing) provided originally by his mother and later by others, and so he has to resort to autistic strategies of seeking order and predictability in order to reduce his anxiety. Attwood (2006), in his comprehensive account of Asperger's syndrome, notes that many of his patients have said they cannot think of a time when they have not felt anxious and that "A means of avoiding anxiety-provoking situations is to develop the kind of personality that is unfortunately perceived as controlling or oppositional" (p. 137). ADHD and Asperger's are both (often overlapping) conditions in which the person finds the ordinary social world traumatically difficult to manage, perplexing, and overwhelming. A person with predominantly ADHD traits will tend to use other people as *enforced selfobjects*, trying to *force* them to provide what is missing for the regulation of his or her mind–brain–body system, while the person with predominantly Asperger traits will tend to withdraw from other people, and turn to the non-human world for soothing, as a means of managing anxiety. Many people show a combination of ADHD and autistic spectrum traits. In both conditions, there is a defective "stimulus barrier", whereby, in terms of Freud's *Project*, there is too much stimulation (creating pain or "unpleasure") entering the system from the outside. Andrew is overwhelmed by exogenous sensory stimulation, while suffering insufficient endogenous arousal. Like many who suffer with this constellation, Andrew experiences both too much and too little stimulation concurrently. He does seek stimulation *actively*, for his underaroused and underpleasured brain, but this is experienced differently from the highly aversive *passive* impingement of extraneous stimuli.

Internal brain arousal is needed to deal with external stimulation

Freud's *Project* (on pp. 296–297) gives some early hints of this balance between the tendency to reduce or avoid stimulation and the need to maintain sufficient stimulation for a well-functioning brain. He draws an analogy with protoplasm as a primitive prototype of a nervous system, whereby stimulation of its irritable surface results in a "muscular" movement, so the Q acquired by the stimulation is then discharged by the movement, with the result that the level of Q in the system is minimised. However, with more complex organisms, the nervous system also receives *endogenous* stimulation from the bodily needs of hunger, respiration, and sexuality. Such internally derived stimulations can only cease when appropriate actions have been performed in relation to the external world, requiring effort and the maintenance of a necessary level of internal arousal for the work to be done. For the person with ADHD and autistic spectrum traits, a sufficient level of internal brain arousal is necessary (but is often deficient) in order to deal with the impingement of stimuli from outside as well as addressing endogenous needs. It is a matter of common introspective observation that when we feel fully awake and alert, it is more easy to focus and concentrate and we are less irritable, but when tired or not fully awake, we might be much more irritable and disturbed by intrusive sounds and other stimuli. Indeed, some adults with ADHD find that their brain function improves significantly with caffeine, in coffee, for example, and an animal study supports this (Prediger, 2005).

Summary and conclusions

People with ADHD may display marked features of primitive destructiveness and primitive defences. These need to be addressed with care and empathy in order to avoid shaming the client and injuring his or her self-esteem further. An empathic perspective, that recognises the person's struggle with a sub-optimum brain state and impaired ego functions, can lead to a more supportive and calming therapeutic stance. Freud's fundamental theorising concerning the functions of the ego provide a helpful framework for supporting and encouraging ego development. Inadequate ego functioning means that the memories and narratives reported by people with ADHD should be regarded with caution, since aspects of the wider context might be omitted. Many people with ADHD also display autistic spectrum characteristics, associated with high levels of anxiety.

CHAPTER FIVE

What is going on in the brain in ADHD?

A DHD might best be viewed as a *deficit in the overall organisation, regulation, and coherence of consciousness, experience, affect, and behaviour*. Whilst attentional deficits are often a prominent feature, the problems are both broader and deeper than this component alone would suggest.

A selfobject deficit disorder

Placing the emphasis upon a deficit in "organisation, regulation, and coherence" puts the condition into line with the functions of the self-object described by Kohut (1971, 1977, 1981), of soothing, stimulation, and regulation provided by the empathic availability of the carer in childhood, and friends and family throughout life. The merging of the word "self" with that of "object" (meaning "other") denotes how these empathy-based functions provided by the other form part of the regulatory functioning of the self. Within a modern attachment neuroscience framework, this can also be viewed in terms of the *social construction and regulation of the brain,* rooted in early attachment—the "dyadic regulation of affect" (Sroufe, 1996). From this kind of perspective, it becomes easier to see ADHD as a *selfobject deficit disorder*, and also to see ADHD as a core in various other constellations where disorders of self-regulation are apparent, such as borderline personality disorder. We can also more easily understand that ADHD may have a neurobiological core, but this can be exacerbated by adverse early experience that contributes to dysregulation.

People with ADHD have enhanced selfobject needs for soothing, stimulation, and regulation to be provided by others and become irritable, agitatedly searching for these, when they are absent. Those with autistic spectrum traits also have enhanced selfobject needs, but these people find relationships and interactions with others to be inherently disorganising, much of the time: thus, for them, other people function as *anti-selfobjects* (Mollon, 2001). Instead, they resort to seeking familiar regularities in the inanimate world as a source of soothing and regulation. Many people show both characteristics, thus complicating the confusing and disturbed presentation of people with ADHD.

Dysregulation is exacerbated by anxiety, stress, and insufficient sleep. It is certainly the case that the functioning of people with ADHD and autistic spectrum problems decreases with anxiety, stress, and sleep deprivation.

Although attentional problems are a prominent feature of ADHD, this is just one component of the broader and deeper dysregulation. The pervasive dysregulation is not easily revealed in neuropsychological tests. Thus, Fisher (2013) reports on twenty years of neuropsychological testing of adults, children, and adolescents diagnosed with ADHD, and finds very little that distinguishes people with ADHD other than attentional problems. It seems likely that being given discrete neuropsychological tasks, mostly taking just a few minutes, in a calm environment, does not sufficiently mirror the real life stresses and distractions and competing agendas that constantly bombard the experience of the person with ADHD. On the basis of her neuropsychological testing data, Fisher concludes that many of what are assumed to be ADHD symptoms are actually caused by comorbid anxiety disorders, but this argument seems to miss the possibility that the anxiety which people with ADHD (and also autistic spectrum disorders) undoubtedly experience is itself a component or consequence of the core dysregulation. It might be that anxiety arises from the dysregulation, and from the person's general awareness of not functioning well, but this anxiety then exacerbates the dysregulation, creating a positive feedback loop whereby dysregulation and anxiety mutually reinforce each other.

Dysregulation of emotion, mood, and motivation

Whilst attentional deficits may be the feature of ADHD most observable in psychological testing, the more prominent aspect apparent clinically, and through self-reports and reports from families, is that of dysregulation of emotion and mood; Sobanski and colleagues (2010) found 75% of ADHD children and adults showed significant emotional lability. For many people with ADHD, moods may shift suddenly and dramatically and emotions easily get out of control. Frustrations and disappointments trigger emotional and behavioural states, including aggression (Thapar et al., 2001) that to others might seem wildly out of proportion. For example, men with severe ADHD are sometimes afraid to venture out because of a worry that encounters with other people in shops, in the street, or on a bus, might trigger rage and result in physically attacking a stranger. Smashing objects in the home when feeling frustrated is a common report among those at the more severe end of the ADHD spectrum. Self-harm similarly is frequently reported. People with ADHD often describes states of (sometimes unpleasant) excitement, as well as plunging into states of despair, or intolerable states of boredom and pervasive feelings of dissatisfaction. Another common experience described by people with ADHD is that when they feel angry or agitated, it takes a long time to come out of that state. They are often in a "bad mood", or clinically depressed (Eyestone & Howell, 1994) and at times might feel suicidal (Hinshaw et al., 2012; Impey & Heun, 2012).

Motivational difficulties are another regularly reported feature. The person with ADHD often cannot get started on a task and will procrastinate, or cannot decide what task is a priority, but once started cannot then stop the activity. Trying to undertake a task that is not inherently pleasurable or rewarding is often near impossible, and sometimes the frustrating and paradoxical effect is that the more effort that is expended the less positive the result. Pleasure and incentive are often elusive. Any activity that *is* found to be pleasurable tends to become addictive.

Addictions, including sex addiction

Addiction and substance abuse are commonly associated with ADHD (Charach et al., 2011; Olhmeier et al., 2008; Van Emmerik-van Oort-merssen et al., 2012), as is sex addiction (Blankenship & Laaser, 2004; Hayden, 2006), as well as Internet addiction (Yen et al., 2007). The rates of ADHD among adults misusing substances are five times the rates of ADHD in the general population (Brown, 2013a, p. 154). It seems that people with ADHD turn to alcohol and substances, as well as to addictive and compulsive activities such as eating and sex, broadly for three reasons: (1) as an attempt at self-regulation of mood and arousal; (2) as part of their general seeking of sensation and novelty; (3) as a consequence of a lowered capacity to delay gratification and a tendency to be "captivated" by immediate rewards. The problems of addiction might assume prominence in the minds of psychiatrists and others providing mental health care, eclipsing the perception of the underlying ADHD. Within an NHS service, I found it was not uncommon for people with very clear ADHD characteristics to be told that their problems were essentially due to their use of cannabis (or other drugs), resulting in a suboptimum provision for their real needs.

Impulsivity

People with ADHD are impulsive. This might not be apparent all the time. In some contexts, an individual might be cautious and restrained, but might suddenly act in a careless, thoughtless, and impulse-driven way. For example, a normally polite and restrained person with ADHD might abruptly lose their temper with the boss or a colleague, or might make a sudden purchase later regretted, or make a risky road manoeuvre. Others, at the more severe end of the spectrum, could display impulsive behaviour most of the time. One man who had recently started stimulant medication remarked that he had noticed, for the first time in his life, that he had thought before opening his mouth and speaking.

Family and interpersonal relationships

Interpersonal relationships of people with ADHD are almost always problematic, fraught with tension, conflict, and high levels of negative emotion. Frequently, the ADHD temperament leads people to be argumentative, rigid, and fixed in their stance, and sometimes physically violent. They can also provoke rage reactions, and other intense emotions, in others. Parents of children with ADHD are much more likely to divorce (Wymbs et al., 2008). Adults with ADHD consistently report lowered levels of marital satisfaction (Barkley et al., 2008). A common observation is that some people with ADHD seem to home in on any potential for argument or interpersonal aggravation, and to chew on this like a dog with a bone. Pursuing an argument by following a person from room to room, unwilling to let it go, is frequently reported. It is as if some hidden pleasure or gratification is experienced, perhaps addictively, in the expression or exchange of rage, or in spoiling another person's peace of mind or happiness. If limited to a psychoanalytic perspective, one might construe the problem as one of domination by feelings of envy (Klein, 1975). Amen (2001a) describes a range of strategies that people with ADD use unconsciously to evoke interpersonal conflict.

People with ADHD may at times be markedly egocentric (Nilsen et al., 2013; Yu & Kim, 2009), unable to appreciate the other's point of view or experience, and seemingly unaware of their sometimes devastating emotional impact on others. Their capacity for empathy may be variable.

Deficiencies of executive function and overall regulation

Many components of ADHD may be considered disturbances of executive function, which Brown (2013a) defines as: "the functions of the brain circuits that prioritize, integrate and regulate other cognitive functions" (p. 21), which he also views as the "self-management system of the brain". Brown (p. 22) lists six areas of interrelated executive functions that tend to be chronically impaired in ADHD:

- organising, prioritising, and activating to work;
- focusing, sustaining and shifting attention to tasks;

- regulating alertness, sustaining effort, and processing speed;
- managing frustration and modulating emotions;
- utilising working memory and accessing recall;
- monitoring and self-regulating action.

It is apparent from this list that ADHD can actually affect most areas of mental functioning and associated behaviour, both cognitive and emotional, and that severe ADHD can be very disabling indeed, preventing a person from working, sustaining relationships, behaving within the law, and taking care of basic needs. People with ADHD require assistance from others to support their self-regulation in the manner of external ego functions. The provision of selfobject functions, of empathy and soothing, emphasised by Kohut as crucial in childhood and, to some extent, throughout life, are required to a greater degree by those with ADHD. This is, no doubt, why patients with ADHD often tend to remain in therapy more or less continually for many years, because the underlying dysregulation cannot be resolved (although it can be alleviated). Stimulant medication can assist the brain's regulation and people with ADHD are often drawn towards illegal drugs for the same reason.

The traditional focus on attentional deficits and hyperactivity, and, indeed, the name itself, might have tended to obscure a perception of the wider dysregulation inherent in ADHD. Once this core of dysregulation is recognised, many of the controversies about ADHD fall away, such as whether it is a genuine and discrete condition, whether it is a response to trauma or adverse early events, whether it is just a term for children who are difficult to manage, and whether it is better thought of as a mixed bag of heterogeneous disorders. It is obvious that such a deep and pervasive problem of a deficit in self-regulation will have multiple repercussions and can present as a variety of clinical problems and on a spectrum from mild to severe. The presentation will also vary greatly according to the environmental context, degree of stress and distraction, sufficiency of sleep, and adequacy of nutrition. Benign *vs.* adverse childhood circumstances and reliable empathic availability of carers will have a significant impact in exacerbating or attenuating the developmental expression of the ADHD core.

So, what knowledge and insights into brain function do we have that might throw light on the causes of these disturbances of regulation, affecting emotion, motivation, mood, impulsivity, and attention?

Four brain regions that are dysfunctional in ADHD

> Anatomical imaging studies of individuals with attention deficit/ hyperactivity disorder (ADHD) consistently point to involvement of the frontal lobes, basal ganglia, corpus callosum, and cerebellum. (Giedd et al., 2001, p. 33)

> Anatomical and psychological evidence suggests that ADHD is characterized by reductions in regions of the corpus callosum, frontal lobes, basal ganglia, and cerebellum. (Murias et al., 2007, p. 1798)

An emerging consensus indicates four brain regions that might play a significant role in some forms of ADHD (Giedd et al., 2001; Murias et al., 2007; Nigg, 2006): (1) the prefrontal cortices (these being the thick outer layer of the prefrontal lobes, which are, in turn, the frontal part of the frontal lobes); (2) the basal ganglia (subcortical nuclei at the base of the forebrain, with strong connections to various parts of the brain); (3) the cerebellum (an area at the base of the brain, thought to be involved in fine coordination and timing); (4) the corpus callosum (the long area of white matter fibres connecting left and right hemispheres, involved in interhemispheric communication). Reduced volumes have been found in all four of these brain areas (Murias et al., 2007). In addition to these four areas, the dopamine pathways, mediating pleasure and reward, are implicated (Volkow et al., 2011), as well as functional connectivity between different brain regions (Konrad & Eickhoff, 2010; Murias et al., 2007).

Frontal lobes

The role of dysfunction in the frontal lobes has long been suspected of playing a key role in ADHD (Benson, 1991). Doyle (2006) summarises the evidence with the succinct conclusion: "The frontal lobes of persons with ADHD behave differently from those of other people" (p. 88). At times, people with ADHD give the impression of functioning like patients with frontal lobe damage, being impulsive, emotionally volatile, easily distracted, and (on occasion) disinhibited. Nigg (2006) comments, "Patients with neural injury to various prefrontal regions exhibit an array of impulsive, unsocialized, emotionally unregulated, and amotivational syndromes, depending on the site of the injury" (p. 55). It is thought that the prefrontal structures are involved in (a) executive functioning (being in conscious charge of one's own behaviour, and directing and coordinating activities towards conscious goals, while avoiding being distracted by irrelevant stimuli and impulses), (b) the organisation of behaviour in relation to time, (c) motivation in terms of working towards rewards that are not immediate, (d) judgement of socially appropriate behaviour, and (e) motor control (Nigg, 2006). The sense of self and self-concept, and "theory of mind" might also be partly a function of the frontal lobes (Stuss, 1991; Stuss et al., 2001), as is the capacity for empathy (Eslinger, 1998). Frontal lobe volume has been found to be smaller in children with ADHD in a number of studies, summarised by Voeller (2004). An MRI study of the brains of a large sample of children aged 10–18 with ADHD, and a comparison group of typically developing children, found significantly slower brain development in the ADHD group, particularly in the lateral prefrontal cortex (Shaw et al., 2007). Rubia and colleagues (1999), using functional magnetic resonance imagery, found that activation of the frontal lobes was lower in boys with ADHD. A crucial finding from the specialist ADD clinics of Daniel Amen, using SPECT scans, is that when a person with ADD tries to concentrate with effort, the frontal lobes shut down even more (Amen, 2001a).

Basal ganglia

The basal ganglia are a group of grey matter neurons, part of the cerebrum, deep in the brain behind the forebrain, connecting to both the thalamus and the cortex. They work with the prefrontal regions to inhibit unwanted behaviours and to keep behaviour on track towards desired goals, thus having an effect on motivation, emotion, and motor control. In addition, they are concerned with "integrating feelings, thoughts and movement . . . [and] setting the body's idling and anxiety levels" (Amen, 2001a, p. 90). Some of the known neurological conditions resulting from basal ganglia dysfunction include Tourette's syndrome, obsessive compulsive disorder, movement disorders, including Parkinson's and Huntington's. The largest part of the basal ganglia is called the striatum, which consists of the caudate nucleus, the putamen and the nucleus accumbens, the latter being part of the limbic area, having a role in motivation. Reduced volumes have been found in areas of the basal ganglia (particularly in the caudate nucleus), as well as differences in shape (Aylward & Reiss, 1996; Nakao et al., 2011; Qiu, 2009; Schrimser, 2002). Teicher and colleagues (2000) found abnormal functioning in the basal ganglia of children with ADHD, particularly in the putamen, which is thought to be concerned with the regulation of motor behaviour through fine balance of excitation and inhibition of movement. The Amen Clinics find the basal ganglia tend to be underactive in classic ADD (Amen, 2001a). When this is the case, a person might respond positively to stress, as if woken up by it. By contrast, when the basal ganglia are overactive, the person might suffer with an anxiety disorder such as OCD.

Cerebellum

Alterations in the structure and function of the cerebellum, an area at the base of the brain, under the cerebral hemispheres and just behind the brainstem, have been found in people with ADHD (Ashtari et al., 2005; Castellanos et al., 2001; Mackie et al., 2007; Schneider et al., 2006; Swanson & Castellanos, 2002). Nigg (2006) suggests that the cerebellum is involved in the judgement of time, processing of temporal information, and coordinating behaviour with events and consequences in time. This is in addition to the more familiar role of the cerebellum in relation to coordinated movement. It is a common observation that people with ADHD are frequently late and have a poor sense of time (Yang et al., 2007), as well as tending to be clumsy and uncoordinated.

Corpus callosum

Nigg (2006) suggests it is likely that abnormalities are present in the corpus callosum of people with ADHD, since interhemispheric transfer of information is important for normal functioning, and the corpus callosum might be involved in attentional processes (Banich, 1998). Hynd and colleagues (1991) and Giedd and colleagues (1994) did find reduced corpus collosum volume in children with ADHD, in the rostral area, which relates to the frontal lobe, and other investigators also provide support for this (Roesnner et al., 2004; Rüsch et al., 2007). However, Overmeyer and collegues (2000) found no difference in total volume of the corpus callosum in children with ADHD and a control sample, so, such differences as there are, may relate to specific areas of the corpus callosum.

Parietal lobe

Less commonly cited these days is the "right parietal lobe theory" of ADD (Aman et al., 1998). Fisher (1998) summarises much evidence suggesting this area might play a significant role in ADD without hyperactivity. The parietal lobe is concerned with the reception and transformation of somatic sensory information, combining discrete elements into meaningful wholes located in space. Fisher points out that many ADD symptoms can be seen as deficits in spatial awareness, neglect of certain elements, and a difficulty in grasping the whole picture, whether this whole be words and sentences on a page, the judgement of the space of time required for a task, or a complex social situation. She proposes that ADHD (with hyperactivity) is a frontal lobe disorder, while ADD (without hyperactivity) "is more characterised by inactive right-hemisphere functions, extensive spatial issues (explaining reading and language problems), and deficits related more to deficient parietal information-processing problems . . ." (p. 148). Support for the hypothesis of a role of underfunctioning of the parietal lobe is provided by an fMRI study by Vance and colleagues (2007), although this was found to be present in both children and adolescents with ADHD (not just ADD). On the other hand, Amen (2001a), using SPECT scans, reports *excessive* activity in the parietal lobes in certain subgroups of people with ADD, resulting in hypersensitivity to the environment: "They tend to see too much, feel too much, and sense too much" (p. 149).

Grey and white matter

Although studies have indicated particular brain regions that are implicated in ADHD, others have pointed to more widespread differences in volume of grey matter, the neural material that is dense with nuclei (Nakao et al., 2011; Proal et al., 2011). Development of the total surface area of the cortex is also delayed in children with ADHD (Shaw et al., 2012).

In addition to reductions in grey matter, there are also differences in the amount and distribution of white matter (Bush, 2009; Konrad et al., 2010; Nagel et al., 2011). This white matter is the long myeli-nated nerve fibres that form connections between regions of grey matter (the nerve nuclei and synapses), like long insulated electrical wires. White matter comprises about half the brain's volume. Among its varied functions, white matter is probably involved in coordination of different brain regions and also in speed of thought and processing of information. In a meta-analysis of fifteen studies of children, adol-escents and adults, van Ewijk and colleagues (2012) found that those with ADHD had impaired integrity of white matter, particularly in connective fibres involved in fronto–striatal–cerebeller neurocircuitry.

It is important to note that abnormalities of white matter can also result from early stress and trauma. Using a primate model, studying adolescent rhesus monkeys, Howell and colleagues (2013) found impaired white matter integrity in those monkeys who had suffered maltreatment or neglect by their mothers, particularly in tracts involved in visual processing, emotional regulation, and somatosen-sory and motor integration. The impairment in white matter was also correlated with raised levels of the stress hormone cortisol in infancy. This provides some hints as to how phenomena of ADHD could, in some instances, arise from early trauma and stress.

Interaction of brain regions and the default mode network

Konrad and Eickhoff (2010) have drawn attention to an evolving shift in perspective in brain studies:

> While the assessment of functional segregation in the human brain, i.e., the localization of regionally specific functions, has been the predominant concept in imaging neuroscience for many years, the pathophysiology of neuropsychiatric disorders is now being increas-ingly treated from a systems perspective in which function emerges from an interaction of regionally specialized elements. (p. 205)

In recent years, interest has developed in the function of the "default mode network" (DMN)—the state of coherent brain activity when the mind is not focused on any particular task. The function of this background default level of brain activity is not yet well under-stood, but it might be somewhat analogous to having a car engine ticking over and ready to move immediately the driver is ready. In order to function well, the activity of this default mode network must subside, so that attention can be fully given to a current task or need. A persistence of DMN activity during performance of a task results in impaired functioning, with more errors and slow reaction times (Konrad & Eickhoff, 2010; Weissman et al., 2006). Intrusion of DMN activity has been postulated as one factor of the impaired attentional efficiency and focus shown by people with ADHD (Sonuga-Barke & Castellanos, 2007). This is very consistent with the experience commonly described of having difficulty focusing, of the mind wandering, and of a multiplicity of extraneous thoughts intruding when trying to attend or listen. To use a psychoanalytic analogy, it is rather like having a hyper-free-associative patient in one's mind while trying to focus on a non-free-associative task. This may occur in a certain rhythm, reflecting the cyclical patterning of the DMN, so that the experience of being with a person who has ADD is that he or she might periodically appear psychologically "not there". Inappropriate dominance of the "task negative" components of the DMN have been linked also with tendencies toward depression, rumination, and a dysfunctional internally focused cognitive style (Marchetti et al., 2012). The DMN can have various positive functions, such as self-referential thought, the processing of autobiographical memory, and social cognition (Buckner et al., 2008), as well as creativity (Baird et al., 2012), and may be enhanced with meditation (Jang et al., 2011). It may be underactivated in autistic spectrum conditions (Kennedy et al., 2006) and overactivated in schizophrenic states (Garrity et al., 2007).

There are several brain regions that generate coordinated activity supporting the DMN: precuneus/posterior cingulate cortex (PCC), the medial prefrontal cortex (MPFC) and the medial, lateral, and inferior parietal cortex (Konrad & Eickhoff, 2010; Mazoyer et al., 2001). However, the exact nature of the impairment of this network is unclear. Tian and colleagues (2008) found higher levels of resting activation in people with ADHD, while Castellanos and colleagues (2008) found reduced functional connectivity between different parts of the network. Wang and colleagues (2009) found decreased global efficiency of brain networks in general in those with ADHD. As Konrad and Eickhoff (2010) make clear, the research findings in relation to DMN are quite varied, but it seems likely that DMN dysfunction could arise either in the connectivity and "working together" of the brain regions that support the network, or in the appropriate attenuation of the

DMN activity when focused on a task. Nagano-Saitoa and colleagues (2009) found that deactivation of the DMN is modulated by dopamine, found to be deficient in people with ADHD (Blum et al., 2008).

Functional connectivity density

Tomasi and Volkow (2012) compared the functional connectivity density between 247 children with ADHD and 304 typically developing control children from a public magnetic resonance imaging database (the ADHD 200 Global Competition for diagnostic neuroimaging of ADHD). They found the orbitofrontal cortex (a region involved in attributing meaning and significance to information) had higher connectivity with reward–motivation regions (striatum and anterior cingulate) and lower connectivity with superior parietal cortex (region involved in attention processing). This may mean, putting it simply, that (a) the ADHD brain will lead a person to respond to immediate reward rather than engage in delayed gratification for more valuable later reward, and (b) immediate reward is given preference over capacities for sustaining attention and grasping a wider context. The authors suggest their data supports the idea of ADHD as resting upon a dual deficiency in both attentional processes and motivation.

Costa Diass and colleagues (2013) similarly found that children with ADHD had increased connectivity between the prefrontal cortex and the nucleus accumbens, which is particularly involved with reward. This was associated with greater impulsivity, which the authors linked to the hypothesis that these children had greater difficulty in delaying reward. They link this to a theory proposed by Nigg and Casey (2005) that greater signalling between the nucleus accubens and the prefrontal cortex would lead to increased "approach" behaviour and a deficit in evaluating future consequences of an action.

ADHD and dopamine

The role of dopamine and abnormalities in the reward and motivation system has gained considerable attention in recent years (Blum et al., 2008; Luman et al., 2010; Starka et al., 2011; Tripp & Wickens, 2008, 2009; Volkow et al., 2007, 2011). The fact that stimulant drugs, such as methyphenidate and amphetamine, increase available dopamine levels and are used both as prescription treatments for ADHD and also as street drugs to achieve recreational "highs", suggests the obvious possibility that ADHD might have something to do with low dopamine levels. Dopamine is a neurotransmitter that modulates pleasure, reward, and feelings of well-being. It is also involved in attentional processes, which depend upon dopaminergic pathways. Dopamine cells in the nucleus accumbens are involved in reward, while those pathways leading to the caudate are concerned with attention, and those leading to the prefrontal regions play a role in executive functions. Tripp and Wickens (2008, 2009) present a slightly different model from that of low dopamine, proposing instead that in people with ADHD there is a failure to transfer dopamine cell firing to cues for *anticipation* of reward as well as to the reward itself, so that there is less pleasure in *working towards* a rewarding goal. As a result there is easier extinction of learned behaviour, and the normal reinforcers of behaviour have less effect. Behaviour is controlled by proximal rather than distal cues, resulting in easy distraction and failure of attention. This is called the "dopamine transfer deficit" theory.

Shaywitz and colleagues (1977) found lower levels of dopamine metabolic products in the cerebrospinal fluid of children with ADHD compared to those without ADHD. Reimherr and colleagues (1984) found that in a sample of adults with ADHD, those who responded well to stimulant medication had low levels of CSF metabolites of dopamine, compared to those who did not respond well. However, Doyle (2006) cautions that these studies do not indicate whether the deficiency in dopamine is to do with too little being synthesised in the brain, or too much being metabolised too quickly, or too much transported back into the presynaptic neuron, and he refers to evidence for all three possibilities.

In an important and innovative study, del Campo and colleagues (2013) used a combination of positron emission tomography and magnetic resonance imaging comparing sixteen adults with ADHD with sixteen matched controls without ADHD, on a computerised attentional task, following administration of methylphenidate or placebo, using a within subject, double blind, cross-over design. As expected, the people with ADHD showed significant attentional deficits. They also showed less grey matter in the fronto–striato–cerebellar and limbic networks. There was no difference in the amount of dopamine receptors (D2/D3) between the two groups, and both groups displayed a similar increase in endogenous dopamine after administration of methylphenidate. However, those with particularly poor attention, in both the ADHD and matched control group, showed lower dopamine activity in the left caudate, which has previously been found to be involved in attentional processes (Benke et al., 2003; Schrimsher et al., 2002; Volkow et al., 2007, 2009) and also in the midbrain, and this was brought to normal levels with methylphenidate, irrespective of diagnosis. Methylphenidate improved performance generally in both groups. The authors argue that their findings support a dimensional view of attentional deficits, with a continuum extending from ADHD into the general population. They also draw attention to a hitherto unknown role of midbrain dopamine receptors in the effects of methylphenidate. Rather curiously, they conclude:

> The absence of significant case-control differences in D2/D3 receptor availability (despite the observed relationships between dopamine activity and attention) suggests that dopamine dysregulation per se is unlikely to be the primary cause underlying attention deficit/ hyperactivity disorder pathology in adults. (del Campo et al., p. 3253)

On the contrary, their findings would seem yet further evidence that dopamine dysregulation plays an important role in ADHD, as well as in attentional deficits among the general population. Their data do, however, suggest that the boundaries between ADHD and the general population are not firm.

What does dopamine actually do? Berridge and Robinson (1998) used a study with rats that had been depleted of dopamine in the nucleus accubens (in the basal ganglia), finding that this did not reduce pleasure responses to reward, but reduced the incentive to pursue a reward: "In other words, dopamine systems are necessary for 'wanting' incentives, but not for 'liking' them or for learning new 'likes' and 'dislikes'" (p. 309). It is known that drugs that increase dopamine activity, such as amphetamines and methylphenidate increase "seeking" behaviour but not necessarily expressions of pleasure, whereas opiate drugs such as heroin increase feelings of pleasure but reduce "seeking". Animals in which the ventral tegmental area of the basal ganglia (the largest concentration of dopamine neurons) has been rendered inactive, will actually starve to death if left to their own activity, but will consume food and show signs of pleasure if it is placed in their mouth (Arias-Carrión & Pöppel, 2007). In a recent human study, Treadway and colleagues (2012) found that those individuals who showed more dopamine activity in the left striatum and ventromedial prefrontal cortex were more willing to work harder and longer for a reward, even when the probability of reward was low. By contrast, a willingness to work hard for low reward was less when there was more dopamine activity in another area of the brain, the bilateral insula.

Genetic differences in dopaminergic activity have been found. The dopamine DRDA1 allele is linked to alcoholism and other substance abuse (Bowirrat & Oscar-Berman, 2005). It is associated with fewer D2 receptors, and it is hypothesised that addicts might use drugs to increase dopamine activation of their reduced DR receptors to provide enhanced feelings of reward (Noble, 2000). Richter and colleagues (2013) also found that carriers of the A1 allele showed different motivational and attentional responses to reward. Blum and colleagues (2008) have linked the A1 allele to ADHD and "reward deficiency syndrome", and to impulsive, compulsive, and addictive behaviours in general, although they have emphasised it must be linked to a further subset of genes for the clinical expression of ADHD.

Dopamine is also known to be involved in cognition and attention, particularly in relation to the prefrontal cortex (Cohen et al., 2002; Nieoullon, 2002). The prefrontal cortex is rich in dopamine receptors, particularly in fronto–striatal areas involved in working memory and cognitive control (Cools & D'Esposito, 2011). Back in 1979, Brozoski and colleagues found that monkeys depleted of dopamine in the prefrontal cortex showed a very severe deficit in working memory. However, various studies have found that either too much or too little dopamine activity in the prefrontal cortex leads to cognitive and attentional impairment (Cools & D'Esposito, 2011). It seems there are different optimal levels of dopamine for different cognitive tasks. In their review of a range of studies of both animal and human subjects, Cools and D'Esposito (2011) draw attention to a dynamic balance between cognitive stability and cognitive flexibility, and suggest that high levels of dopamine in the prefrontal cortex might enhance cognitive stability but be detrimental to cognitive flexibility, while high levels in the striatum might enhance flexibility at the expense of stability. Thus it is not a simple matter of "lots of dopamine is good".

Dopamine also plays a role in mood (Diehl & Gershon, 1992; Dunlop & Nemeroff, 2007; Nutt, 2006; Robinson, 2007). People with ADHD tend to be low in mood, grumpy, miserable, and irritable.

Norepinephrine and serotonin

Interest has also grown in the role of another neurotransmitter, norepinephrine (Spencer, 2006). In a review, Prince (2008) summarised evidence that patients with ADHD have depleted levels of both dopamine and norepinephrine (adrenalin). It is known that medications that help with ADHD symptoms, such as both stimulants and tricyclic antidepressants, increase levels or availability of both dopamine and norepinephrine (Doyle, 2006). A genetic study found differences in the epinephrine transporter gene in some people with ADHD and a difference in the transporter gene for dopamine in others, and the action of different medications, affecting dopamine and epinephrine availability, suggest that inattention and distractibility might relate to low levels of norepinephrine, while impulsivity might relate to low levels of dopamine (English et al., 2009). In this same study, alterations in the transporter gene for choline, which is a precursor of another neurotransmitter, acetylcholine, was found in some people with combined hyperactivity and attentional problems, although currently no medication specifically targets this neurotransmitter.

Regarding the interplay of dopamine and epinephrine, it might be considered (crudely) that epinephrine (adrenalin) is needed to power up the brain, enabling it to be attentive and focus on a task, while dopamine is needed to inhibit impulses and keep a person working towards a goal. A notable feature of many people with ADHD is a compulsive or addictive pursuit of stimulating or stressful activities that create adrenalin. These might include dangerous sports, driving fast, attending loud music events, or getting into fights.

A number of studies also relate a third neurotransmitter, serotonin, to features of ADHD, particularly aggression (Clarke et al., 1999; Flory et al., 2007; Halperin et al., 1994; Halmøy et al., 2010; Kruesi et al., 1990). Nikolas and colleagues (2010) note that both abnormally high and abnormally low levels of serotonergic activity have been linked with ADHD symptoms, and they hypothesise that it is serotonin dysregulation that confers vulnerability. These researchers also found that both high and low levels of serotonin were associated with higher levels of self-blame for parental conflict, as well as ADHD symptoms, in a group of adolescents. Serotonin is known to affect both mood and impulse control (Young & Leyton, 2002).

A further point of interest is that the left hemisphere is more dependent on dopamine, while the right is more dependent on norepinephrine and serotonin (Glick et al., 1982; McGilchrist, 2009; Tucker & Williamson, 1984; Wagner et al., 1983). Previc (2009), in his wide-ranging study of dopamine in human evolution, concludes that serotonin and norepinephrine are involved in physically "close in" and emotional activities involving downward gaze and touch, such as feeding a baby, while dopamine is involved in upward gaze, scanning the horizon, and distant view. This distant perspective has evolved to include distance in time, so that dopamine is deeply involved in pursuit of distant goals.

Brain laterality in ADHD

Since it had been noted that damage to the right hemisphere can produce symptoms similar to ADHD (Heilman et al., 1986), there has been speculation that ADHD reflects a dysfunction of the right hemisphere, particularly since attentional research has indicated that the right hemisphere plays a significant role in directing and sustaining attention and in regulating arousal (Stefanatos & Wasserstein, 2001). However, Hale and colleagues (2009, 2010) indicate that this hypothesis had not been well supported. Their findings suggest abnormally *increased* use of the right hemisphere in ADHD, this hemisphere being harnessed for tasks normally undertaken by the left hemisphere, which is underfunctioning, with impaired functional connectivity and interaction *between* the hemispheres. If the right hemisphere is having to do more work than it can cope with, as a result of having to compensate for left hemisphere underperforming, it might function inefficiently, thus contributing to the impression of a right hemisphere dysfunction. Since the left hemisphere depends particularly on dopamine, these findings are consistent with the beneficial effect of dopaminergic stimulant medication, which might boost left hemisphere functioning. A right hemisphere processing bias could explain aspects of the strong association between ADHD and dyslexia, which also displays this RH bias, as well as impaired interhemispheric communication (Hale et al., 2010; Dhar et al., 2010).

Normal brain development produces a well-known asymmetry, whereby there is an increase in the right frontal lobe and the left occipital lobe, as if the brain has been slightly twisted to the right, through a process called torque. This development reverses an opposite twist shown in infancy. It is generally assumed that asymmetry plays an important role in the combined work of the two hemispheres. Shaw and colleagues (2009) have found in their sample that this normal asymmetry fails to occur in those with ADHD. They suggest this links with studies showing abnormal lateralised brain activation in ADHD (Langeleben et al., 2001; Rubia et al., 2005). These studies tend to be viewed as supporting the right hemisphere deficit hypothesis, in contrast to the findings of Hale and colleagues, discussed above. It seems all we can be certain of regarding brain lateralisation, from the overall neurobiology research so far, is that the brains of people with ADHD show atypical features in terms of asymmetry, lateralisation of function, and interhemispheric connectivity.

In using methods of energy psychology (Mollon, 2008), it is possible to gain some impression of brain function through procedures of "therapy localisation", which allows the body to signal areas of dysfunction (although these are not necessarily accurate!). From such enquiries (for what they are worth), I have the impression that sometimes a person with ADHD may be in a state of right hemisphere dominance, and sometimes a state of left hemisphere dominance— although often it does seem to be the left that is underfunctioning. What they cannot do is move easily *between* these modes of functioning, and draw upon both for optimum engagement with a task. The two hemispheres do not cooperate, but exist in a state of competition, like a kind of interhemispheric warfare. It is the communication and cooperation between the hemispheres that is dysfunctional (Hale et al., 2009; Roessner et al., 2004). This creates internally generated frustration, rage, and chronic stress. I find that this condition seems to be helped by exercises that stimulate interhemispheric communication, such as eye movements and other forms of bilateral stimulation (Mollon, 2005).

Emotional lability

Emotional lability is a crucial feature of ADHD and prevalent throughout the lifespan (Barkley, 2010; Barkley & Fischer, 2010; Martell, 2009;

Shaw et al., 2014), although it is often given less emphasis than other cognitive and attentional features and is not part of the core diagnostic *DSM* or *ICD-10* criteria. People with ADHD tend to be more anxious and more angry than others, and are easily frustrated, erupting in temper outbursts or tears. Because the emotional lability tends not to be recognised as a core feature of ADHD, additional "comorbid", or alternative, diagnoses are often given, such as oppositional defiant disorder (ODD), or antisocial personality disorder, or disruptive mood dysregulation disorder, or even bipolar disorder (Kaplan, 2011). Merwood and colleagues (2014) found a strong correlation between emotional lability and ADHD symptoms of hyperactivity–impulsivity and inattention in a large child and adolescent sample of twins, supporting the hypothesis that emotional lability is part of the "core ADHD phenotype".

There is relatively little published research on the neurobiology of emotional lability dysregulation in ADHD, other than the obvious role of deficiencies in the frontal lobes. Brotman and colleagues (2009) found hyperactivity in the left amygdala in youths with ADHD. On the other hand, Posner and colleagues (2011) found enhanced activity in the *right* amygdala in adolescents with ADHD, when presented with emotionally arousing stimuli. They also found greater connectivity between the amygdala and the lateral prefrontal cortex in this group. These effects were normalised when the subjects were given stimulant medication. Some studies implicate lowered activity in the anterior cingulate cortex in both attentional (Bledsoe et al., 2013; Bush et al., 1999) and emotional aspects of ADHD (Stevens et al., 2011), but the latter may be particularly to do with social emotions and empathy (Decety & Jackson, 2004; Jackson et al., 2006). Amen (2001a) reports that *overactivity* in the anterior cingulate gyrus is found in people with over-focused, obsessive, and rigid forms of ADD.

Abnormal brain waves

Several studies have found abnormal brain waves in people with ADHD (Amen & Carmichael, 1997; Chabot et al., 1995; Lubar, 1991; Mann et al., 1991; Mazaheri et al., 2013). People with ADHD tend to have excessive slow waves (delta, slow theta, and sometimes excess alpha) in the frontal executive area, associated with difficulties controlling attention, behaviour, and emotions. Lubar and colleagues

(1995) found a higher theta/beta ratio in those with ADHD, which was *not* modified when methyphenidate was administered. Thus, it is as if people with ADHD tend to be in a dreamy state even while awake.

The work of Dr Daniel Amen

Arguably the most interesting and important work on the neurobiology of ADHD is that of Daniel Amen, outlined most clearly in his popular book *Healing ADD* (Amen, 2001a) and through his website, www.amenclinics.com/. Dr Amen also has a number of publications in peer-reviewed journals, as well as being the author of many books aimed at the general reader. In addition to his Board Certification in Psychiatry and Neurology, he holds a range of further qualifications, including in nuclear medicine. His particular contribution involves the use of SPECT scans (single photon emission computed tomography), which use radioactively tagged compounds, injected in small amounts into the body, which then act as a "beacon of energy", emitting gamma rays that can be tracked to reveal areas of greater and lesser activity (blood flow) as the subject is engaged in mental tasks or is resting (Carmago, 2001; Holman & Devous, 1992). This technology can be used to reveal more clearly and precisely what is going on (or not going on) in the brain of people with a range of psychiatric and neurological conditions and can, thus, be invaluable in diagnosis in relation to ADD, as well as head trauma, mood disorders, strokes, seizures, dementia, and the effects of alcohol and drug abuse (Amen et al., 2008a,b; Amen & Willeumier, 2011). According to Dr Amen, "The brain SPECT studies of today, with their higher resolution, can see into the deeper areas of the brain with far greater clarity and show what CAT scans and MRIs cannot: how the brain actually functions" (Amen, 2001a, p. 48). He makes the point that psychiatrists are the only medical specialists that never look at the organ they treat (2001a,b).

Despite (or because of) Dr Amen's impressive achievements, he appears to be a controversial figure within his profession, as he readily acknowledges and describes in his book (2001a). He recounts how he was told by a SPECT specialist (Dr Thomas Jaeger), in the early 1990s, that he should not use this kind of brain imaging procedures clinically, since they were only suitable for research. It has been argued that SPECT imagery is not part of the normal standard of care for psychiatric and neurological conditions, is very expensive for patients, and potentially dangerous (Adinoff & Denous, 2010; Leuchter, 2009), and that clinical claims might exceed the scientific data (Chancellor & Chatterjee, 2011; Farah & Gillihan, 2012)—all challenges which Dr Amen refutes. ADD specialist Dr Joel T. Nigg, clinical psychologist, does make reference to Amen's work, clearly finding it of interest, but comments, "This work has received only very limited exploration in the published, peer-reviewed scientific literature, and so cannot yet be formally evaluated" (Nigg, 2006, p. 190). As far as I can judge, the only clinics using SPECT scans in the way he describes are those run by Dr Amen, and his methods are not available in the UK, but he does provide an online treatment programme, called "Healing ADD at home in 30 days", based on a questionnaire analysis of the person's type of ADD.

Whatever cautions might be appropriate in relation to Dr Amen's work, his brain imaging findings, and his writings and clinical recommendations, seem to me highly illuminating. I have read many books and papers about ADHD, and have worked with a large number of clients with these problems, and Dr Amen's text for the general reader (2001a) astonished me with its depth of understanding of the nature and manifestations of different forms of ADHD, which seems far beyond that of other accounts. Two of his insights strike me as particularly important: that mental effort causes ADD symptoms to worsen (the frontal lobes shut down even more), and people with ADHD might unconsciously seek out arguments and conflict, and might be addicted to negative thoughts because these all stimulate the brain (see Amen's discussion of "The games ADD people play", Chapter 14 of 2001a).

Dr Amen (2001a) describes six different types of ADD (and an additional one listed later on his website), based on SPECT scan data and how it links with clinical presentation. He takes a scan when the person is in resting mode and another when he or she is concentrating.

1. *Classic ADD.* The SPECT scan shows the resting brain appears normal, but with concentration, there is decreased activity in the underside and lateral prefrontal cortex and in the cerebellum. Primary symptoms of this common form of ADD include being inattentive, easily distracted, disorganised, hyperactive, restless, and impulsive.

Dr Amen recommends: stimulant medication, such as Adderal, Ritalin, Dexedrine, and Cylert, a higher protein diet, intense aerobic exercise, herbal supplements L-tyrosine, EEG biofeedback to enhance beta and suppress theta over the prefrontal area.

2   *Inattentive ADD*. People with this condition show primary ADD symptoms, but also appear unmotivated, dreamy, and "spacy". The SPECT scan is similar to that of classic ADD.

Dr Amen's recommendations are the same as for classic ADD.

3.   *Overfocused ADD*. People with this condition show primary ADD symptoms, but in addition are somewhat obsessive, rigid, and inflexible, over-controlled, argumentative, and oppositional, tend to hold grudges, be fixed on negative thoughts, and need routines. Their SPECT scans tend to show decreased activity in the underside and lateral prefrontal cortex during concentration, but, in addition, there is increased activity in the anterior cingulate cortex both at rest and during concentration. It is common among people with alcohol and substance abuse problems.

Dr Amen recommends: serotonin enhancing antidepressant medication, combined possibly with a stimulant; a lower protein and higher carbohydrate diet; intense aerobic activity; herbal supplements, St John's Wort, 5-HTP, L-tryptophan, Inositol with L-tyrosine; EEG biofeedback to enhance alpha over the anterior cingulate gyrus.

4.   *Temporal lobe ADD*. People with this condition tend to have a short fuse, are prone to temper and rages and dark thoughts, can be somewhat paranoid, misinterpreting comments, sometimes suffering headaches and abdominal pains, might have memory problems and difficulty reading. SPECT scans show decreased activity in the prefrontal cortex with concentration, but also abnormal activity in the temporal lobes (both increases and decreases).

Dr Amen recommends: anticonvulsant mood stabilising medications, a higher protein and lower carbohydrate diet, intense aerobic activity, herbal supplements GABA, ginkgo biloba, phosphatidyl serine, vitamin E, Piracetam, EEG biofeedback to enhance SMR (sensory motor rhythm) and suppress theta over the temporal lobe.

5.   *Limbic ADD*. People with this condition show a more depressive presentation, with sadness, social isolation, low self-esteem, irritability, negativity, poor appetite, and sleep problems. SPECT data

show low prefrontal activity, both at rest and with concentration, but in addition show high deep limbic activity.

Dr Amen recommends: stimulating antidepressants, higher protein and lower carbohydrate diet, intense aerobic exercise, herbal supplements DL-phenalalanine, L-tyrosine, SAMe, EEG biofeedback to enhance beta and suppress theta over the left prefrontal area.

6. *Ring of fire ADD*. People with this condition show primary features of ADD, with moodiness, anger, excessive talking, fast thoughts, oppositional responses, and sensitivity to sound and light. The term "ring of fire" derives from the appearance of an intense ring of overactivity across the cortex, especially in left and right parietal lobes, left and right temporal lobes, and left and right prefrontal cortex. Dr Amen finds that many "really difficult cases" have this pattern (2001a, p. 66). It is made worse by stimulant medication.

    Dr Amen recommends: anticonvulsant medications, as for Type 4 ADD, or atypical antipsychotics (e.g., Risperdal or Zyprexa), higher protein and lower carbohydrate diet, herbal supplements GABA, omega-3 fatty acids, EEG biofeedback to enhance sensory motor rhythm over the parietal and lateral prefrontal areas and high alpha over the anterior cingulate gyrus.

7. *Anxious ADD*. This type was not listed in the 2001a book, but is an additional category listed on Dr Amen's website. People with this condition are anxious, predicting the worst, tending to freeze in test-taking situations, are socially anxious, experience headaches and gastrointestinal symptoms, as well as displaying the common ADD symptoms of distractability, inattention, and disorganisation. The SPECT data show decreased activity in the underside of the prefrontal cortex and cerebellum when concentrating, as well as increased activity in the basal ganglia both at rest and when concentrating.

    Dr Amen has not published recommendations specifically for this group.

His general recommendations for all forms of ADD include:

*   30–45 minutes a day of intense aerobic activity;
*   turning off the television and video games, or limiting these to half an hour a day;

- eliminating caffeine from the diet;
- dietary attention—high protein and low carbohydrate for most types (except overfocused, where he recommends low protein and high carbohydrate);
- high quality fish oil supplement—2000–4000 mg per day for adults;
- avoiding overt expressions of anger with people with ADD—their brains find this stimulating and addictive;
- focused breathing for calming;
- cognitive–behaviour therapy strategies for overcoming automatic negative thoughts;
- ADD coaching, to facilitate clarifying and focusing on goals, and what resources and behaviour are required to reach these goals;
- the use of self-hypnotic programming;
- strategies for going to bed at a reasonable time and getting up and getting going in the morning (including avoiding early morning starts)
- The use of neurofeedback, such as that developed by Dr Joel Lubar and others, to modify abnormal brainwave patterns

What does the neurobiology explain about ADHD?

So, what do these varied neurobiological findings begin to explain regarding the experience, behaviour, and mental functioning of people with ADHD? It seems there are several different types of ADD, with different neurobiological patterns, but there is also much common ground among the variants, particularly in relation to dysfunction in the frontal lobes.

The dysfunctional frontal lobes/prefrontal cortex explain a great deal about ADHD. Diminished capacities for inhibition of impulse and emotion, as well as general impairment of executive function, mean that the person with ADHD is impulsive, acts without thinking at times, cannot restrain or adapt an emotional response or impulse to suit the context, and cannot modulate emotional experience and expression. He or she is captivated by external stimuli, pulled in a multitude of directions without an internally derived goal. Emotions, particularly of anger or catastrophic anxiety, tend to amplify and expand to their maximum. If the ADHD person were a vehicle, it would be capable of high speed, have an oversensitive and difficult to control accelerator pedal, and defective brakes. Like others who are disinhibited, through alcohol or brain injury, people with ADHD can cause great embarrassment and discomfort to others.

Adequately functioning frontal lobes are necessary for "theory of mind"—the capacity to understand the mind of self and other. People with ADHD are often unaware of both their own mind and motivations, and those of others. They often have great difficulty in decentring from their own perspective to understand the other's point of view; they are egocentric and may, at times, lack empathy. Social awareness and emotional intelligence may, at times, be impaired. Their own self-concept, and sense of self and identity are often shaky, and they might have a diminished sense of personal agency, continually blaming others and circumstances for their difficulties. When not agitated, these deficits may subside.

Good frontal lobe activity is essential for executive functioning, the capacity to work towards a goal and to harness and regulate body and brain to this end. People with ADHD have difficulty doing this. They are continually distracted by both external and internal stimuli, so that, instead of the sense of being an agent pursuing goals, the experience is of continually reacting. As a result, the person can feel bombarded, pushed, and pulled, creating an agitation that further undermines their functioning.

The deficit in executive functioning means that people with ADHD have an enhanced need for selfobject support from others, a provision from outside of the functions that are insufficiently established within. Such assistance will often take the form of provision of reminders of appointments and schedules, helping think through priorities, stimulating motivation, but, particularly, talking through emotional distress. While necessary, all of this might be deeply resented by the person with ADHD, provoking angry and punitive outbursts against the one who functions as a selfobject.

Because the frontal lobes in people with ADHD can have higher than normal connectivity with reward centres of the brain, the prospect of immediate reward has greater salience, adding to the tendency to go for immediate gratification at the expense of long-term goals and health. Inadequately functioning frontal lobes create a deficit in evaluating future consequences of actions.

A feature of ADHD that seems particularly frustrating, and almost perverse, is the tendency for the frontal lobes to under-function even more when the person tries to put effort into attending or concentrating. To return to the vehicle analogy, it would be as if pressing the brake pedal or trying to manoeuvre the steering wheel resulted in the car becoming even more out of control and travelling faster.

The under-performing frontal lobes are accompanied by slower than normal brainwaves—a prevalence of theta. It is as if the person is "asleep and dreaming", or in a deep state of meditation while awake, and perhaps required to attend to a task involving attention and goal-directed activity. The ADHD brain is, in certain ways, a "dozy brain", not quite awake, even when seemingly very agitated and aroused.

The dreamy-daydreamy, distracted and "spaced out" appearance of some people with ADHD might be due partly to the intrusion of the "task negative" activity of the default mode network (DMN). When the person is meant to be focusing on a task, the "task negative" activity, associated with free-associative internal processing, should attenuate and the contrasting "task positive" activity should predominate. For a person with an ADHD brain, the "task negative" DMN stays active, keeping them in "daydreaming" mode. Its activity might also be cyclical, so that withdrawal from an external reality focus occurs in a somewhat regular pattern. The experience of others could be that the person with ADHD appears at one moment to be engaged and listening, and then, at some later point, appears psychologically "not there".

The insufficiently active frontal lobes are fed by "underpowered" basal ganglia. These lead to impaired motivation and uncoordinated movement (including poor handwriting). Stress or excitement can enhance functioning by "waking up" the brain. Unfortunately, this often leads a person with ADHD unconsciously to seek out conflict, arguments, and interpersonal drama, and to become addicted to these. This is not so much an unconscious desire, in the psycho-analytic sense, but more of an addictive brain state, the function of which is entirely unknown to the person concerned. For similar reasons, the person may be "addicted" to emotionally negative thoughts because these are more stimulating to the brain than positive thoughts (Amen, 2001a). George and colleagues (1995) found, using PET scans with a group of emotionally healthy women, that transient sadness significantly activated bilateral limbic and paralimbic structures (cingulate, medial prefrontal, and mesial temporal cortex), as well as brainstem, thalamus, and caudate/putamen, whereas happy thoughts did not lead to increased activity in any part of the brain and actually reduced activity in the prefrontal cortex. It is as if the person with ADHD feels more alive when there is drama, danger, or something big to be concerned about. He or she is continually hungry for stimulation. This will clearly play a part in addiction to sexual fantasy and pornography, and these might tend toward the sadomasochistic because the strong component of aggression or violence provides additional brain stimulation. Boredom is very highly aversive to the ADHD brain.

Optimum brain functioning is dependent on being able to draw upon the resources of both hemispheres: the linguistic, "logical", and categorising left hemisphere and the more visual and global mode of the right hemisphere (McGilchrist, 2009). People with ADHD seem to get stuck in one or the other mode, try to use one hemisphere for functions that are best performed by the other, and cannot efficiently engage with the task before them. There is impairment in the taking in and processing of information: language and meaning are not fully integrated. The lack of cooperation and communication between the hemispheres leads to intense frustration and rage, as well as chronic and cumulative stress that can culminate in chronic fatigue. It is like a split brain, containing two inhabitants, like two occupants of a prison cell who refuse to acknowledge or speak to one another, but the dissociation between the hemispheres is functional and anatomical rather than to do with gross brain damage. These states of interhemispheric apartheid seem to be relieved by exercises to facilitate bilateral communication, such as eye movements (as in EMDR) or systemic energy methods such as collarbone breathing and cross tapping, as well as interhemispheric imagery exercises.

The negativity and moodiness of people with ADHD, along with their potential for addiction, is partly mediated by the low levels of dopamine (and, in some cases, serotonin) in crucial parts of the brain. This results in a general "negative outlook", as if nothing is worth doing or working for, with reduced motivation to get out of bed in the morning. There is an irritable seeking after stimulation and arousal, perhaps in the form of coffee and a cigarette to start the day, as well as other addictive activities that provide some immediate reward and provoke release of dopamine. For the ADHD person, ordinary life might lack sufficient reward or stimulation. There is no incentive, or even capacity, to pursue long-term plans, or work towards a distant goal, or to take account of future consequences of present actions or inactions. Abuse of alcohol or other substances, resorted to in an unconscious attempt to counter this problem, could greatly exacerbate the situation, depleting the person of dopamine yet further and leading to an ever more entrenched state of depression. Low levels of available norepinephrine mean the person is easily distracted and cannot focus. Inadequate availability of serotonin might further contribute to low mood, irritability, and negative social interactions. A combined deficit of norepinephrine and serotonin may result in an underpowering of the right hemispheric capacities for empathy and tender connections with others. The overall combined effect of these neurotransmitter deficits might be a person who is highly irritable, unmotivated, moody, lacking in capacities for empathy or affectionate interactions with others, easily distracted, unable to complete tasks or pursue goals, exhausted by unproductive random or compulsive activity (or lying around apathetically), and sometimes prone to aggressive (or even violent) outbursts against others or their own property, in rage-filled frustration at their own limitations. The person might blame others, parents, or circumstances for these problems, often lacking full insight into the contribution of his or her own temperament and brain function.

An awareness that one's perception of the external world of other people is coloured by our own inner emotional and mood state is a significant later achievement. The primary response is to perceive our state of feeling as somehow "caused" by other people or external circumstances. Therefore, the depletion of neurotransmitters (dopamine, serotonin, and norepinephrine) leads the person with ADHD to feel unloved by others—originally by the parents. The lack of neurotransmitters is perceived as a lack of love. In family interviews, I have observed adolescents with ADHD vehemently complaining that the parents do not love or care about them, when it is obvious that the parents have been struggling for years in a deeply loving and caring way—but this is not registered by their child.

As well as being depressed, people with ADHD are often anxious, congruent with the finding of higher levels of activity in the amygdala. It might also be that anxiety itself, although unpleasant, can be addictive since it stimulates the basal ganglia and prefrontal cortex (George et al., 1995). A common observation is that people who are frequently anxious will appear to search for something to be anxious about, as if the state of being without a focus for anxiety is itself anxiety-evoking. The deficit in executive functioning, and the general sense of *chaos* resulting from under-functioning frontal lobes, as well as the disorganisation and resulting crises in the person's external life, may all conspire to fuel anxiety.

The ADHD person's relationship with time is commonly noted to be problematic (Tartakovski, 2014), and lateness might be a chronic difficulty. Time might be felt to be *too much*, resulting in highly aversive boredom, or *too little*. Coordinating inner processes with external time might be a continual challenge. Estimates of time to undertake a task might be wildly inaccurate. Tasks might be endlessly put off, but then, once started on an activity, the person might find it hard to stop. Going to bed at a normal time is often resisted, but then getting up in the morning could also be a struggle. These deficits in relation to time might be due to a combination of dysfunctions in the prefrontal cortex and the cerebellum.

Thus, although the current neurobiological understanding of ADHD is inevitably partial and patchy, there is enough discovered already to throw a great deal of light on the deficits and struggles of people with these problems and the effects on those who have relationships with them. It is also possible to see the potential advantages of the ADHD brain, and how it might have been adaptive in certain evolutionary contexts (Hartmann, 2003). Several features, such as impulsivity, disinhibition, and both inner and outer "chaos" may contribute to creativity. Impulsivity and the search for stimulation might encourage adventure and aggression. Thus, Blum and colleagues note:

> . . . we wish to emphasize there are many examples in which the rest-less, workaholic, always-have-to-be-doing-something, I-need-to-be-my-own-boss, characteristics of ADHD subjects result in very successful lives. Thus, in the right combination, some of the symptoms we have been discussing in a negative light can be used to great advantage. (Blum et al., 2008, p. 901)

Altered brain waves and default mode network might facilitate artistic work, as well as mystical and spiritual experience. In many ways, the ADHD brain might function as an adaptive "irritant" to established beliefs, routines, and the accepted order. The world would be a duller place without ADHD!

CHAPTER SIX

Principles of psychotherapy with ADHD

In pondering the principles of psychotherapy with this client group, it may be helpful first to explore some basic psychoanalytic considerations. Whilst cognitive–behavioural therapy (CBT) is generally assumed to be the most appropriate therapy for people with ADHD (Philipsen, 2012), a broadly psychoanalytically informed approach, taking account of ego functioning more generally (Bellak et al., 1973; Blanck, 1966; Blanck & Blanck, 1974, 1979; Hurry, 1998; Mollon, 1979), has much to offer as an encompassing framework and can take us more deeply into core aspects.

In his final account of psychoanalysis, Freud (1940a) summarised the therapeutic task as one of assisting a weak ego:

> The ego is weakened by the internal conflict and we must go to its help. The position is like that in a civil war which has to be decided by the assistance of an ally from outside. The analytic physician and the patient's weakened ego, basing themselves on the real external world, have to band themselves together into a party against the enemies, the instinctual demands of the id and conscientious demands of the super-ego. (p. 173)

The ego (the organ of adaptation to reality) has "been developed out of the id's cortical layer, which through being adapted to the reception and exclusion of stimuli, is in direct contact with the external world (reality)" and

> its constructive function consists in interpolating, between a demand made by an instinct and the action that satisfied it, the activity of thought which, after taking its bearings in the present and assessing earlier experiences, endeavours by means of experimental actions to calculate the consequences of the course of action proposed. (p. 199)

In its task of self-preservation, the ego "makes use of the sensations of anxiety as a signal to give a warning of dangers that threaten its integrity" (p. 199). The ego must, while awake, make a clear distinction between *memories* that arise in consciousness and *perceptions*, since their coexistence creates the possibility of "a confusion that would lead to a mistaking of reality" and so the ego "guards itself against this possibility by the institution of reality-testing" (p. 199). However, the ego is threatened not only by dangers from outside but also from its own id:

> an excessive strength of instinct can damage the ego in a similar way to an excessive "stimulus" from the external world. It is true that the former cannot destroy it; but it can destroy its characteristic dynamic organisation and change the ego back into a portion of the id. (p. 199)

In all these functions, the ego of the person with ADHD is certainly weakened and, in severe cases, may seem almost non-existent. The drives are too strong, inner regulatory functions are impaired, the superego might be foreclosed or defective, and the relationship with reality is compromised. The crucial *interpolation of thought*, between impulse and action, often fails completely. Perceptions, memories, and imaginings are sometimes confused. The ego fails to make constructive use of signals of anxiety. In its attempts to negotiate between the inner world of impulses and emotions and the external reality of other people, rules, and limits, the ego requires help. We can frame this help to the ego in a variety of ways and it can include pharmacotherapy, psychotherapy, nutrition, modification of the environment, skills training, and brain training.

Some of the discussion below might prompt comparisons with therapies for people with borderline personality disorder. This reflects the close similarity between these conditions and the possibility that

BPD often is developed around a core of ADHD (Matthies & Philip-sen, 2014; Philipsen et al., 2009).

Defusion of the aggressive and libidinal drives

Although deficits in the regulation of drives/energy/impulses are often a prominent feature of ADHD, the abnormal or regressive nature of the energy and impulses is also striking. The person with ADHD is often very destructive. This destructiveness can take varied forms, including attacks on others, smashing objects and possessions, physical attacks on the self (hitting, cutting, overdoses, and other forms of self-harm), psychological attacks on others (e.g., relentless criticism, hurtful and provocative remarks, mockery), psychological attacks on the self (self-critical ruminations, internal shaming remarks), self-damaging and risky behaviours (e.g., drug taking, alcohol abuse, driving recklessly), and self-sabotaging behaviour of various kinds. If we consider these phenomena from the point of view of classical psychoanalytic "dual drive" theory (Freud, 1923b; Hartmann, 1939, 1952; Hartmann et al., 1949), of the libidinal and aggressive drives being fundamentally in conflict from the beginning, but in the course of development becoming fused, with libidinal and loving elements in ascendance, their raw energy "neutralised" for the purpose of higher cortical and cultural functions, it is apparent that the person with ADHD appears to display a failure of drive (or "ener-getic"[8]) development, or has undergone an "energetic regression".[9]

The raw "disintegrative" aggression of the child with ADHD is not of a more "neutralised" kind that can be used to promote growth, independence, and higher ego functions, as described by Solnit (1966) and Hartmann, Kris, and Loewenstein (1949). It is not harnessed to Eros, in the service of life, love, and achievement. Instead, it adds to the child's helplessness, low self-esteem, and general failures of ego functioning.

Edith Jacobson (1965), a significant figure amongst the psycho-analytic ego psychologists of the 1950s and 1960s in the USA, makes the point that ". . . drive fusions appear to result in an absolute preva-lence of libidinal drive energy, while drive defusions bring about libidinal impoverishment and absolute predominance of aggressive drive energy" (p. 16).

The point here is that when a trauma, separation, or developmental insult of some kind brings about a regression and "defusion" of the libidinal and aggressive drives, the resulting behaviour, impulses, and emotions are predominantly aggressive and destructive. It is apparent that highly regressed and pathological states rarely (if ever) seem to result in a preponderance of feelings of love and loving behaviour, but in various forms of destructiveness, either towards the self (self-harm, suicide, psychosomatic states, malevolent hallucinatory voices), or towards others and the external world.

It is notable that children and adults with ADHD (more so than ADD without hyperactivity) seem more than usually inclined to say no, to be uncooperative and defiant. This seems to be another component of the aggression that dominates the ADHD psyche, and reminds us of Freud's comment in his paper on "Negation" (1925h):

> Affirmation – as a substitute for uniting – belongs to Eros; negation – the successor to expulsion – belongs to the instinct of destruction. The general wish to negate, the negativism which is displayed by some psychotics, is probably to be regarded as a sign of a defusion of instincts that has taken place through a withdrawal of the libidinal components. (p. 239)

The person with ADHD appears to be continually inclined to negate, to repudiate, all external prohibitions and limits, and the aggressive drive has gone on the rampage!

The foreclosed superego: the pervasive "No"

The pervasive ADHD "No!" undermines the normal regulatory processes of the establishment of the superego. Freud (1940a) describes this normal developmental process as follows:

> A portion of the external world has, at least partially, been abandoned as an object and has instead, by identification, been taken into the ego and thus become an integral part of the internal world. This new psychical agency continues to carry on the functions which have hitherto been performed by the people (the abandoned objects) in the external world: it observes the ego, gives it orders, judges it and threatens it with punishments, exactly like the parents whose place it

has taken. We call this agency the super-ego and are aware of it in its judicial functions as our conscience. (p. 205)

In normal development, the superego, as an internalised regulatory agency, has an important stabilising effect, enabling greater independence of the individual, since prohibitions that were once provided externally are now established internally. This seems not to happen with (some) people with ADHD. Rather than taking in an external authority, there is a continual expulsion of all prohibitory intrusions, which, in children, can, at times, almost take the form of a prolonged scream of "No!"

Psychotherapist Gabor Maté (1999), viewing the oppositional stance of the ADHD child as an attempt to protect a "fragile threatened sense of self" (p. 188), comments,

> Counterwill has many manifestations. The parent of a child with attention deficit disorder will be familiar with them. . . . Like a psychological immune system, counterwill functions to keep out anything that does not originate within the child himself. (Maté, 1999, p. 186)

However, the streaming evacuation of images and signifiers of prohibition then creates further problems—a terrifying sense of being suspended in space without boundaries or limits. Delinquent acting out, in both children and adults, might be unconscious attempts to seek the reassurance of regulatory external control, even though this is rejected and expelled (Winnicott, 1956).

Disruptions of attachment and deficits in the selfobject functions

A further aspect of such processes is that rage and destructiveness often seem triggered by separations and disruptions of attachment, experiences of rejection and feeling unloved, states of insecurity in relation to a needed person, or failures of empathy. Kohut (1972, 1977) described "narcissistic rage" as a "disintegration product" when the world of others (the "selfobjects") fails to respond with empathy. Aggression is held in check when libidinal connections are secure. In general, people are not filled with rage or aggression when they feel safe and secure in a relationship characterised by empathy. Those who are in love, and feel reciprocally loved, are rarely aggressive or destructive. On the other hand, narcissism (when in opposition to love of others) is almost always destructive. It seems that the factors that trigger regression in a person's psychological development (resulting in "neurosis", according to the classic psychoanalytic theory) are the same ones that release destructive aggression.

The aggressive drive is held in check by the libidinal connection to others, or, to put aspects of this in more modern terms, by secure attachment. Love and care towards and from others tempers the potential for aggression. For the infant and young child, the source of loving energy is the mother, originally the breast. Without this, according to Melanie Klein, the infant is left in terror of the "death instinct" within: "I hold that anxiety arises from the operation of the Death Instinct within the organism, is felt as fear of annihilation (death) and takes the form of fear of persecution" (Klein, 1946, p. 100). Bion (1962) describes how the baby takes in both milk and love at the mother's breast and the mother's capacity to be receptive to the baby's fear and distress, and to respond thoughtfully, helps promote the development of the baby's mind and embryonic thought. Problems can arise either through the mother's incapacity to tolerate her baby's distress—deficiencies in her empathy—or through the baby's fear of its own projected aggression:

> The infant receives milk and other creature comforts from the breast; also love, understanding, solace. Suppose his initiative is obstructed by fear of aggression, his own or another's. If the emotion is strong enough it inhibits the infant's impulse to obtain sustenance. (Bion, 1962, p. 10)

The baby then might fear that the breast or mother contains his or her projected aggression, giving rise to a feeling that both the baby and the mother are full of aggression. This is a situation that is likely to further fuel aggression, resulting in an intensification of the fear. If the mother responds with actual aggression in reality, then this will tend to confirm the baby's phantasy. Following Klein (1957), Bion (1962) postulates that the infant's aggression may be further fuelled by primary envy accompanying feelings of love:

> Love in infant or mother or both increases rather than decreases the obstruction partly because love is inseparable from envy of the object

so loved, partly because it is felt to arouse envy and jealousy in a third object that is excluded. The part played by love may escape notice because envy, rivalry and hate obscure it, although hate would not exist if love were not present. (p. 10)

Fear of the mother and her breast is in conflict with fear of starvation:

Fear of death through starvation of essentials compels resumption of sucking. A split between material and psychical satisfaction develops . . . The need for love, understanding and mental development is now deflected, since it cannot be satisfied, into the search for material comforts. Since the desires for material comforts are reinforced the craving for love remains unsatisfied and turns into overweening and misdirected greed. (p. 10)

Bion is describing a situation where the infant is driven to feed from the breast out of fear of starvation, but is unable to make use of the mother as a source of love, empathy, and solace. Mental development (embryonic mentalization) is shut down, because love gives rise to envy. In its place is substituted an insatiable greed for both food and sensation.

Whilst the Kleinian concept of primary envy, as explored here by Bion, is probably not accepted by the majority of psychoanalysts and its evolutionary adaptive value is far from obvious, it provides a pointer to another factor that might play a role. If the infant is deficient in neurotransmitters, such as dopamine, serotonin, and norepinephrine, he or she will not find feeding, and other interactions with the mother, pleasurable or fully engaging. There will be no inner feeling of well-being. The experience could be perceived as if the mother and her breast are withholding love, a situation later expressed by the adolescent who proclaims (despite evidence to the contrary) "you don't care about me".

In such circumstances of neurobiological deficit, the mother's love will not be sufficient to hold the infant's aggression at bay, because *it will not be perceived and registered*. Abnormal levels of certain neurotransmitters are known to increase both aggression and depression, and even the potential for suicide (Flory et al., 2007; Nikolas et al., 2010; Young & Leyton, 2002). The explosive aggression sometimes shown by both children and adults with ADHD has qualities of discharge, fragmentation, loss of coherence, and despair. Perhaps it is not too much of an exaggeration to say that what is being conveyed in these states is a sense of disintegrating and dying, similar to the dread or terror that Klein and Bion postulated as part of the experience, at times, of the young infant. Rage that is expressive of disintegration of the self (Kohut, 1972, 1977) might be a plea for help with an inchoate sense of dying. It is known that a loving hug—a tangible expression of Eros—will often calm an agitated child (or adult) with ADHD.

It follows that an insecure or disorganised pattern of attachment, rejection by parents or other carers, or early loss, or repeated separations, may all exacerbate the potential for expression of ADHD. Such factors might not *cause* ADHD, but would function as loss of the "self-object" functions, of empathic responsiveness and soothing, required to regulate the child's affect and self-esteem (Kohut, 1971, 1977) and contain the potential for aggression that is always likely to emerge as a "disintegration product" (Kohut, 1972). We might say that destructive aggression emerges when love departs, but the person with ADHD might be unable to perceive or feel love because of their biochemistry. The problem is compounded by the common negative interaction between the child or adolescent with ADHD and the family environment. Hyperactive and aggressive behaviour can be extremely difficult for a family to tolerate and contain, particularly since the child will not respond normally to ordinary sanctions but is likely to react with ever more intensified rage. The family of a child with ADHD becomes increasingly exhausted, angry, and despairing. Not surprisingly, the parents might at times react with counter-aggression, resulting in a spiralling feedback loop of mutual aggression and intensely dysphoric interactions. Such processes contribute further to the child's (and later adult's) sense of being unloved and unlovable. The child (and adult) with ADHD has exceptional needs for soothing, empathic "selfobject" responses from others, but has great difficulty in registering and receiving these and his or her behaviour tends greatly to repel and discourage these needed responses. In this respect, ADHD is created neither by neurobiology alone nor by parental behaviour and family dynamics, but is located in the self-object space between these.

Deficits in ego functions (primary and secondary process), pleasure principle, and reality principle

Along with abnormalities in the qualities of the aggressive drive, its defusion from the libidinal drive, and its unsuitability for sublimation in the service of development and higher mental functions, there are deficits in those aspects of ego functioning to do with management and containment of the drive, and its harnessing in the service of engagement with reality—in the realm of what Freud called the "secondary process" (1911b, 1950a).

Lustman (1966) describes the problems presented by hyperactive children at school as follows:

> The ability to learn, to use a school experience, to relate to a teacher or a toy in a constructive way, depends directly on the progressive ability to sit still (at least for short periods), to attend, to resist distraction (from within and without), and to invest in the task. In short, it depends on those aspects of secondary process function put forth by Freud as delay, detour, binding, control of access to motility, regulation of discharge, and control of attention, all of which we attribute to the ego. It is precisely this developmental defect that makes school so unrewarding for these children and overwhelms their teachers. (p. 191)

The person with ADHD is compromised in his or her ability to make the transition from Freud's "pleasure principle" and the "primary process" to the "reality principle" and "secondary process". Freud (1911b) refers to the "older, primary processes" which are governed by the "pleasure principle", striving towards experience of pleasure and avoidance of "unpleasure". Initial hallucinatory gratification of internal needs (as may still occur during dreams) is confronted by the non-occurrence of the expected satisfaction in reality. As a result,

> the psychical apparatus had to decide to form a conception of the real circumstances in the external world and to endeavour to make a real alteration in them. A new principle of mental functioning was introduced; what was presented in the mind was no longer what was agreeable but what was real, even if it happened to be disagreeable. This setting up of the *reality principle* proved to be a momentous step. (Freud, 1911b, p. 219)

In order to engage with external reality, consciousness has to be adapted with a new function of *attention*, whose task is to search the external world. In addition, Freud argues, "a system of notation was introduced, whose task it was to lay down the results of this periodic activity of consciousness – a part of what we call *memory*" (1911b, pp. 220–221). Motor discharge

> which under the dominance of the pleasure principle, had served as a mean of unburdening the mental apparatus of accretions of stimuli . . . was now employed in the appropriate alteration of reality; it was converted into action. (1911b, p. 221)

In order to impose restraint on action, the process of thinking was developed "which made it possible for the mental apparatus to tolerate an increased tension of stimulus while the process of discharge was postponed . . . essentially an experimental kind of acting" (1911b, p. 221).

Thus, in this succinct account, Freud describes how the psyche shifts from an initial primary pleasure seeking, pain avoiding, and tension discharging mode of operating to one that makes use of attention, memory, and processes of thought as deferred action, in order to engage with external reality in such a way that brings real satisfaction of needs. All these ego functions are compromised in the person with ADHD (Jones & Alison, 2010).

The capacity to postpone gratification and to tolerate frustration, subordinating the pleasure principle to the reality principle so that an eventual, more desirable, satisfaction can be attained, is a crucial and momentous development, underlying all personal and cultural achievement. It is, however, not always easily established and is problematic for those with ADHD. Anna Freud (1966) comments,

> Experience shows that a child's chances of remaining mentally healthy are closely connected with his reaction to the unpleasure which is released whenever drive derivatives remain unsatisfied. Children are very different in this respect, apparently from the outset. Some find any delay or rationing of satisfaction intolerable and protest against it with unhappiness, anger and impatience; they insist on unchanged fulfilment of the original wish and reject all substitute satisfactions and compromises with necessity. Usually this shows first in the feeding situation, but is carried over from there to later stages as a habitual response to any thwarting of desires. In contrast, other children

stand the same amounts of frustration with comparative equanimity or systematically reduce whatever tension they experience by accepting substitute gratifications. . . . Children of the second type either remain undisturbed under the same conditions or find relief in healthy displacement and neutralisation of drive energy, which they direct to aim-inhibited, available goals. There is no doubt that the capacity to sublimate acts as a valuable safeguard to their mental health. (pp. 134–135)

In his paper "Two principles of mental functioning", Freud (1911b) gives three examples of healthy ways of supporting the reality principle, which also, perhaps, provide some clues as to what may help a person with ADHD. He regards the pursuit of *science* as the best means of subordinating the pleasure principle through the explicit examination of reality, whilst, at the same time, science "offers intellectual pleasure during its work and promised practical gains in the end" (pp. 223–224). Similarly, he sees *education* as "an incitement to the conquest of the pleasure principle, and to its replacement by the reality principle", and "To this end it makes use of an offer of love as a reward from the educators" (p. 224). His third example is that of *art*. He views the artist as "a man who turns away from reality because he cannot come to terms with the renunciation of instinctual satisfaction", but, rather than remaining lost in phantasy, the artist "finds his way back to reality . . . by making use of special gifts to mould his phantasies into truths of a new kind that are valued by men as precious reflections of reality" (p. 224).

These capacities for subordinating the pleasure principle to the reality principle depend on the fusion of the libidinal and destructive instincts, with neutralisation of aggression, and "aim-inhibited" sublimation of Eros, to provide "displaceable and neutral energy" (Freud, 1923b, p. 44). This neutralisation and sublimation is "an important function of the ego" (p. 46).

Making use of signal anxiety

Management of anxiety is an important part of engagement with reality. Hartmann (1956) draws attention to the way in which Freud's (1926d) account of "signal anxiety" actually makes use of the pleasure principle in the service of the reality principle. The child learns to make use of a small "dose of unpleasure" to mobilise the pleasure principle to avoid a more overwhelming or catastrophic experience of anxiety. Hartmann comments, "What interests us in this connection is that through a special device, an aspect of the pleasure principle itself (avoidance of unpleasure) is made to serve one of the most essential functions we make use of in our dealings with reality" (p. 250). A striking feature of many children and adults with ADHD is a relative absence of usable signal anxiety and a tendency to progress immediately to catastrophic anxiety.

Object relations

In addition to the obvious attentional problems, deficits in regulation of impulse and affect, and incapacity to delay gratification and tolerate frustration, a marked feature of many children and adults with ADHD is an egocentric attitude towards others and an impairment in the capacity for empathy and recognition of the other as an independent being with his or her own feelings, perspective, and needs. This can be particularly marked in relation to parents, but is usually a feature of most relationships. People with ADHD have a tendency to be fixated at the level of relating to others as a "need satisfying object", for others to be emotionally meaningful only when, and in so far as, they meet a need; others are not seen as having a constant life of their own irrespective of the moods or needs of the one who is relating to them (Anna Freud, 1952). This may also be framed in terms of a failure to reach the "depressive position", described by Klein (1935), wherein the aggressive and libidinal drives are fused, ambivalence is tolerated, and the mother is perceived as having a life separate from the child's needs and phantasies. It may also be formulated as Winnicott's (1945) account of the *ruthless* nature of the baby's relating to the mother, which can also evoke the mother's hatred because the baby is "ruthless, treats her as scum, an unpaid servant, a slave" (Winnicott, 1949, p. 73). Many mothers of adults with ADHD might feel that their offspring continues to treat them in just this way.

It is well known that, for people with ADHD, those tasks and considerations that are not a matter of immediate interest tend to lack salience, as if they have no emotional and motivational meaning or significance. This same pattern appears to be reflected in the ADHD perception of other people, who are "lit up" on the emotional screen when they are needed or are of interest, but at other times fade back into the emotional darkness.

The "need-satisfying" mode of perceiving others—an essentially exploitative stance—may itself be projected, or, at least, becomes a lens through which all interpersonal relations are viewed. As a result, the person with ADHD might expect to be treated exploitatively and will assume that love is conditional upon being what the other person wants. It will contribute to a perception of not being loved by the parents.

Narcissistic disturbance

People with ADHD are often grandiose, their assertions of their talents, skills, and abilities being starkly at odds with their actual achievements. This gap between the potential that they assert and the reality of their often relatively limited accomplishments might be ascribed to the obstructions or failings of parents, workplace colleagues, or other circumstances. For example, one young man whose ADHD was very marked, with severe attentional difficulties, low frustration tolerance, and inability to sustain work towards a goal, declared, in a tone of absolute conviction, that he *knew* he was going to be a millionaire, although, when pressed, he was unable to indicate how this might come about. It is similarly common for people with ADHD to claim unusual levels of intelligence, or to appear to believe that they could successfully turn their attention to more or less any task or line of work if they really wanted to. The gulf between the raw grandiose self and actual reality can be huge and painful and confrontation with this gap can evoke shame and rage (Kohut, 1972).

However, for the person with ADHD, grandiosity may coexist with chronic low self-esteem. Maté comments,

> Guilt, shame, and self-judgement are commonly heard in interviews of adults with attention deficit disorder. While features of many other chronic and troubled psychological states, such as depression, for example, low self-esteem and merciless self-criticism are so much part of the ADD personality that it would be difficult to know where ADD ends and low self-esteem begins. (Maté, 1999, p. 236)

The important contributions of Heinz Kohut (1971, 1977, 1981) help us to understand the vicissitudes of narcissistic development in both its healthy and pathological developments. Kohut describes how grandiosity and the desire to "show off" and be admired and to receive parental interest is a natural feature of childhood. It is closely linked with the continual need for empathic responses from carers and other significant figures. In normal development, this empathic mirroring, along with opportunities for the child to parti- cipate in the sense of power, strength, and wisdom attributed to the father and others, enables an optimum disillusionment and gradual modification of the narcissistic lines of grandiosity and idealisation. When such benign developments are aborted, for whatever reason, narcissism remains primitive and unmodified by harnessing with reality. This infantile raw narcissism is then a source of shame and rage. The adult with such intense inner narcissistic demands cannot simply transform them into love of others (as implied in Freud's 1914c theory of narcissism): these inner demands can at best be repressed, but, more commonly, find noisy and embarrassing expres- sion that results in continual humiliation and rage against both self and others.

We might say that for the person with ADHD, their narcissism functions like another intense and peremptory drive, alongside those of aggression and libido. In severe cases, the person cannot contain the pressures for expression of aggression, for seizing of immediate pleasure, and the assertion of grandiose self-importance and desires to be admired. Sometimes, this is hidden. For example, a man with ADD (without hyperactivity) used to speak and write of his extreme failings, and lack of worth, proclaiming himself to be the most worth- less human being who had ever existed. He refused to wear normal men's suits of the current fashion, declaring them to be far too exhibi- tionistic for the likes of him. As a result, he wore clothes that actually drew attention to him through their unusual nature. His grandiosity was expressed in its negative: he declared himself to be the most worthless and useless person ever, and also revealed his hidden sense of superiority over those who wore "flashy" contemporary suits. In such an example, the repressed narcissistic drive follows the classic Freudian psychodynamic paradigm—the repressed is manifest in disguised form, and its repudiation ("I am worthless") simultaneously gives it expression ("I am exceptionally worthless").

Kohut's gift was to point out what is obvious once stated: that narcissism follows its own line of development and cannot be eliminated, any more than can sexuality, but can only be encouraged to develop along more mature lines. In the case of people with ADHD, their narcissism has often remained highly immature, along with most other areas of their personality. Like other emotional and instinctual "driving forces" within the ADHD personality, their narcissism retains an overwhelming and forceful quality that can be painful both for others and the person who is helplessly driven by these opprobrium-evoking and potentially shame-inducing needs.

According to Kohut's account, modification of infantile narcissism in normal development occurs through numerous tolerable challenges and disillusionments. The gradual and optimally titrated encounter with reality, over the years of childhood and adolescence, precipitate a building up of internal structures of persisting ambitions and ideals —a process Kohut (1977, 1981) called "transmuting internalisation". This can occur not only during normal development, but also through the psychoanalytic process. The problem for the child with ADHD in relation to this is that their narcissistic challenges are never tolerable. All narcissistic injuries are experienced as overwhelming and intolerable, evoking rage. For the ADHD child, there is no cushioning of their emotional experiences. As a result, the structure-building processes of transmuting internalisation do not take place, and narcissism remains primitive and peremptory.

The normal results of transmuting internalisation—the persisting structures of ambitions and ideals, harnessed to the reality of the person's skills and talents—constitutes Kohut's (1977) concept of the Self. It is perhaps partially as a result of the failure of this structure to develop that people with ADHD often indicate a deficit in their sense of who they are, what they want to do, and what values they hold. This can give a certain chameleon-like, or "false self" quality to their presentation in different contexts and at different times, and their lack of deeply held values and ideals can even, in some cases, give the impression of psychopathic traits. Values, ideals, and ambitions may change fluidly in accord with temporary identifications with different individuals, groups, cultures, or employment organisations, all of which might, in a brief time, be aggressively discarded as restrictive and constrictive "mirror stage" images (Lacan, 1948, 1949). On the other hand, some with ADHD traits develop a kind of belligerent integrity, and perhaps identity as an "outsider", based around a questioning and rejection of all authority. In relation to some artistic and creative pursuits, the combination of rebellion against rules and limits, with a relatively unmodified narcissism, can be of some advantage.

The insubstantial, fluid, and fragile sense of self in ADHD may contribute to deficits in empathy and "theory of mind" (Ensink & Mayes, 2010), the capacity to understand both self and others. It is quite common for the person with ADHD to declare, at times, a certain bafflement at their own behaviour, particularly following destructive rages. In a therapeutic context, such a person might ask the therapist for ready-made external understanding, or might look for clues as to how the therapist expects or wants them to behave or think. The possibility and value of exploring the mind, as opposed to having a template presented from outside, might not immediately be apparent to the person with ADHD.

Some hints from analysis of a child

Some indications of therapeutic possibilities are provided in an early paper by Lustman (1966), describing work with a five-year-old boy called Tim who would certainly be viewed today as displaying marked features of ADHD, and probably also some autistic spectrum traits. Lustman describes the situation as follows:

> The presenting complaints were persistent encopresis and sporadic enuresis in a behaviorally uncontrolled child. Tim was given to severe temper tantrums, could tolerate no frustration, would not accept any substitute gratifications, was violently destructive of all property, and could not be controlled by any form of parental prohibition or punishment. (p. 194)

Lustman felt that Tim's faecal soiling expressed severe aggression towards his parents. He would shake faeces out of his trouser leg and carry on playing "unmindful of whether he stepped in it or not—but always managing to step in it" (p. 195). When the parents had attempted sanctions or efforts to persuade Tim to take more responsibility for his toileting, these had resulted in extensive smearing of faeces and smashing of property, including walls and the door.

In the consulting room, Tim's behaviour was frenetic, taking all the toys out of the box in a mess on the floor, then he would lie in it and masturbate with both hands, one on his penis and the other rubbing his anus. Lustman reported that the chaotic and disorganised quality of Tim's behaviour quickly settled after the first few hours of treatment, but problems of impulse control remained the central theme. However, Lustman noted that Tim displayed great intelligence, and also sensitivity and a capacity for psychological insight. During an analysis lasting four years, Tim achieved control over his enuresis and encopresis and other areas of behaviour and fantasy sufficiently for him to become an outstanding student and a participant in his peer group. However, when Lustman saw him later, in adolescence, he noted a quality of continuing impulsivity, as well as "his chronic level of excitement, his periodic difficulty in restraint, and his propensity for violence . . . (and) a characteristic trait of 'impulse buying' . . ." (p. 195). Tim's wish to see the analyst again was to do with his worry about sadistic fantasies and his fear that he would not be able to control his impulse to touch girls and provoke sexual fights with them.

Lustman reports a significant event during the childhood analysis that played a key role in Tim's achievement of greater control over his impulses. The sessions took place within a playroom, which Tim subjected to his typical abuse of violence and mess as part of his relentlessly frenetic and hyperkinetic behaviour. At a certain point, it was necessary to carry out repairs to the playroom and the work was transferred to Lustman's own office. Although there had been previous talk of the new room, Tim was visibly shocked by the difference between it and the playroom, and his behaviour changed markedly. He was no longer destructive and messy when in Lustman's office, but engaged in strenuous efforts to control himself, such as trying to sit still, or lie still on the couch, and progressing to playing chess. The playroom was soon refurbished, but Tim preferred to have the option of the two settings. When in the playroom, his behaviour remained restless and frenetic, with difficulties in attention and concentration, and motoric discharges and the creation of mess. In the office, his behaviour continued to be very controlled. Lustman comments, "In the home and the playroom, impulse always won the day. In my office, control became ever more pronounced and continuous" (p. 197). Lustman was able to help Tim understand that the changed behaviour was not a result of the office controlling him, but it showed his own capacity for control. As a result, he became able to tolerate longer and longer periods in the office without resorting to motoric discharge in the playroom. His restlessness and distractibility decreased, and he was able to concentrate more and more on chess. Soon, all the work was transferred to the office and he became an accomplished chess player.

Lustman noted the striking change in Tim's quality of play:

> The sequence of his play went from amorphous, restless, highly distractible, impulsive play, which was frequently the vehicle for making a mess, to highly organized, thoughtful, controlled planning such as is necessary for a good chess game. This became his favorite game and would on occasion take up the entire hour, with Tim sitting quietly for long periods, immersed in the intricate strategy of the game. (p. 199)

He points out that in one setting, Tim's functioning followed the primary process of immediate instinctual motoric discharge, and in the other setting it expressed the secondary process and showed sublimation: "As treatment progressed, his aggression, curiosity, and the need for violent struggle underwent a sublimation into highly competitive scholarship and well-controlled, remarkable chess playing" (p. 199).

However, this change was not due to a "reaction formation" of repudiating the messiness and adoption of an opposite stance. Tim remained far from excessively tidy, clean, and neat, and he continued to experience some problems with impulsivity and worries about sadistic sexuality. Thus, the changes expressed authentic and healthy sublimation, processes of displacement, and aim-inhibition, rather than mechanisms of defence.

Lustman makes the point that during Tim's frenetic and impulsive period, the "fully instinctualized" nature of his energies "not only disrupted intellectual development, but seemed to cripple all ego functions" (p. 198). His initial "almost heroic efforts to just lie still or sit still" took such "heavy investment of the limited attentional cathexes available that for the moment all other functioning was impoverished and blotted out" (p. 198), but, with sublimation, much more energy became available to the ego generally.

The sudden change in Tim's demeanour and behaviour when shown into the analyst's office in place of the playroom is striking. Lustman postulates that this functioned as a kind of developmental "shockwave", producing "a sudden and conspicuous awareness of difference and of self" (p. 196) and creating a "functional differentiation" within the psyche analogous to that within embryo development:

> That is to say, as soon as a function becomes structuralized, i.e., as soon as it begins to function with a degree of stability, its further differentiation will tend to be modified by its own activity, in addition to other forces. The classic biological example of this is the circulatory system of the vertebrate embryo. As soon as the heart starts to beat, a momentum in development is established via the hydrostatic pressure and its effect on all of the blood vessels. (p. 203)

Lustman goes on to consider the prevalence of impulse disorders among "culturally deprived" children of nursery school age, in comparison with children from more "middle class" backgrounds. He argues that this increased prevalence could not be due to a skewing of congenital variations in children's drive endowment (Alpert et al., 1956), but must reflect their cultural and familial environment, and that therefore "the internalization process of structuralized regulation and the crucial quality of its underlying object relationships are the most significant factors" (p. 207).

Lustman extended his enquiry with a study of impulse control among children at a middle-class nursery school, using an experimental situation that involved working with two puzzles, one of which was impossible to solve, and contained the potential for winning prizes and opportunities for cheating. In this way, he was able to observe a variety of interwoven phenomena, including strength of impulse, capacity for impulse control, ego functioning, and internalised morality. Some children were excessively impulsive, explosive, distractible, and showing low frustration tolerance. Others were excessively controlled and showed evidence of much internal conflict, such as child S, who sat quietly, listened to the instructions, looked at the prizes, but did not touch any of them, and announced that he did not want to eat any of the candy because it would give him cavities. S managed the easy puzzle and "seemed a model of the secondary process in his work" (p. 211), but, after making a great effort with the impossible puzzle, he actually stole a piece and put it in his pocket, and then became calm. While working on the puzzles, S made repeated references to paternal prohibitions in his chatter. Although he did not take a prize without completing the easy puzzle (thus following the rules), he displaced the conflict by stealing a piece of the impossible puzzle. In his nursery school behaviour, S showed great concerns about morality, often playing the policeman, and being "the most vociferous advocate of following all the adult rules and regulations, and yet was also a sly instigator of getting other children into trouble" (p. 211). The importance for S of this inner conflict over impulse control and morality was indicated by the fact that, for weeks after this experiment, he would bring puzzles and prizes with him to school to "play the game" with other children, clearly in an attempt at mastery. Lustman provides descriptions of various other children's behaviour in this experiment, illustrating different degrees of partial internalisation of originally external regulation and morality, and the development of impulse control, steps along the way towards the establishment of a functioning superego.

Lustman draws an analogy between the development-provoking shock experienced by Tim (when the therapy room was changed) with the normal shock of the oedipal crisis, giving momentum to ego and superego development. We may remember that Freud (1925j) described this momentous development as follows:

> In boys . . . the complex is not simply repressed, it is literally *smashed to pieces by the shock* of threatened castration. Its libidinal cathexes are abandoned, desexualized and in part sublimated: its objects are incorporated into the ego, where they form the nucleus of the super-ego and give this new formation its characteristic qualities. In normal, or rather, in ideal cases the Oedipus complex exists no longer, even in the unconscious; the super-ego has become its heir. (p. 257, my italics)

Thus, in this brief extract, Freud describes the giving up of infantile sexual aims, the alteration of the libidinal drive to make it available for non-sexual purposes, and the internalisation of external control to form the new structure, the superego—all provoked by the oedipal crisis. Lustman implicitly draws upon Freud's account in suggesting that "shock as a special instance of crisis mobilizes intrapsychic tensions of such magnitude that it imposes the need for resolution"

(p. 214). He further hypothesises that the "disorganised family of the culturally deprived family, the distortions and inability to enter into or to resolve oedipal conflicts may account for the failure of the super-ego development as an integrant in impulse control" and that "the disorganization of the family does not permit the oedipal phase to reach the crisis intensity necessary to induce further ego and superego development" (p. 214). Lustman's ideas here are of interest because they highlight the potential role of shock and crisis in stimulating ego and superego development, in contrast with the more common idea of trauma as an event that causes a collapse or regression in ego functioning. The internalisation of functions of regulation of impulse, and the creation of inner structure, may be compared with the process of "transmuting internalisation" described by Kohut (1977, 1981), although the latter is seen as developing from innumerable small micro-traumas rather than from a shock or crisis.

Lustman's account illustrates how a very severe deficit in impulse control can be overcome through a process of gradual internalisation of function, in the context of a supportive relationship, and this process can be activated by shock, challenge, or change of environment.

The therapeutic tasks in ADHD

Finding words and speech for impulse and affect

One of the fundamental components of most forms of psychotherapy is that of helping the client find words for his or her impulses, moods, emotions, and worries. In place of action, there is speech. People with ADHD are often confused about what they feel and think. Impulse might often proceed straight to action without intervening awareness of thought or feeling. When asked "why did you do/say that?", following some destructive or hurtful action or verbal outburst, the person might truthfully reply that he or she does not know why. The client might begin a session with words such as "I'm really fed up" (or more expletive-laden variations on this theme), without being able to elaborate any further on the nature of the emotion or on its causes or triggers. It is only after the client is helped to continue speaking that the underlying emotional themes, thoughts, and conflicts gradually become apparent. In some instances, the client's speech during the session is itself a form of motor discharge. This is apparent in those instances where speech is rapid, repetitive, and heavily laden with expletives. The task is to help the client move from speech as a form of action to speech as a means of communication (to self as well as other) about the contents of his or her mind.

For example, a woman typically began her session with incoherent talk conveying a general state of undifferentiated agitation. We found that as each session progressed it was possible for me to make one or two brief comments about her emotions and thoughts, and how she might have experienced certain situations. She would find such interventions soothing and helpful in facilitating her thinking. On the other hand, lengthier, more complex, or more frequent comments from me seemed unhelpful, generating confusion and further agitation. In the case of people with ADHD, it can be very important for the therapist to keep his or her sentences short, succinct, and coherent because a person with attentional difficulties might not be able to follow and understand a lengthy or complex sentence.

Although there is one currently popular brand of therapy that focuses exclusively on the task of helping the client identify their thoughts and feelings, and those of other people, there seems little merit in extracting this one ingredient and elevating it to the status of an entire therapy in its own right. Recognition of the importance of this component is not new. It is a crucial feature of any feasible psychotherapy, but assumes particular importance in all conditions where ego functioning is impaired, as is clearly the case with ADHD. For example, Anna Freud (1966), writing about certain kinds of children whose psychic structure was insufficiently developed to make use of psychoanalytic interpretation, advised that

> therapy is best served . . . by verbalization and clarification of internal and external dangers and frightening affects which are perceived preconsciously but which his weak and helpless ego, left to itself, cannot integrate and bring under secondary process dominance. (p. 230).

Promote fusion of the drives through selfobject attachment

As described above, defusion of the normally "fused, blended and alloyed" (Freud, 1923b, p. 41) dual drives of libido and aggression, with a resulting release of raw destructive aggression, is a significant problem for many people with ADHD. The defusion is triggered by disruptions in attachment relationships, and, in particular, a breach in the required empathic connection that provides external regulation for the inner state of mood, affect, and self-esteem—the functions that Kohut (1977) designated by the term "selfobject". Because of the inherent disorganisation and underfunctioning of the ADHD brain, the person with this condition has an enhanced need for selfobject responses. When these are insufficiently available, as they always will be at times, the person feels abandoned, dropped, discarded to their helplessness and chaos. Moreover, there is also a tendency to attribute all misfortune or adversity to a failure of the selfobject, so that the main attachment figure is blamed and is expected to resolve the problem. Sometimes, particularly in adult attachment relationships, this can lead to escalating violence of emotion and, sometimes, physical violence.

These tendencies can be countered by empathic exploration of the triggers, experience, and consequences of disintegrative rage. People with ADHD will become calm when the therapist shows empathic appreciation of their experience and perspective but will tend to become increasingly agitated if the therapist speaks from a non-empathic position. Alternative perspectives, from the other's point of view, can be presented, and it might be important to do so, but these must follow the communication of an empathic perspective. As these situations of potential release of defused aggression are explored and slowly mastered, there is a gradual building up of internal structures of regulation through "transmuting internalisation" (Kohut, 1977).

For example, one woman (Henrietta), with marked attentional deficit problems, displayed an intense yet fickle "object hunger", using her physical charm to engage many different men, finding another one as soon as tensions and difficulties developed in the relationship. She could not bear to be bored and seemed addicted to drama. In some instances, she would become very attached to a man, in a needy and demanding way. If the man was not emotionally available at some point, she would turn to alcohol as a substitute selfobject. Her behaviour would then deteriorate and she would become even more demanding. Some men would try ever harder to meet her selfobject needs, before eventually giving up. In other cases, her behaviour would elicit counter-aggression and rejection from the

130 THE DISINTEGRATING SELF

man. On occasion, her rage would become out of control, and she would engage in physical attacks on the man, destruction of property, and severe self-harm through cutting. At times, she would be enraged with the therapist for not helping her sufficiently, and blame him when things were not going well for her. Helpful work with Henrietta revolved around exploring and giving words to her emotional needs, her experience when these were not met, and the effect on the other person of her demanding behaviour. Her rage with the therapist was met with an empathic grasp of her feelings of helplessness, frustration, and shame, while also pointing to her own responsibility for her life and emotions. It was pointed out that blaming others was not helpful. In this way, we helped facilitate empathy for both self and other, and also awareness of other people as separate beings with their own needs, emotions, and perspectives. We also explored the damaging effects of her use of alcohol as a maladaptive chemical self-object that undermined, rather than supported, her ego functioning. Gradually, Henrietta gained more control over her impulses, with more awareness of the nature of her emotional needs, became more realistic in her expectation of what others could provide, and learned better ways of communicating her needs. Her aggression, while still frequently present, took on a less raw and unusable quality, and became more available for constructive self-assertion and pursuit of goals (including persistence in seeking a change of apartment from her housing association, a task that required repeated controlled aggression in the form of assertive verbal and written communications).

Exploration of how projection of aggression and egocentric relating colours the perception of others

Klein (e.g., 1946) and Bion (e.g., 1962) described ways in which the infant's own rage and hatred colours the perception of the feeding breast and the mother, creating highly conflicted and ambivalent relational states. For many people with ADHD, this dynamic continues, generating expectations of rejection and counter-aggression. Another aspect that is less commonly recognised is that the egocentric and need-satisfying mode of relating that can be typical of those with ADHD leads to the assumption that others will relate in the same way. Thus, the person will tend to assume that everyone is motivated from essentially selfish concerns and perceptions, and is engaging in manipulation rather than a loving exchange, generating a bleak and despairing outlook.

This was the case for Henrietta, described above. She did not expect to be understood empathically, or cared about, or related to honestly. While remaining very needy of her parents (although she was in her thirties), she seemed convinced that they did not care about her and that they used her essentially to meet their own emotional needs (despite much evidence to the contrary). She would complain that they did not love her. Modification of this perspective required careful elucidation of her assumptions and beliefs, and of her partic-ular bias in interpreting the motives behind her parents' (and others') behaviour. The concept was presented to her of a possibility that human beings might relate sometimes on the basis of love rather than pure self-interest, of wanting what is the best for the loved person rather than what would be preferred by the other. Henrietta had felt she had always been under pressure to conform to her parent's expec-tations, even though there seemed little substantial evidence of this from her accounts or from family meetings involving her parents. This assumption of their conditional love appeared more based on her projection of her own egocentric and need-satisfying mode of relating. Once this assumption was questioned, and its possible basis in her own exploitative stance towards others had been explored, Henrietta was able to be somewhat freer of this rather imprisoning schema concerning the nature of her interpersonal world. Like many with this spectrum of problems, she was able to be curious about her own mind, and that of others, when challenging and interesting alternative perspectives were put to her—and it is, indeed, crucial to engage the ADHD person's curiosity.

It was also important to assist Henrietta in understanding that sometimes her expectation that another person (such as the therapist) was angry with her was based on her projection of her own state of anger, and that this in turn tended to evoke further anger within herself. For example, on some occasions, Henrietta arrived at her session in an angry mood and appeared sullen and irritable towards the therapist. Eventually, she might give some clue that she had engaged in behaviour that she felt the therapist might disapprove of. What we were able to unravel was that her expectation of disapproval had evoked her anger towards the therapist, which was then also projected so that she expected the therapist was angry with her, which, in turn, further provoked her own defiant anger, and so on, in an intensifying projective spiral.

Encourage dominance of the "reality principle"

Regarding the importance of achieving dominance of the "reality principle" over the "pleasure principle", Freud (1911b) comments:

> The superiority of the reality-ego over the pleasure-ego has been aptly expressed by Bernard Shaw in these words: "To be able to choose the line of greatest advantage instead of yielding in the direction of least resistance". (p. 223, fn. 1)

Every human achievement, other than those that are most pathological and perverse, depends on dominance of the reality principle, even though this may ultimately serve the pleasure principle by providing greater reward later. People with ADHD have great difficulty with this. For them, the pleasure principle is often dominant, so that doing what gives immediate pleasure, or avoiding doing what might give immediate "unpleasure", has priority over engaging with what is needed for long term satisfaction and success. Very often, the person with ADHD complains of not fulfilling their potential, of not achieving anything, and of being bored because they have no satisfying occupation. While some do manage to find a form of work to which they are suited, others squander their time on daytime television, computer games, drugs, alcohol, excessive eating, or masturbation.

It is important to draw the person's attention to the disadvantages of following immediate pleasure at the expense of reality and to point out that achievement of any kind usually involves effort, struggle, frustration, perhaps pain, and basically requires *work*. Whilst this may be obvious to most people, for the person with ADHD it might not be obvious. Although self-disclosure about the therapist's own life is not required, it can be helpful to provide such expressions of the reality principle in a manner that conveys a hint of the therapist's own struggles with the pain and frustration of reality, in a spirit of "We're all in this together—it is difficult for all of us". I have found this quite a natural stance to take at times, and it seems to foster a benign temporary idealisation that facilitates internalisation of a more reality-based attitude (Kohut, 1971), even though this idealisation is not deliberately evoked.

The client can be helped to consider scenarios in which positive benefits ensue as a result of work towards goals, and, on the other hand, to see more clearly the damage resulting from short-term pursuit of pleasure and avoidance of discomfort. Harmful effects of alcohol and drugs can be outlined, as well as those of certain kinds of avoidance, such as failing to attend to bills and official documents. Stealing, and other instances of superego lacunae, can be juxtaposed to consideration of consequences if caught. The corrosively damaging effect on self-esteem of a pervasive dominance of the pleasure principle is a crucial and fundamental point to emphasise.

Support strategies of sublimation

People with ADHD tend to be deficient in the capacity for sublimation, the desexualisation, neutralisation, and aim-inhibition of raw instinctual energy, and the use of this for higher cultural or scientific pursuits. Lustman's (1966) case of Tim, described above, is a vivid example of the dramatic value of sublimation, illustrated by his development of an intense interest in chess. All forms of engagement with science and the arts, and community activities, including politics, and all forms writing or skilful use of speech, as well as sports, are expressions of sublimation. They make use of fused libidinal and aggressive instinctual energies to make a contribution to personal pleasure and the good of society. We might note, however, that some forms of "art", such as highly aggressive rap music and certain forms of very crude "heavy metal" music with extremely aggressive and sexual themes, as well as many forms of pornography, express minimally sublimated libidinal and aggressive energies, with a preponderance of destructive aggression. Unfortunately, it is these minimally sublimated forms that often appeal to people with ADHD.

The therapeutic task is to prompt and encourage the client in undertaking any form of learning, study, artistic pursuit, sport, gardening, or community activity. Men who have difficulty managing aggression might benefit from competitive sports, martial arts, or even just working with a punch bag. I have known people with ADHD benefit from taking up activities as diverse as gardening an allotment, writing poetry and short stories, working out in the gym, joining the (volunteer) Territorial Army, studying social science, writing an extensive complaint to an NHS Trust, and playing a guitar. Most forms of work and employment contain opportunities for sublimation, and this, of course, includes voluntary work. Sometimes, these possibilities need to be raised with the person, while in other cases he or she might speak of them spontaneously, and these initiatives can then be affirmed as positive developmental steps. The value of sublimatory interests, and their necessity for mental health—of having some focus of interest outside the self and its immediate bodily gratifications—can be explained to the person. He or she can be asked if they can think of any potential interest or activity they might like to explore. If they can identify a potential interest, the next step is to help them think about what they could do to pursue this, how they might find out more information: for example, by looking on the Internet, visiting a library, or obtaining a college prospectus. This further step is important, since the person with ADHD might not be able to think this through on their own.

Very often, people with ADHD are isolated. Joining a group of others with similar interests, or engaging in a community project, can help to alleviate this and foster a sense of social inclusion.

Support the function of signal anxiety

Freud (1926d) drew a distinction between anxiety that is a direct response to trauma—a state of being overwhelmed—and "signal anxiety", which is a warning of potential trauma. Because people with ADHD have difficulty in thinking ahead in a constructive way, they are often deficient in the capacity for signal anxiety. They do not always anticipate the outcome and consequences of actions and, thus, are more likely to be assailed by unexpected events that are experienced as traumatic. On the other hand, some people with ADHD will endlessly worry and ruminate about future dangers, but not in a way that leads to constructive action. This can easily become a generalised anxiety disorder. Moreover, because of the ADHD brain constellation that does not dampen emotions, there is a tendency for any anxiety to escalate to critical levels.

The client can be helped to think realistically about dangers in terms of both anticipating likely situations and also containing the potential for anxiety to spiral out of control. This work involves careful attention to the details of the client's thoughts and fantasies, in so far as these relate to anxiety.

This task, of managing anxiety and promoting the development of signal anxiety, is one in which the client with ADHD will naturally seek to engage the therapist. Problems with anxiety are commonly what bring people with ADHD to seek therapy.

Tactfully counter grandiosity

As with other aspects of the psyche, the narcissism of the person with ADHD is often relatively unmodified. Grandiosity may coexist uneasily with low self-esteem and the reality of limited achievements. Unrealistically grandiose expectations can make it difficult for the person to pursue more ordinary forms of employment, all of which might be seen as "beneath" him or her. For example, a young man with ADHD stated that he could not find any line of work that appealed to him because he did not want to be "one of those 9–5 people going to an office every day doing some mind-numbing job" because he felt he was destined for better things, although he could not say what those better things might be. A woman with ADHD complained that there was no form of work or activity that attracted her because of the "boring town" in which she lived. She felt she could be much happier living in another country, where she felt sure she could be successful in running a guest house, although she took no steps towards making this a reality. By contrast, a man with severe ADHD found great satisfaction in taking a course in plumbing. He experienced significant difficulty with attention during the teaching and would often need to get up and leave the class in order to walk around, but, with understanding from the staff and his own persistence, he was successful and justifiably proud of his achievement.

Modifying grandiosity is another aspect of enabling greater dominance of the reality principle. Of course, this confrontation with a gap between grandiose aspiration and reality needs to be undertaken tactfully and with care for the person's vulnerable self-esteem and potential for shame. Gentle enquiry about what steps the person has taken towards their goal will often be sufficient. Reality itself often intrudes, providing an opportunity for empathic addressing of this issue. More forceful challenge might be experienced as an aggressive narcissistic assault by the therapist (Kohut, 1971) and is best undertaken only in the context of a secure therapeutic relationship of established trust.

Sometimes, a client will establish an idealising selfobject transference towards the therapist (Kohut, 1971). The therapist might be perceived as a source of wisdom, knowledge, or calm, and the client experiences peace and well-being in his or her presence. This will often be a benign station along the line of development of internal ideals and other regulatory structures of the psyche (Kohut, 1971) and it will naturally fade as reality gradually impinges.

Clarification of oedipal conflict and the "law of the father"

Many people with ADHD have not internalised the regulatory function of the father's authority (the internalisation of Lacan's (1957) symbolic function of the "Law" through the signifier of the "Name of the Father" (Lacan, 2013)), that crucial process of establishing limits and boundaries, of separating mother and child, and of setting the primacy of the *reality principle* and the *secondary process* (of language and law) over the *primary process* realm of imaginary satisfaction. In normal processes of development, the child traverses the oedipal crisis (of desire and rivalry) and comes to accept that he or she cannot possess the mother or remain fused with her; there is a boundary and limit to fulfilment of desire. Moreover, satisfaction of desire is not immediate and hallucinatory, but must be mediated by the language shared with others and must engage with what is possible in external (as opposed to psychic) reality.

In the case of people with ADHD, all these functions could be insufficiently established. He or she might display a general rejection of all forms of authority—a stance that contributes to difficulties with any form of employment. The clear pattern in childhood might have been that any parental attempt at sanction or imposition of authority would simply evoke an ever more intense rebellion (as described above in Lustman's case of Tim), and this is then continued into adulthood, albeit with somewhat less violent expression. A general reluctance to acknowledge limits and even an attempt to repudiate reality in all its forms might be apparent. This does not quite amount to a fully developed psychotic illness, although at times people with ADHD can, indeed, appear a little psychotic. In addition, I have often had the impression that some people with ADHD, both male and female, have never fully given up the illusion that they possess, and have a right to possess, their mother. While the mother is treated with distain and contempt, and is complained of as if she were the source of all problems, she is also regarded as rightfully having a duty to prevent or resolve all difficulties that her offspring encounters. A naïve therapist listening to the discourse of a person with ADHD could conclude that the mother is, indeed, the cause of the client's difficulties—perhaps by being over-indulgent, over-protective, judge-mental and critical, and so forth. All such alleged characteristics of the mother can be, at least in part, a response to the abnormal tempera-ment of her child and his or her rejection of the "law of the father". The actual father is often regarded highly ambivalently, and inter-actions might be acrimonious.

The father, as carrier of the symbolic signifier of the "law of the father", provides *structure* and *space*. As the "third", coming between the dyad of mother and child, the father opens a triangular space. When this fails, if there is an oedipal triumph whereby the father and his authority are dismissed, or if the father leaves, or dies, the child is left trapped in the claustrophobic dyad with the mother, unable to think or plan clearly and his or her potential for independent func-tioning aborted (Mollon, 1985, 1993). One man (Jim) with ADD had his mother to himself for his first few years. When Jim was seven, his mother married a rather fierce man from the Far East, whose appear-ance, language, and manner appeared strange and terrifying to him. Jim's reaction was to have as little to do with this frightening figure as possible and it really seemed that this man had taken up no symbolic place in Jim's psyche at all. Other than acknowledging, during an initial assessment enquiry, that this "foreign body" had been present in his childhood from age seven, Jim made no reference to the stepfather's behaviour or attitudes whatsoever—he had been excluded from Jim's psyche. As I put to him, "There is no father in your mind!" It seemed to be partly as a result of this "missing signi-fier", like a missing piece of software code, that Jim was left startlingly passive, seemingly unable to take any initiative or work towards any goal, and also with limited capacity to think clearly. His inner oedi-pal structure was incomplete. In general, he was unable to approach women in any active way, but he did have fantasies of gaining the favour of the very attractive wife of the chief executive of the company he worked for! When he talked of these fantasies, the fact that this lady was already married to a man in a position of significant authority and power seemed not to enter into his conscious thoughts. Useful therapeutic work with Jim, over several years, involved repeated and firm challenges about his passivity, self-neglect, and pervasive avoidance of many of the normal tasks of life, such as cooking food and attending to basic and routine cleaning and maintenance of house and garden. Each such challenge seemed to function as a development-provoking shock, as if the therapist had introduced a startlingly novel idea. For example, when I pointed out that his neighbours might be distressed to have to view his grossly neglected garden, he appeared utterly astonished, repeatedly asking if I really thought this could be true, and saying that such a possibility had never occurred to him. He developed a benign idealising transference, the therapist becoming a highly significant paternal figure for him, contrasting starkly with the absence of significance of his step-father.

Another man with ADHD traits, Paul, had lost his father through death when Paul was aged twelve. Prior to this, Paul had experienced his father as very controlling and restricting. Following this, Paul had become markedly more hyperactive, constantly busy, until, some years later, he collapsed with exhaustion that became a state of chronic fatigue. In part, this hyperactivity had obviously been a manic defence against his grief and a block on the necessary mourning, all of which were addressed in subsequent psychotherapy. However, we found there was more to the hyperactivity than a defence against mental pain. It expressed Paul's sense of liberation from all control. As he looked back, he was able to see that it was as if he had no internal control; he did not know when or how to stop. He realised that the only way he had been able to impose any limit or control on himself was by becoming ill. It seemed that the excessively controlling nature of Paul's father, followed by his abrupt and premature death, left Paul without any internalised structures of control. His mother had not been a source of limits or control, and continued to be entirely indulgent of Paul following his father's death. Thus, like Jim, there was no father in Paul's mind. When he thought about the future in terms of work and career, he was clear that he did not want any kind of boss or authority over him.

People with ADHD often become addicted to computer games, as well as Internet pornography. The widespread contemporary use of screens, games, and pornography could be contributing to deficits or regressions in psychic structure and functioning, luring people away from the Freudian reality principle and the Lacanian realm of the *Symbolic*, seducing the psyche with temptations of the (Lacanian) *Imaginary*. All that is desired can instantly appear on the screen at the click of a mouse. The Symbolic register, of language, separation, and limits, is replaced by the quasi-hallucinatory gratifications of the *image* on the screen. It can be helpful to point out to people with ADHD that too much time spent in this way can be harmful for the mind. Other current contributions to undermining the reality principle include the ubiquitous availability and use of street drugs, the seductive lure of money to be made through the drug trade, and the rise of "celebrity culture", whereby people become "famous for being famous" by doing nothing more than drawing attention to themselves. All such culture-corrosive and destructive phenomena are fuelled by *images*, and, thus, belong in Lacan's register of the Imaginary.

Alongside the failure to establish the function of the "law of the father", adults with ADHD often display an ambivalent desire for paternal authority. In men, this might take the form of desires to join the Territorial (volunteer) Army or the Community (volunteer) Police, and to be guided by benign male authority. A woman with ADHD might show an ambivalent desire to be taken care of by a strong male figure, might complain that all the men she meets are "too weak", and might describe a longing for a man who is "strong enough" for her. In these ways, adults with ADHD express a need to establish, or compensate for, the missing internal structure of the Lacanian "law of the father".

These problems appear to be the psychic structural correlate of the impaired frontal lobe functioning at the neurobiological level. Some clients are able to appreciate an explanation along these lines—that they are psychologically impaired by their childhood rejection of authority. Simply speaking of these things introduces into the client's psyche important elements (signifiers) that were not there before, thereby allowing new development to take place, rather analogous to the way a nutrient-deprived plant might start to grow if the missing substance is supplied. In a perhaps grossly simplistic parody of Lacan, we might say that carefully chosen words, in a psychotherapeutic context, help structure the mind and promote its growth.

Encourage the synthetic function of the ego

An important aspect of ego functioning is to draw together and unite the different and sometimes conflicting desires, thoughts, perceptions, and needs within the person. In a classic paper, Nunberg (1931) discusses this synthetic function.

> Children and primitive men have not developed a unified ego. They are able to harbour contradictions not only of thought, but also of feeling and action. With further development the ego becomes more unified in its aims and endeavours; with the total disintegration of the personality the ego's synthetic function fails altogether. (p. 129)

On the other hand, Nunberg argues that an *indiscriminate* fusion or linking of ideas is a key process in schizophrenia and many other forms of mental illness:

> This brings us back to our hypothesis that the synthetic capacity of the ego is derived from Eros, whose function is not only to unite and to bind, but also to create from this union a new living being. In most forms of illness, symptoms do not remain stationary: they grow and increase (phobias, obsessional neurosis), and in certain morbid conditions, such as schizophrenia, they threaten to strangle with their growth what is left intact of the personality. Neurotic like all other psychic productivity is stimulated by the synthetic activities of the ego. (p. 132)

Nunberg is describing here an uncontained proliferation of Eros that is not balanced with a necessary amalgamation with the aggressive drive. Once again, we see the importance of the fusion of the drives. One without the other leads to pathology. Intellectual work, for example, requires a bringing together of information and ideas (Eros), but then we also have to bring our aggression to bear, to "get our teeth" into the material, breaking it apart and drawing distinctions, in order for anything useful to be done with it.

People with ADHD often seem to display both an uncontrolled proliferation of thoughts and ideas (which potentially can give rise to creativity) *and* a lack of integration of conflicting and contradictory contents. For example, one young man's early sessions consisted of rapid discourse around diverse and incompatible elements, such as his lack of achievement, his superior intellect, his guilt about depending on his parents, his complete independence from his parents, his wish to be a university professor, and his scorn for academics. His thoughts would flow so fast that he could not keep up with himself, an uncontained stream of consciousness in which contradictory elements coexisted, much as Freud described as being characteristic of the primary process of the unconscious mind.

By listening, and from time to time making careful succinct comments on what is said, drawing attention to contradictory and conflicting themes and statements, the therapist assists the client's ego in its balanced synthetic function. In struggling to understand and think about the client's speech, the therapist is actually demonstrating and modelling this important ego function. As a result, the person with ADHD does, in time, become more thoughtful, and more able to examine his or her thoughts.

A related point is the client's use of dreams. Whilst a person who does not have ADHD (or, at least, does not have it severely) might report a dream as a useful mental production whose meaning can be explored, the person with severe ADHD is more likely to report a dream but not wait to look at its meaning, or might even go on to discharge dream after dream in the session, resulting in a completely overwhelming and indigestible pile of words and images that leave the therapist speechless. In such instances, it might be best to interrupt the client's quasi-urinary flow and try to create a space for thought. This can take a simple form such as: "Stop! You are presenting too much for us to think about at once. Let's go back to your first dream and try to think together about what it might be telling us. Let's think about how it might relate to what is going on in your life at the moment."

Acknowledge and support the positive aspects of ADHD

The positive aspects of ADHD are expressed most strongly in the writings of Thom Hartmann (e.g., 1993, 2003), who has advanced the "hunter–farmer" theory of ADHD. Basically, Hartmann argues that traits of ADHD have been useful in a society of hunters, while unhelpful in a society of farmers (or in a modern school classroom). For example, he considers how the following brain and behaviour characteristics might be beneficial in a hunter society.

- Short attention span, with the ability to become intensely focused on objects of interest. This can enable constant monitoring of the environment with the potential for engaging intensely in hunting.
- Poor planning and impulsivity can enable entering the chase at a moment's notice.
- A lack of awareness of how long a task will take can enable a flexibility of response.
- Impatience can enable sustaining drive when "hot on the trail".
- A difficulty following directions can facilitate independence.
- A tendency to daydream may be associated with being bored with the mundane and being excited by what is new—the "hunt" and "being hot on the trail".
- Acting without considering the consequences may be associated with a willingness to take risks and face danger.
- Lacking social graces may be associated with an orientation towards urgent decisions and actions.

According to this perspective, people with ADHD could be the excitement- and sensation-seeking hunters, explorers, and warriors. Hartmann finds some support for his theory in genetic studies by Ding and colleagues (2001), who conclude their paper by suggesting "the very traits that may be selected for in individuals possessing a DRD4 7R allele may predispose behaviors that are deemed inappropriate in the typical classroom setting and hence diagnosed as ADHD" (p. 313). Not all ADHD specialists agree with Hartmann's positive perspective. Hartmann quotes Russell Barkley as remarking in a talk, "Let me tell you something. The last person I want to go hunting with is an ADHD individual off their medication!" (quoted in Hartmann, 2003, p. 79).

Hartmann (2003) further hypothesises that children with the "hunter" brain and the DRD4 7R allele gene might be chronically stressed by educational systems for which they are not suited, and which generate "predominantly punishment, criticism, and other fear- and anxiety-inducing feedback from the world around" (p. 110). The resulting excess cortisol could stimulate development of the survival-orientated reptilian brain at the expense of the prefrontal areas:

> After a few years of this daily stress in school, the child's brain has been sculpted into something different from what it could have been: It's more functional for survival—fight or flight—and less functional

for deep or long-lasting thinking processes. She now has attention deficit disorder. (Hartmann, 2003, p. 111)

I find some plausibility in Hartmann's argument. Certainly, his hunter–farmer theory presents a positive reframing of ADHD, and I have found it helpful to offer this perspective to clients. It highlights the way in which ADHD traits may be more problematic in some environmental contexts than others.

The further ADHD trait I find helpful to emphasise is creativity. A number of typical ADHD characteristics may contribute to this.

- The search for novelty and sensation facilitates discovery and exploration of the unknown.
- Boredom with routine leads to experimentation.
- The inherent "chaos" of the ADHD mind, and its free-associative flow, allow for possibilities of new combinations of ideas and knowledge.
- The capacity for hyper-focus when something is of interest enables prolonged pursuit of a new possibility.
- Rejection of limits and external authority facilitates exploration and adventure, as opposed to conformity.
- Slower brainwaves and failure to shut down the default mode network facilitate a creative brain state.

The therapeutic task is to help the person engage their creativity with reality. This can be done by careful questioning and prompts to thinking about how he or she might carry a potential idea forward to manifest in reality. For example, one woman realised she had a certain skill in finding old clothes in charity shops that she could modify, with changes to shape and buttons, etc., or combining pieces from different garments, so as to create a novel product that she could potentially sell. With questioning and discussion, she decided she could market these via an online auction, and she began to consider how she would name and style her "brand" and also to think through the logistics of time, postage, and pricing.

Cognitive–behavioural approaches

It should be apparent that the psychoanalytic approach described so far is not mere "insight-orientated psychodynamic therapy". Rather, it emphasises multi-faceted processes of ego support and of ego function development and general maturation of the personality, all mediated via the relationship with the psychotherapist. This includes helping the person achieve a clearer understanding of the nature of their brain function, its strengths and deficits, and a knowledge of what drives their behaviour. Identifying and examining thoughts and feelings, considering different behavioural strategies, understanding interpersonal interactions, trying out different perspectives, modifying unrealistic beliefs and assumptions, appreciating the experience of others, and many other components form part of the therapeutic tapestry.

Although it is possible to consider these different aspects, they do not easily divide into specific techniques. As Blanck (1966) comments,

> Most analysts agree with Freud that, essentially, technique is unteachable in its specifics, nor can many rules be promulgated. The essence of what is teachable is an attitude or philosophy based on psychoanalytic theory of personality development and of the pathological consequences of the human condition. From this, technique flows naturally. (pp. 7–8)

By contrast, cognitive–behavioural approaches tend to tease different therapeutic elements apart and develop specific strategies for each. These strategies tend to be viewed as "skill-based interventions". In relation to ADHD, the assumption in such work is that the condition has a neurobiological basis, but that CBT strategies can help intervene and break the link between the core brain processes and the repeated dysfunctional patterns of behaviour. Typical CBT strategies involve:

- identifying and questioning automatic negative thoughts (Wilens et al., 1999);
- noticing negative cognitive bias—modifying the tendency to see the worst;
- learning to notice and modify thought processes that lead to anxiety and depression;
- psychoeducation about ADHD;
- structuring daily life tasks—making lists, planning, goal setting, time management, etc.;

- dialectical behaviour therapy skills training for affect management, impulse control, and self-esteem (Hesslinger et al., 2002; Linehan, 1993);
- group therapy with skill modules including time management, behavioural activation, procrastination, organisation, and planning (Hirvikoski et al., 2011, 2014; Philipsen et al., 2007);
- mindfulness-based skills (Zylowska et al., 2008).

There is no doubt that CBT interventions can be helpful. In a review, Philipsen (2012) concludes,

> To date, CBT-based treatment is the most extensively tested psychotherapeutic approach in adult ADHD in individual and group settings. All CBT treatment programs examined have resulted in significant improvements in ADHD. (p. 1223)

Philipsen (2012) also notes that structured group interventions have been found to be helpful, and that CBT is more helpful that medication alone for persisting ADHD problems.

Energy psychology targets in ADHD

Those readers who have some training and experience in energy psychology approaches, such as thought field therapy (TFT), emotional freedom techniques (EFT), advanced integrative therapy (AIT), Tapas acupressure technique (TAT), psychoanalytic energy psychotherapy (PEP), will find many potential targets for these techniques. Specific energy psychology techniques, which can be incorporated into psychotherapy (Mollon, 2005, 2008, 2014a), are described in Appendix III.

All energy psychology procedures follow the basic principle that (1) a troubling event, state of anxiety, or dysfunctional emotion is activated by thinking of it, while (2) the body's energy system (of acupressure meridians, chakras, etc.) is stimulated in such a way as to induce calming of brain, body, and mind. In some approaches, the body is included in the therapeutic conversation by using energy signalling systems. Some aspects are easy to learn and apply, while others are deeply subtle and require years of practice. All these methods work very well (Feinstein, 2012), although they are far from being considered "standard care" and, therefore, at the time of writing are regarded by many as still "experimental".[10]

Areas of trauma, anxiety, and injuries to self-esteem that can be targeted include (with typical phrasing used to access the relevant experience):

- "All the times and ways I was overwhelmed by my own emotions";
- "All the times and ways my mother/father/siblings were enraged with me because I was out of control and driving them nuts";
- "All the times and ways I was criticised and humiliated by teachers because I could not attend, focus, or concentrate";
- "All the times and ways I felt stupid and ashamed because I could not take in information";
- "All the times and ways I felt stupid and ashamed because I jumped to the wrong conclusion, or got hold of the wrong end of the stick";
- "All the times and ways I felt there was something wrong with me because my learning style was different";
- "All the times and ways my peers made fun of me";
- "All the times and ways I felt stupid and ashamed because I could not control what came out of my mouth";
- "All the times and ways I felt frustrated because my brain would not work properly";
- "All the times and ways I felt rage and despair because when I tried to focus my frontal lobes shut down";
- "All the times and ways my frontal lobes were not working properly and I could not focus, or keep on track, or inhibit inappropriate speech and behaviour".

This is far from an exhaustive list and would need to be adapted to the specific experiences of the individual, and also using, as far as possible, the client's own language and phrases. The latter is very important; too often, therapists create a paraphrase of what the client said, translating the client's speech into something the therapist might say, but in the process this loses a great deal of connotative richness and specificity. I find that if we listen to the client's speech, now and again he or she will utter a particularly evocative sentence or phrase, usually some kind of metaphor, which corresponds to what I call a "succinct dynamic statement". Examples of these are:

- "I have to put on this front—but all the time I am worried *they will see I'm just an idiot!*";
- "My mother said I was a horrible brat";
- "My father said I was a waste of space";
- "It is like I have to keep going—like *I am afraid to stop*";
- "Often my brain just feels like a storm of mush";
- "When I get angry *it is like an explosion inside me* that just has to come out";
- "When something attracts me, I am like a child grabbing for a sweet";
- "When someone says no to me, it is like a road barrier I just have to accelerate and drive through";
- "Often it is like my body is on the ground but my mind is in orbit";
- "I've never been able to complete anything—*I just feel I've wasted my life*".

All such phrases can be used in verbal formulae such as "Every time that . . .", or "All the times and ways that . . .",[11] or "Even though . . . I completely accept myself".

Some energy approaches, such as EFT, emphasise the importance of targeting very specific experiences, while others (such as TAT and PEP) do not. It is very much a matter of the practitioner's training and experience.

Whilst one important application of energy psychology methods is towards the traumas and other experiences that have overwhelmed, distorted, or undermined the person's development and mental equilibrium, another highly relevant consideration is the "systemic" disturbances in a person's subtle energy system. The energy system is that which is addressed in acupuncture and all forms of "energy medicine", and relates to the meridians, chakras, and other components of this complex system (Eden & Feinstein, 2008; Keown, 2014). This energy system can be disturbed or malfunctioning—not necessarily for any psychological reason—and this is then reflected in sub-optimum brain function and behaviour. The energy systems of people with ADHD are commonly compromised (with reversed polarity, non-polarity, or homolateral flow), but these problems can be quickly and easily corrected with simple exercises. Subtle energy (Keown, 2014; Swanson, 2010; Tiller, 2007) has quasi-bioelectrical qualities, and for optimum functioning, the palm of the hand and top of the head should have opposite polarity, so that there is a strong energy flow when tested (like batteries inserted correctly in a device), and there should be a good *cross-flow* (as opposed to homolateral flow) of energy across the body and brain. These systemic disturbances are not, in themselves, psychological in nature, but they do have repercussions at the body, brain, and mental level. We find that people do not function at their best when their energy system is not correctly polarised and flowing well and, crucially, they cannot respond well to other therapeutic interventions when this is the case.

I have found that people with ADHD can benefit particularly from the following energy techniques (found in Appendix III): collarbone breathing (modified version); cross crawl and cross tap; Wayne Cook postures. These are all extremely simple, comfortable, and promote calm and coherence.

For further information generally, and in more detail, regarding systemic energy disturbances, I strongly recommend *Energy Medicine* by Eden and Feinstein (2008). This finely written and well referenced book, citing research evidence, provides many techniques for promoting health, optimum functioning, and stress relief.

The systematic research of William Tiller (2007), over a number of years, indicates that if we enter a meditative (altered) brain state, or if we activate the human subtle energy system, we engage with a realm of reality that is responsive to our intention. His basic research paradigm was to have a group of meditators enter an altered state of mind, and then to direct an "intention" (to bring about a measurable physical or biochemical change in a target item) into a simple electronic device. The "intention-imprinted electrical device" would then be shipped a long distance away, perhaps to another continent, but it would consistently be found to generate the intended effect. Moreover, other unintended effects would occur in the "conditioned space" created by the presence of one of these devices: the normal laws of physics would subtly change. Tiller found that the human energy system also operates at this same level of reality that interacts with human consciousness and is responsive to intention.

The reason for including this brief outline of Tiller's work here is to provide some rationale for therapeutic phenomena that might otherwise appear implausible and, frankly, preposterous. Many practitioners find that in using energy methods, we seem to be able to bring about changes in the functioning of body and brain, simply by using intention and words while the subtle energy system is activated. What this means in relation to ADHD is that we can target different brain regions and functions, and neurotransmitters, and appear to bring about positive changes. When the energy system is activated, then, provided that the internal objections (the "psychological reversals") have been identified and modified, the desired effect will tend to materialise. Experienced energy psychotherapists will understand these points, and how to focus the relevant procedures, which would require an entire large book to describe in detail (e.g., Mollon, 2008) and can only be learnt through direct workshop training and much practice. However, we cannot at present provide tangible and objective measures of these effects of energy and intention on the human body and brain, and sceptics would argue that any such effects must be entirely due to suggestion.

Another way of using energy psychology is for reaching goals and establishing new habits. The principles of these are essentially simple, consisting of (1) clearing trauma, stress, and unhelpful beliefs, and (2) stating an intention, or goal, and using visualisation of achieving this. More details are provided in the Appendix.

Brain-training technologies

Various commercial brain-training technologies are available that are claimed to improve functioning in those with ADHD. Since I do not have personal experience with these, I cannot vouch for their effectiveness, but it seems entirely plausible that they could be of benefit to some people and there is research evidence supporting them. At least four approaches are available: cranial electrotherapy stimulation; neurofeedback; working memory training; interactive metronome.

Cranial electrotherapy stimulation sends small electrical currents to the brain, via a battery-powered device, aiming to alter brain electrical activity in a positive direction.[12]

Neurofeedback uses EEG measurements of brainwaves to produce a signal of brain activity that can be used to provide feedback for learning self-regulation of the brain. There is research suggesting that this approach can be effective for ADHD. In a review, Arns and colleagues (2009) concluded that neurofeedback was efficacious for ADHD, with a large effect size for inattention and impulsivity and a medium effect size for hyperactivity, and in a later pilot study (Arns et al., 2012) found that personalised protocols for neurofeedback produced even better results. A more recent review (Lofthouse et al., 2012) concluded that neurofeedback with *children* with ADHD was "probably efficacious".

Working memory training uses software on a home computer to train the brain in memory tasks. This has been found to be effective (Gropper et al., 2014).[13]

Interactive metronome teaches people with ADHD to synchronise a range of hand and foot exercises to precise computer-generated tones heard through headphones. Schaffer and colleagues (2001) found that in a study of boys with ADHD, this method facilitated a number of capacities, including attention, motor control, and selected academic skills.

Summary and conclusions

This chapter has explored psychoanalytic drive theory, defusion of the drives and the ensuing predominance of aggression, the importance of sublimation, the functioning of the ego and its need for support, the dominance of the pleasure principle over the reality principle, deficits in the superego and the missing paternal signifier, the *selfobject* provision of empathy at the interface between external and internal regulation, the immature narcissism, impaired appreciation of other people' emotional reality, and the role of the ego's synthetic function. We have considered various components within the psychotherapeutic relationship and process that support development in these areas of deficit, taking the concept of facilitating ego function as a helpful overall therapeutic framework. We have looked at the importance of acknowledging the positive aspects of ADHD, such as its link with creativity. With a passing glance at CBT techniques, we moved on to consideration of the various ways in which the knowledge and skills of energy psychology can be applied to ADHD, making use of the principle whereby the stress and dysfunction within the mind and brain are mirrored in the body's energy system. Finally, we noted the availability of several commercial brain-training programmes that have been demonstrated to be efficacious for some people. All these diverse, yet interrelated, perspectives reflect the multifaceted nature of ADHD.[14]

CHAPTER SEVEN

The porous personality (and the "apparently normal" persona)

From time to time, in a clinical practice of seeing several thousand patients over a period of over forty years, I have encountered people with what I eventually recognised to be a particular constellation of characteristics that I have come to think of a "porous personality", because of the combination of inadequate boundaries between self and other and between conscious and unconscious mind. It has taken a very long time for me to grasp the nature of this constellation, but eventually I realised that many of the more puzzling and apparently obscure personality presentations seem to correspond in certain ways to this description.

The patients I have in mind often present with a pattern of regular or occasional self-harm, but this is not always the case. Such episodes of self-harm might seem to occur without any obvious precipitating event. The person might seem very disturbed in ways that are not easy to understand. States of extreme self-loathing, associated with self-harm or vomiting, might suggest the possibility of repeated adverse experiences during childhood, such as sexual abuse, but none is found in the patient's narrative. Whilst aspects of the person's childhood experience might seem less than ideal, these do not seem sufficient to account for the severity of disturbance. The person might seem in some ways quite communicative, but in other ways rather private. Gradually, she or he might reveal some odd states of mind, with unusual imagery, fantasies, or thought processes. These might appear to follow the Freudian "primary process", the language and thought patterns of dreams and the unconscious.

The emerging impression (perhaps developing over a considerable period of psychotherapeutic time) is that the person's boundaries— between self and other, and between conscious and unconscious mind—are *porous*. Primary process material, that in other people is screened off from the conscious awake mind, tends to leak into awareness, giving rise to cognitive experience that does not easily find a place in social discourse and is, thus, essentially autistic. For example, a patient reported a fantasy (accompanied by much reticence and shame) of slicing her arms in multiple places and walking down the street dripping with blood, and, on another occasion, of cutting out her eyeball. Another described an aversive fantasy that the plate of food she was eating had turned into a plate of faeces. Yet another reported an urge to swallow a handful of sewing pins. The person's humour might appear quirky. At times, his or her perceptions, and interpretations of perceptions, could be eccentric, bordering on the psychotic and paranoid, but never enough to attract a diagnosis of schizophrenia. In some cases, however, the concept of schizotypal personality may be of relevance. Sometimes, hallucinatory voices might be experienced, during childhood as well as when adult, but, again, not in a way that would typically lead to a diagnosis of schizophrenia (although occasionally such an illness may develop). When highly stressed, brief periods of more florid psychosis or hallucinosis may occur, but these are rarely sustained. The person might present outwardly, and superficially, as "normal", yet hidden autistic and psychotic characteristics can gradually be discerned. In these ways, the boundary between conscious and unconscious mind, secondary and primary processes, is more porous than in other people.

The second area of "porosity" is in relation to other people. Boundaries between self and other seem flimsy, and a quality of appearing "thin skinned" is apparent (Rosenfeld, 1987). The person with a "porous personality" may correspond, in part, to the concept of "highly sensitive person" (Aron, 1999), and Eigen's (2004) account of the "sensitive self", as well as Kohut's (1971) description of narcissistically vulnerable people who are easily upset and wounded by seemingly small slights, criticisms, or rejections by others. These wounding events could be so subtle that their impact might seem puzzling. Examples might include: an absence of a sufficiently warm smile, or lack of sufficient enthusiasm in responding to the person, or mild criticism or teasing. These might trigger strong internal reactions of shame, withdrawal, and rage. The person's narcissistic vulnerability and sensitivity seems raw, with little of the normal buffering that allows others to weather the emotional rough and tumble of social interactions.

A crucial period for the development of disturbance in response to this vulnerability seems to be primary school, from age seven. At this time, children are becoming more concerned with the peer group, and rejections and other narcissistic wounds experienced within peer social life take on greater significance. The child may come home each day full of intolerable and toxic feelings of shame and rage as a result of repeated painful interactions, but will not be able to explain to parents or teachers what is wrong.

The adults who develop the porous self constellation described here seem always to have felt (but are not always perceived by others as) somehow odd, different, not fitting in. The idea of feeling like "an alien in a human body" is often apt, but this can also, paradoxically, coexist with a capacity for unusual empathy. As a result, the person can experience understanding *of* others, but not *by* others. The "oddness" is essentially part of the autistic spectrum, which, in females, can be less apparent overtly than in males, since it is covered by a greater social skill and relational seeking (Attwood et al., 2006). Social interactions are stressful for these people, at the same time as some contact with others is needed. The claustro–agoraphobic conflict is dominant, of experiencing too much contact as oppressive and "claustrophobic" whilst finding too little contact results in loneliness. Disrupted expectations and changes of routine are also a source of stress and anxiety. All of this means that the child, and later the adult, with these problems exists in a chronic state of high anxiety. This might not be apparent to others because it is so constant, albeit with periodic intensification. It is, therefore, a "normal" part of that person's experience. In an attempt to cope, the child learns to override the anxiety, creating a split between the outward, socially performing persona and the inner state of chronic intense anxiety combined with shame. The outward, "apparently normal" persona will lack grace and ease, appearing at times slightly brittle or awkward. Sometimes, tell-tale signs of the underlying autistic spectrum qualities may be glimpsed, such as repetitive bodily movements, including hair stroking or pulling, and compulsive smoking, particularly when stressed.

Although traumatic experiences might have occurred during childhood, in the case of these patients the adverse events seem not to have been the primary cause of the disturbance, but function more to emphasise and entrench the sense of being different—or of being inadequate because of not coping—and to intensify the shame.

A third area of porous sensitivity is in relation to sensory stimulation. In keeping with their characteristics as "highly sensitive persons", these people feel easily impinged upon by noises, smells, unaesthetic sights, commotion, and "too much going on". When overwhelmed with sensory and emotional stimulation in this way, the "porous" person feels a need to withdraw and be alone. Too much contact with others is experienced as over-stimulating and emotionally and energetically draining. Change or disruption of routines or expectations might be highly aversive and disturbing.

Yet another area of porosity that is sometimes present is a tendency towards "clairvoyant", "telepathic", or other "psychic" abilities (Brottman, 2011; Williams, 1998b). An unusual awareness of other people's thoughts, feelings, and intentions, or of future events, can be confusing to both self and others. Autistic writer, Donna Williams, comments,

> One can respond to the body-mapped pattern of energy sensed and that response may demonstrate a "knowing" that is seen as "psychic". So, for example, I seemed constantly to surprise people who were closely involved with me when I would phone them up out of the blue – very often this would coincide with their just having mentioned me or been writing to me or thinking of me. By contrast with their other friends or acquaintances, the number of such occurrences was very high, leading people to believe there was some kind of psychic occurrence happening. Someone summed this up by saying, "you don't have to call Donna, you just have to think loudly about her." I would have said it was not about thinking loudly but feeling strongly. In those days my "doors" were wide open, too open, and too often. I've fortunately learned how to shut those doors and to use them at least more by choice than purely by resonance. (Williams, 1998b, pp. 121–122)

The ego of the "porous personality" feels threatened by both internal and external stimuli. This vulnerability evokes shame and rage, usually directed against the self.

The "porous personality" has struggled with this sensitivity and vulnerability from the beginning. Some develop what is recognised relatively easily as overt autistic spectrum qualities, such as extreme shyness, social avoidance, preference for routine and predictability, and aversion to strong emotions. Of these, a smaller proportion may attempt to create a mode of being that is based entirely on rational considerations and an avoidance of emotions and attachment. One such person remarked that she did not want anything to do with people or emotions because these cause pain, and she did not want to be attached to anyone because people "either hurt you or they die". Not surprisingly, she struggled with a constant sense that life held no meaning, purpose, or pleasure.

However, the patients I am focusing on in this account are those who develop an extensive concealment of their sensitive autistic core. Outwardly, they present as "normal". Teachers might not identify any abnormality, and might perceive the child as happy and outgoing. Family, too, might not recognise the problem, until some degree of disturbance becomes overt during adolescence. What appears to develop is a split between an "apparently normal" outer persona and the inner realm of shame and rage.

The inner realm is indeed a cauldron of toxic shame. By "toxic", I mean shame of a quality and intensity that cannot be psychologically metabolised. This is hidden. It is in the nature of shame that the wish to hide is evoked, and also that shame is itself shameful (Mollon, 2002b). The person's sensitivity is concealed, covered by a social façade. However, the sensitivities, vulnerabilities, and narcissistic wounds experienced in the course of ordinary social and relational interaction evoke not only intense shame, but also rage. The target of rage is the self (although there are some who express this outwardly at others, such as toward the mother or a partner). A tirade of self-directed abuse may in this way be continually stimulated, resulting in hostile inner self-talk and attacks on the body (which might also be hidden, such as cuts on parts covered by clothing, self-inflicted blows, or overdoses that do not require hospital treatment). The attacks on both body and mind cause further shame, although the assaults on the body could be experienced as soothing. This spiralling and intensifying "shame about shame", with its associated self-directed rage, may reach panic proportions, but all of a nature that the person finds near impossible to explain to others, or, indeed, to gain any clarity or distance for internal understanding. All the person feels is panic, shame, and compulsions to self-harm.

Introspection into these states of mind may be alarming for the person experiencing them, creating panic about panic, and shame about shame. It is a self-fuelling system of disturbance, whereby each increment in shame distress evokes a further increment, somewhat akin to a nuclear explosion and with similar, but psychological, devastation.

Giving up the torrents of shame-fuelled rage against the self is not a simple matter. This self-directed aggression might have formed a crucial structuring function within the personality, providing a kind of "strength" and keeping the person's behaviour in line. Thus, the messages of internal abuse may be along the lines of "you are pathetic—they will think you are stupid—you must not show how you feel—stop being such a wimp" (albeit with more colourful and vicious language). The person believes such voices are correct and that he or she needs them. One patient described her voices as like an exoskeleton—without them she would be formless and would have no direction. In extreme cases, the streams of self-abuse take on stable forms as quasi (or even actual) hallucinatory voices that appear to assume effective control over the personality. Such voices never take kindly to being discussed. They are like a military junta that has taken control of an otherwise weak or disintegrating country, maintaining order and power through aggression, cruelty, and intimidation.

Self-harm and the prey–predator dynamic

Self-harm, such as cutting the body, is often driven by shame, rage, and anxiety, and apparently can provide immediate relief for some. This relief appears to result from a sudden shift from the position of "prey" to that of "predator". Some hints concerning this dynamic are provided in a remarkable book, *Blood Rites*, by Barbara Ehrenreich (1997). She traces the history of humankind, exploring the roots of fears of the predator, deriving from primordial terrors of being eaten by carnivores: "The transformation from prey to predator, in which the weak rise up against the strong, is the central 'story' in the early human narrative" (p. 83).

According to her thesis, the hard-wired terror of predators of other species gradually shifted to a fear of human predators, fuelling the human compulsion to engage in continual warfare and in other ways playing out the prey–predator dynamic.

An awareness of this came to me during a particular session with a young woman who fitted the porous personality pattern. She was speaking of her anger and scorn regarding her own feelings of vulnerability and sensitivity, remarking that the only time she felt safe was when she was in bed at night, curled around her large husband, adding, with self-contempt, "how pathetic is that?!" I tried to speak to her, in what I misguidedly intended to be an empathic way, about her general sensitivity. She became increasingly agitated, and told me that her urge to self-harm was feeling stronger and stronger as we spoke. As I continued to try to talk to her of her sensitivity, her agitation escalated, until she stated that at that very moment her urge to run away and self-harm was stronger than she had ever known it. At that moment, I realised my stupidity and what she was trying to convey. Her feelings of sensitivity and vulnerability were completely intolerable for her because in that state she felt herself to be in the position of "prey". Self-harm has its relieving effect because it instantly shifts the person's identity from that of "prey" to that of "predator". By harming the body, the person steps into the position of predator, even though it is her or his own body that is the prey. Once I had articulated this to her, she began to calm down.

What makes psychotherapeutic work with this kind of porous personality organisation very difficult is that the whole structure of inner disturbance, with its core of vulnerability around which is organised a "Mafia-like" patrol engaging in self-directed aggression, is hidden, split off from the "apparently normal personality" presented to the world, including the therapist. It is possible to work with a patient for a long time without getting much glimpse of this hidden structure.

Moreover, the "voices" will emphasise to the person the foolhardiness of trusting anyone other than them—particularly the therapist. This message is easily received internally, since the person with a porous personality will have spent years in childhood of feeling inwardly very alone, not understood, and subject to rejections or bullying from peers (or even teachers). Even a kindly and loving mother may be experienced as failing to understand or protect the child.

Sometimes, the impression is that the person's emotional connections with others have been so severed, through pervasive distrust, that hallucinatory voices have become their only real companion. Their link with earlier precursors, such as imaginary friends, may become apparent.

Summary of characteristics

The people I am describing may or may not potentially attract a diagnosis of Asperger's or high functioning autism. In general, I am wary of categorical diagnosis, since mental and behavioural states exist along continuums. Moreover, the developmental and compensatory overlay and adaptations complicate the clinical picture enormously. However, it is possible tentatively to state the characteristics of the hidden autistic–hypersensitive core as follows.

- Chronic high levels of anxiety, often unfocused, but exacerbated in social situations, particularly in response to demands for social performance.
- A preference for order, routine, and predictability.
- A life-long unease and inherent awkwardness in social interactions and relationships, strongly concealed in some who have learnt social skills through observation, mimicry, and practice.
- A life-long sense of being "different"—like an alien in a human body.
- Puzzlement at the motives, emotions, and thought processes of others, although, paradoxically, this can coexist in some with a marked capacity for empathy.
- Hypersensitivity to both social and sensory stimuli.
- Hypersensitivity to emotional injury, rejections, slights, humiliations (narcissistic injuries)—"thin skinned".
- A tendency to "decompensate"—severe (but usually temporary) deteriorations in mental state, with psychotic, paranoid, or suicidal reactions—in response to rejections or narcissistic injuries.
- A tendency to avoid relationships because of this sensitivity.

- Porous boundaries—easily affected by other people's moods and emotions—sometimes resulting in high levels of empathy and interpersonal sensitivity.
- Intrusions of "primary process" thinking—images, fantasies, and "thoughts" that are difficult to translate into social discourse.
- A great propensity for shame.
- Some propensity for rage (often hidden and directed toward the self).
- Clairvoyant and other "psychic" or "paranormal" abilities.

Some people show these characteristics overtly and, thus, can more easily be recognised as falling within the autistic or "highly sensitive" spectrum. It is possible to achieve a healthy adaptation and self-acceptance in relation to these core traits. However, the people I am particularly describing have overlain this core with an "apparently normal" personality which makes recognition of the hidden problem much more difficult. This apparently normal personality shows the following characteristics.

- Outwardly sociable, may be pleasant and charming.
- Functions to conceal and protect the hidden autistic–hypersensitive core.
- Can be sensitive to others, displaying empathy and tact (but not always).
- At times might display behaviour or reactions that strike others as "odd".

The "outwardly normal" personality functions as a cover for the autistic–hypersensitive core. It is what most people, including, for a long time, the therapist, will encounter. Hidden behind it is not only the autistic–hypersensitive core itself, but also the shame, rage, and sense of inadequacy associated with this core. These are only gradually, if at all, revealed to the therapist. Family members, who have had most exposure to the patient from the beginning, might have some partial awareness of the more hidden aspects of the personality, but much may also be concealed from them.

Whilst this formulation might appear superficially similar to Winnicott's (1960b) theory of the "false self", the difference is that this is a response not to an intrusive or insufficiently adaptive mother, but to the inherent vulnerability of the autistic–hypersensitive core and its difficulties in the sensory and social world.

Clinical example[15]

Josephine presented to mental health services in her mid twenties. Her main area of distress concerned her daughter having been taken from her and placed in care. This had come about because a health visitor had noticed Josephine sometimes seemed distracted and not attuned to her young daughter's needs, and there was concern that the child was failing to thrive. Josephine expressed deep anguish about the loss of her child and hoped in time to resume her role as mother. However, she acknowledged that she had not wanted or intended to become pregnant. She had not maintained a relationship with her boyfriend, on the basis of her conclusion that involvements with others would only lead to pain and she preferred to avoid this. Despite her bias against relationships, Josephine did experience strong emotions of longing to have her daughter back with her, but she found these desires puzzling and disturbing since they conflicted with her preferred mode of living without emotion or desire. Josephine had achieved part qualifications in accountancy.

Josephine reported that her problems became manifest in her adolescence. At age fifteen she began making herself vomit and restricting her food. She said she did not like her body, which she considered fat, and found her breasts repulsive. In retrospect, she thought perhaps she had wanted to reverse puberty and recreate her thin child body. It was clear that the changes in her adolescent body, and the emotional impact of hormones, were extremely alarming for her, challenging her profound need for control and predictability. At age sixteen she had made a suicide attempt with an overdose of Paracetamol. She was quite unable to recall why she had done this, other than to say that she had been unhappy.

Josephine's clear unhappiness during her adolescence contrasted with her social involvement. She had friends, played sport, and was given a leadership role at school. This outward appearance disguised the turmoil within. She was constantly anxious—a background dread which would also become focused upon numerous aspects of her daily life as a teenager. Her school grades were a major target of fear, as well as her various social engagements. It seemed that from an outside perspective, she was viewed as charming and socially successful. However, she did not settle with any boyfriend, unlike many of her peers, although she did have brief involvements. Those who knew her well might also observe a certain rigidity in some of her habits, in relation to eating, for example.

During psychotherapy, Josephine spoke of having always felt different, and somehow fraudulent. She was unable to offer much further explanation of this, except to allude to seriously negative self-images, apparently viewing herself as worthless and incompetent. Although she recognised that she had friends and had been seemingly socially successful at school, she believed this simply indicated that people were "taken in" by her. If anyone really knew her, she argued, they would not want to have anything to do with her. Despite the vehemence and rigidity with which she held this view, she could offer little justification for it.

Josephine's account of her childhood background did not reveal much that would seem to explain the extent of her hidden disturbance. Both her parents were still alive and appeared supportive. She had a sister three years older, who apparently had no mental health problems. Josephine's birth had been prolonged, owing to her being breech. It seemed likely, from what Josephine had been told, that her mother suffered depression after the birth—and, indeed, that her mother tended toward a chronic low mood and lack of enthusiasm. For a long time during the psychotherapy, it was hypothesised that her mother's characterological low mood had cast an emotional shadow over Josephine's development, giving rise to a core belief that she was "not good enough" and could never please her mother. Moreover, our speculation was that a relative emotional *absence* of her father, due partly to his very demanding work schedule, had combined with the oppressive emotional *presence* of her mother to create a self-image in Josephine of being unlovable. We explored the possibility that, as a result of these experiences with her mother and her father, she had felt she must conceal her inner self and present a false "cheerful and outgoing" persona in order to be acceptable. Furthermore, we assumed that perhaps her perfectionism and intense academic and social striving at school had resulted from her attempts to meet what she perceived to be her parent's high demands and expectations. This line of enquiry did not, however, lead to any positive change or new understanding and eventually came to be seen as, in part, a "red herring". The more crucial explanatory understanding emerged from consideration of her inherent autistic spectrum sensitivity and her struggles against this.

After some months of meeting, Josephine revealed that she was in the habit of taking small overdoses of Paracetamol when she felt anxious and upset. On enquiring why, she said she did this to "punish" herself. She appeared to like the idea that the repeated toxic amounts of Paracetamol might be doing cumulative damage to her system—even reporting "enjoying" the feeling of a pain in her side. Another form of self-harm was her pattern of cutting herself with a razor, on her upper legs or other places that would not be visible when clothed. When asked why she wanted to punish herself, she said it was because she was a bad person and was "pathetic". It was a long time before it emerged that what she condemned herself for was her sensitivity and tendency to be upset by changes in routine, subtle slights and rejections by others, and failures to achieve perfect results in any task she set herself. She conveyed that somehow these acts of self-harm provided a sense of control, as well as being a channel for her rage. One point to emphasise here is that the whole inner picture—of her sensitivity, her shame and rage, and her self-harm—was hidden. None of it would be known to most of the people who had dealings with Josephine.

Josephine gradually explained that in her early twenties, she began a relationship with a boyfriend, thinking that he seemed to embody desirable qualities (such as stability, loyalty, and a lack of being overly demanding) and that such a relationship was part of the agenda for being "normal". She had not intended to become pregnant, but did so as a result of contraceptive failure. However, instead of this event leading her to feel more dependent on her partner, as it might with other women in that position, she reacted paradoxically by rejecting him. She reasoned that since they had not planned the pregnancy together, he would not be committed to her and the baby, and, therefore, it would be better for her to be without him rather than be vulnerable to his abandoning her. However, after the birth of the baby she had been depressed, which took the form of withdrawal and an absence of emotion and feeling of bonding with her daughter. When her daughter was removed from her care, Josephine reacted with shock and became extremely distressed. However, she found her emotions disturbing. Her feelings for her baby coexisted incongruently with her preference for walling herself off from emotions.

Gradually, Josephine became more able to reconstruct her early development and to speak of this in her therapy. She realised that she had made a choice early in her life, as a result of painful encounters with her peers at school, that she would conceal her inner feelings, even from herself. She would "pretend" to be like others, and developed an outer persona as happy and outgoing. By carefully observing others, and paying attention to portrayals of human interaction in films, Josephine became skilled at putting on a permanent "act" in all her social contexts. Her natural tendency to be strongly affected by other people's moods and emotions was used to develop a highly attuned empathy that gave her good information about her social world, even though she did not feel she was really part of this world. Painful experiences with others were kept in dissociated compartments—closed to others and (mostly) to herself. This strategy of social survival seemed to work for her until adolescence. At that time, under the impact of onslaughts of hormones and the turmoil of the adolescent process, she began to experience a terrible anguish that she felt she must desperately struggle to conceal. This anguish was very difficult for her to put into words, even though she kept a private diary of her thoughts and feelings. She recalled her writings from this time, of feeling she was an alien, that she had come from another planet, or that she was playing a part in some broader scripted theatre where the sense of personal choice was an illusion (somewhat like the idea of the Matrix films). It emerged that she would also, on occasion, hear a voice telling her she was a worthless and fraudulent person, and that she must punish herself by cutting. Josephine felt increasingly "unclean" (like a biblical leper), one who was not fit to be part of human society. At the same time she felt she must maintain the façade of normality, since she was sure that no one would be able to understand or accept her inner experience. She believed she was going mad, and yet was terrified of being seen as such by others, and of being put in that societal place of "invalid", of no longer having "validity". As a result, she desperately strove to suppress and conceal her inner torment and confusion. She settled on a plan of aiming to live without emotions, hoping that in this way she could avoid mental pain and achieve clarity of mind. Immersing herself in the works of Sartre and other existentialists seemed to help her in this process. Her private strategy for survival remained hidden from others.

Josephine's attempt to live without emotions was severely undermined by becoming pregnant. She alternated between numbed, "switched off", dissociative states, and times when she was overwhelmed with maternal feelings. When her baby was born, she went through the motions of care, but mostly in a state of emotional detachment until her daughter was removed from her. The shock of this intervention by the authorities caused her again to be flooded with maternal feelings and intense longing for her baby. Not only did she then feel her strategy had failed, but also she felt helplessly at the mercy of the inner turmoil that she had tried so hard to suppress.

Josephine's autistic avoidance of relatedness was apparent in the psychotherapeutic process through her subtle impression of fundamentally not liking to talk of her thoughts and feelings. There were frequent silences, and at times it would feel that facilitating her speech was like "pulling teeth". She did not display any eagerness for her sessions, and yet she always attended and was never late. Her reactions to breaks were of a superficial nonchalance, accompanied by an implied stance (sometimes stated explicitly) that she was used to looking after herself. Indeed, the whole idea of sharing her inner world with another person seemed to horrify her. She explained that she had never done this, and that it seemed fundamentally foreign to her. Moreover, she found introspection itself highly disturbing, evoking dread, shame, and sometimes panic. Her encounter with these feelings would evoke further anxiety, shame, and self-condemnation, thus generating a psychic "nuclear explosion", whereby each increment of distress triggers a further increment, spiralling into an ever more intense vortex of turmoil. Sometimes, these states could only be ended through some kind of self-harm or self-inflicted pain. She revealed that she had a habit of pinching herself so hard with her fingernails that blood was drawn, in parts of her body hidden by clothing.

Thus it was that psychotherapy was a profoundly torturous process for Josephine. It felt to her highly dangerous and foolhardy. She felt she was losing her fundamental strategy of survival, discarding her psychological armour, leaving her sensitive and shame-laden inner core exposed, and all her repertoire of self-condemnation activated. Her dread of a potential state of "resourceless dependence" (Khan, 1972) became apparent, expressed in a dream in which she was lying injured and helpless, in a snowy landscape, surrounded by predatory wolves. Inner voices told her to stop, declaring that she was fraudulent, "pulling the wool over (the therapist's) eyes", worthless, that she could not trust the therapist (or, indeed, anyone), and that nothing good could come of the therapeutic endeavour. Her mask of the happy and outgoing Josephine had slipped, and could not so easily be restored. At the same time, her distress and need compelled her to continue. It was a long and slow process, whereby Josephine gradually became more accepting and tolerant of her sensitive autistic spectrum core. A crucial part of this revolved around the therapist's explanation of autistic spectrum sensitivity, and the concept of the "highly sensitive person", showing this to be not only a recognised trait, but also one that in some ways is desirable and advantageous. This more positive perspective on her sensitivity was obviously not available to Josephine as a young child, and so the therapeutic process involved bringing this new information to bear on her childhood reasoning and self-perception. Some lessening in her feelings of shame, the fuel of self-hatred, modified the intensity of the fiery torment inside her. She became more able to accept her sensitivity and to adapt to this, no longer feeling so compelled to try to pretend to be like "everyone else". Her emotional self-protection could be more conscious, overt, and thoughtful. The psychotherapy lasted five years.

Commentary

I think there are many people like Josephine, who struggle with a highly sensitive core, which they perceive as being abnormal, wrong, and shameful. If not concealed, this sensitivity can render the person vulnerable to bullying by both peers and teachers. Sensing their difference from others, the highly sensitive person might embark on a developmentally fateful process of concealment of his or her authentic self, needs, and emotions, which is internally sequestered and attacked. An external "apparently normal" self is presented to the social world and, thus, a terrible inner "divided self" is born. Under stress, this kind of person might display psychotic features, reflecting the relative ease of access to "primary process" mental content. This, too, adds to the sense of being different. The stress that is experienced is, in large part, due to a barrage of sensory and social stimulation, impinging on the sensitive core. This combination of being porous, to both internal (primary process, dream-like) material and external social and sensory stimuli and their emotional impact, leaves the ego overwhelmed from inside and outside, struggling with an extreme form of "narcissistic vulnerability" (Mollon, 1993). Josephine attempted to survive not only by developing an "apparently normal" persona, but also by attempting to live without emotions. This fragile and doomed developmental endeavour did sustain her for a few years, but fractured under the impact of adolescent hormonal, social, and emotional pressures. Her repudiation of emotion was also shattered by the eruption of maternal feelings when she had a baby.

The three main psychotherapeutic dangers with patients like Josephine seem to be as follows. The more naïve forms of therapy, such as certain kinds of CBT, would tend, unknowingly, to reinforce or reinstate the failing "apparently normal" persona. A second danger is that an assumption is made that the level of disturbance is due to severe abuse or neglect during childhood, which might not have been the case (although this obviously does sometimes take place and can weave its malign influence through the clinical picture). This psychotherapeutic focus will ultimately not be fruitful. A third danger is that the defensive nature of the "false self" is recognised, but the intense turmoil and vulnerability that it defends against is not understood, with the result that the patient is left with his or her protective defences undermined, but without a supportive understanding of the nature of the threat. Related to this is the danger that the "false self" is perceived not as a protection against inner danger, but as a response to an insufficiently adaptive mother (as described by Winnicott, 1960b). It is important to recognise that the turmoil of the "porous personality" is not anyone's fault—no one is to blame and no one need feel shame—but without a good understanding of the problem, the suffering and sense of isolation and alienation are immense.

Positive aspects of the "porous personality": Donna Williams

The characteristics of the porous personality are rather close to some of the accounts of her autistic experience provided in the remarkable writings of Donna Williams, particularly in her book *Autism and Sensing* (1998b). Williams describes a primary mode of being that consists of *sensing*, without *interpretation*. It is the interpreting mind that ascribes meaning and categories to the sensing experience, establishing boundaries and separation. Her description is somewhat reminiscent of McGilchrist's (2009) account of the contrasting and complementary roles of the right hemisphere (apprehending the living moment without assigning it to a category) and the left hemisphere (judging and categorising experience, and destroying its life). Williams lived for years of her childhood much more in the sensing realm, resulting in many social and psychological difficulties.

For Williams, the boundaries between self and other could be flimsy or non-existent:

> As a young child, people would enter my room and sometimes, without even looking, I'd merge with them and my sense of "entity", perhaps the energy I identified as "mine", left the room as them when they left again. When my body called me back, it was as though I'd had a sharp perceptual shift. It was as if I was surprised to find myself back with my own body. (Williams, 1998b, p. 60)

This porous quality gave her an immediate empathy with others, in the sense of feeling their emotions:

> Walking through the supermarket, I physically felt the pain when someone banged themselves. Around someone with a broken leg, I felt their pain in my leg. The prickles or shivers would get me when I stood too close to someone without walls, as though their energy was affecting me. I could feel when people had real connected emotional pain whether they displayed it or not and I could feel when they were putting it on, when the display had no connection to the energy it was meant to come from. (1998b, p. 59)

Her empathy and loss of personal boundaries could be frightening:

> Some people, however, would capture me emotionally without trying. Merely to be touched by them or looked at could overwhelm me with feelings, sweeping my selfhood away as easily as cobwebs with a duster. With objects, this felt enclosed, taken in, warm and insular. With humans, this felt out of control and frightening. The lightning speed and enormity with which the "self-connectedness" of mind gets washed away by such tidal waves felt like the threat of death . . . (1998b, pp. 59–60)

Williams recognises the value of the human social system of inter-pretation, but she regards the image of the self that it creates as a "false self", not dissimilar to Lacan's (1949) view of the false ego arising from the "mirror stage" and the identification with images and signifiers. She writes of the positive potential for society of retaining both modes of being:

> Imagine a world where all had the flexibility of both systems, where the social cancer born of false-self was not as pervasive nor promoted as natural, where true empathy born of resonance took at least equal place with learned "manners" and the performance of socially expec-ted empathy behaviour. In such a world, one would retain the ability to lose separateness and feel not just for someone or something but *as* someone or something. (1998b, p. 118)

CHAPTER EIGHT

The psychology and neurobiology of the autistic spectrum

"The autistic child and the autistic part in all of us hanker after certainty, after freedom from doubt, after complete knowledge, after unalloyed satisfaction. The hard fact that this is unobtainable is the sharp rock upon which . . . psychic development has foundered. Their emotional and cognitive development has been crippled by the umbrage aroused by it"

(Tustin, 1986, p. 168)

The usual description of autistic spectrum disorders as characterised by deficits in social and communication skills, and in the display of repetitive and stereotyped behaviours, may be supplemented by reference to a number of other aspects of behaviour and experience that become apparent when such people are seen in psychotherapy.

High levels of anxiety and shame

Many (but not all) people on this spectrum are assailed by continual high levels of anxiety. This may worsen when in situations involving proximity to other people and particularly those requiring interaction with others. Psychological contact with other people, including eye contact, may be overstimulating, causing physiological arousal, confusion, irritation, and panic. This may be described as extreme shyness and social anxiety. It might become suffused with shame.

Some of the higher functioning people on the autistic spectrum might manage to conceal this inner turmoil and present outwardly and superficially an "apparently normal" social persona. This split between the inner cauldron of anxiety, confusion, and shame and the outer "apparently normal" personality might begin early. I once asked an extremely troubled lady, with marked autistic spectrum features and intense anxiety and shame, whether she had felt this way as a child. She replied that inwardly she had felt like this for as long as she could remember. I then asked how her teachers might have described her. She said they would have described her as a happy, outgoing, and confident child. Because the world is experienced by the person on the autistic spectrum as inherently assaultive and traumatising, the ground is laid for the development of dissociative disorders (as described in Donna William's autobiographical book *Nobody Nowhere* (1998a)).

It is not only the social world that can seem frightening. People on the autistic spectrum often feel generally unsafe in the physical world. It can seem too big and too open. There can be a preference for familiar enclosed spaces. One woman managed to take the step of purchasing a house, much larger than the small flat where she had lived for some years. She found it "too big" with "too much space", and preferred to sit in a corner with furniture surrounding her. On the other hand, claustrophobic anxiety can occur in unfamiliar enclosed spaces, such as a lift, or a new car.

The continual anxiety and physiological arousal (albeit sometimes hidden from others) tends to take its toll on the body, resulting eventually in psychosomatic illness of various kinds, particularly gut problems, headaches and migraines, and fibromyalgia.

Need for routine, predictability, and certainty

Changes in routine, for example in the workplace, tend to be highly aversive and disturbing for the person on the autistic spectrum, causing marked increases in anxiety and ruminatory apprehension. Adaptation to change is slow. Buying and wearing new clothes is notoriously difficult for such people. Clothes that are unfamiliar can feel irritating and somehow "not right". One man told me of how he tended to avoid having a bath or shower, not because he disliked bathing but because he found the process of putting on clean clothes highly aversive.

A single mother with pronounced autistic spectrum features, widowed with three children (all of whom also were on the autistic spectrum) was able to cope so long as she had a clear routine and schedule in relation to school, mealtimes, bath and bedtimes, but would be triggered into great anxiety by the endings of school terms. She would also become extremely agitated if social workers (or indeed any visitor) turned up unexpectedly without having made an appointment.

The requirement to shift attention can similarly be challenging. If the person is focused on one task, it can be difficult to shift to another task. The overall context of a situation might be missed because the focus is on some detail—examining the individual tree so much that there is no view of the overall forest. This can be helpful in highly technical pursuits, but can cause inefficiency in undertaking more complex work.

The lack of flexibility and the rigidity of attentional focus seems related to perfectionism and "black and white" thinking. Thought and perception are categorical, phenomena are placed in clear categories, rather like the left hemispheric dominance described by McGilchrist in his book *The Master and his Emissary* (McGilchrist, 2009) and Tweedy (2013). One man was highly diligent in his work requiring careful sorting of technical documents, but he was slow because he could not tolerate any possibility of error. His supervisor urged him to work faster, resulting in errors. This caused him great stress, resulting in more errors. A vicious circle ensued, as his anxiety spiralled and his work performance deteriorated, resulting eventually in his resignation from his job with great despair and collapse in his self-esteem.

A state of not knowing, or of uncertainty, can be highly aversive for people on the autistic spectrum and can sometimes provoke an illusory or confabulated certainty. Memory for events might be unreliable, with source monitoring errors (mistakes over the source of a memory or idea) and transposition of elements from one scene to another (Hala et al., 2005), all of which are not necessarily uncommon amongst the general population, but this inherent uncertainty of memory might be displaced by a false certainty. Similar positions of certainty and intolerance of ambiguity might be taken up in the realm of aesthetic, cultural, and political attitudes. One man had been a fanatical and absolutist communist in his political views, until a later point when he decided that capitalism is an inescapable reality, so that he then espoused a position whereby the requirements of a business company took absolute and total precedence over any needs of the individual worker. He would become highly animated and agitated as he articulated this view, and he could tolerate no disagreement. Not surprisingly, this rigid and extreme stance led to recurrent difficulties in his relationships.

Affect regulation: repetitive activities and the sensation-dominated world

Any increase in anxiety and stress is liable to trigger the autistic spectrum person's affect management behaviours. These are often repetitive and somewhat compulsive activities, sometimes involving their "special interests" or current obsessions. For example, one woman would have periods of purchasing numerous boxes of transparent tape or plastic ducks for the bath, none of which she actually needed or used. She would resort to this activity whenever her stress, from whatever source, rose above a tolerable threshold.

In the case of those who are further along the autistic spectrum, there can be a retreat to a "sensation-dominated world" and the non-living in place of connection with human beings. Frances Tustin, in her wonderful book *Autistic Barriers in Neurotic Patients* (1986) comments: "His is a sensation-dominated world in which he seeks *sensations* rather than objects as such. He is not responsive to people as people, but mostly in terms of the sensations they engender" (p. 54).

Slow processing; literal thinking

Processing of social and conversational information might be markedly slow. In the case of people with quite severe traits on this spectrum, the delay in responding to a question or conversational gesture may appear disconcertingly odd, as the person shows no verbal or facial reaction for ten or more seconds. Sometimes, this problem of slow and incomplete processing of conversational information is hidden by an "apparently normal" and immediate response in words that obscures the reality that the person has neither understood what was said nor provided an accurate reply. The words used do not necessarily convey a true meaning. This can make clinical interviews somewhat misleading.

Recurrent confusions and frustrations can occur in social and familial interactions with people on the autistic spectrum as a result of their (sometimes) literal interpretation of verbal messages. It is as if words lose their emotional and connotative meanings, and become devoid of cultural allusions. An invitation such as "Would you like to come round for coffee?" might be responded to on the basis of whether the autistic person likes coffee, thus possibly resulting in the answer "no" when a reference to "tea" would have evoked "yes". An urgent knock on the bathroom door and the enquiry "will you be long?" might result in a precise estimate of the amount of time left to be taken by his or her ablutions, rather than an understanding that a family member is experiencing an urgent need for the lavatory.

In their struggles with social and sensory information, people on the autistic spectrum might be having to cope with a continual threat of chaos, confusion, and disintegration (Ogden, 1989). Many common features of this spectrum—such as social withdrawal, rigidity, imposition of certainty, etc.—might seem to be attempts to cope with, or compensate for, this threat.

Prisoners of the moment

Some (but by no means all) people on the autistic spectrum seem to be prisoners of the present moment. The past and the future are dim. Working towards a future goal does not engage their attention and energy. The outcome of a current activity may appear unclear or irrelevant. Perhaps related to this is a paradoxical tendency to be, on occasion, impulsive. For example, one woman bought a new car on her way home, although she had not planned or intended to, or even thought about doing so beforehand. She had driven to a garage for petrol and her attention had been caught by an offer on a new car. Later, she was extremely agitated because she could not afford this car. Such behaviour clearly has some similarity with the impulsivity shown by people with ADHD.

Empathy, "theory of mind", and turning away from others

The autistic spectrum person's psychological understanding of both self and others might be deficient, or patchy (Baron-Cohen, 2003; Ozonoff et al., 1991). Self-awareness, and the capacity to gauge how he or she appears to others, might be limited, or at least uneven. It is not that the person is completely lacking in "theory of mind" skills, but these might have a less immediate and automatic quality. Possibly this is why a surprising proportion of psychologists seem to display autistic spectrum traits, as they perhaps seek to supplement their deficient "theory of mind" skills by academic learning about the mind!

It should not be assumed that people on the autistic spectrum (especially those who may be described as having Asperger's) do not wish for contact and relationship with others, or that they are lacking in emotional reactions to others. People with autistic traits can feel very emotionally needy and vulnerable, and may potentially experience intense emotions, including both pain and rage. He or she might accurately and realistically recognise their "narcissistic vulnerability", the fragility of their mental organisation and the potential for disintegration if exposed to too much relational trauma. This leads to a protective turning away from others and shutting down emotionally. For the person on the autistic spectrum, contact with others needs to be titrated according to what can be tolerated.

Whilst it is commonly thought that people on the autistic spectrum are deficient in the capacity for empathy, I have found that some are very highly empathic, but in ways that can be overwhelming. Such highly emotionally sensitive people can be flooded in identification with another person's distress. Meltzer (1975) describes the temperament of some autistic children treated psychoanalytically as follows:

> . . . the children present an emotional sensibility which we would wish
> to describe as a kind of gentleness of disposition. Their awareness of
> the mental states of the person to whom they feel intimately related

... is in the nature of a primitive permeability to the emotions of others ... the special nakedness to the emotional winds emanating from others. (pp. 9–10)

When carefully managed, this capacity for feeling the other's pain can prove highly valuable in the profession of psychotherapy. However, what tends often to happen is that the powerful infusion of emotion from another person is experienced as "too much", potentially causing panic or somatic reactions, and triggering emergency shutting down of empathy. The person then appears cold, unfeeling, and "non-relating". Such reactions also have some similarity to the schizoid responses to narcissistic injury, described by Kohut (1971).

Meltzer (1975) observes that the emotionally sensitive person on the autistic spectrum might have initially tended to assume that others are as easily permeated by empathic emotion as he or she is, and so any evidence to the contrary is experienced as a hostile rejection.

This tendency to be bombarded by awareness of the pain in others, coupled with the inclination to interpret emotional obtuseness in others as rejection, makes for a very special vulnerability to catastrophic modes of depressive experience. (p. 10)

Tustin (1986) describes evidence that, in some cases, "autistic children have experienced an agony of consciousness in early infancy" in which too many feelings "were experienced precociously and in a compacted way" (p. 118), as a result of which the human world is felt to be terrifying, invasive, collapsing, or disintegrating. In an attempt to manage these intolerable experiences, the child turns away from the human world: "People are experienced as particularly contrary objects which get out of his control; window panes and suchlike inanimate objects are felt to be much more satisfactory" (p. 145). A patient with marked autistic spectrum features told me that after disturbing interactions with her volatile mother, she would lose herself in a calming state of communing with a radiator, a reassuringly hard and inanimate object that would not shout at her. Tustin notes that such processes "result in a negation of the mother and her human qualities" and that the resulting sensory objects "are not a *substitute* for the mother which enables the child to wait for her return. They are a tangible *replacement* for her which blocks imaginative representation" (p. 145).

Tustin (1986) concludes,

> The trouble with psychogenic autism is that once it has started it easily becomes a rootless, empty way of life, kept going by endless manipulations. Used in a massive way, it leads to a devious psychopathic character and to a devious psychopathic culture. I am coming to the conclusion that many of us—some more so than others—have a bit of psychogenic autism which has shied away from the pains and difficulties of relating to other human beings, and has resorted to devious and manipulative means to avoid these pains. (p. 56)

Although Tustin makes a distinction between autism due to brain abnormalities and what she calls "psychogenic autism", it seems to me that probably what is happening in the processes she describes is that a person is trying to deal with autistic spectrum sensitivities and functional deficits, with all the anxiety and confusion resulting from these, and resorts to these typical autistic defences of turning away from the human world and finding comfort and relief of anxiety in the sensory and non-human realms—processes also described similarly by Ogden (1989).

Feeling "different" and being different.

People on the autistic spectrum experience themselves as *different* from others. This perception is true. The processing style of their brain, their perception of the world, and their general attitudes tend to be atypical. I have found it helpful to say to such people that they are indeed "different" from the majority but they are part of a *substantial minority* who share these characteristics. Processing of information is slower (in certain respects), less verbal and more visual, and there is a bias towards logical reasoning in place of emotional perception and social intelligence.

Because people on the autistic spectrum are actually different in their inner processing and outward behaviour, they are prone to being bullied or rejected. Even when the person is relatively high functioning, subtleties of difference—in social manner, body posture, mode of walking (slightly stiff, and sometimes arms and legs swinging homolaterally)—are subliminally perceived by others and can lead to rejection or abuse, sometimes seemingly random and casual. For example, one man reported that as he walked around the town where he lived, strangers would give him hostile looks or make disparaging remarks as they passed him on the pavement. His account could have been perceived as paranoid, until a relative followed him a little distance behind, and verified that what he described was indeed the case.

Sometimes, people on the autistic spectrum have unusual and somewhat compulsive sexual interests, and, indeed, I have come to view bizarre and compulsive sexual preoccupations as highly indicative of autistic spectrum characteristics. These can include all manner of rigidly fetishistic and auto-erotic interests and behaviours, perhaps occurring more frequently among men. Such compulsive engagements are resorted to particularly in response to increased stress, but can also function to increase stimulation when this is lacking.

In my perception, autistic spectrum characteristics have some overlap with those of the "highly sensitive person" (Aron, 1999). Both descriptions include sensitivity to loud, noisy, and discordant environments, a need to spend time alone, and a preference for solo working environments. The sense of not belonging, or of being "an alien in a human body", or of "being too sensitive for this world" can apply in both.

Chronic mood of depression

The sense of being different, of being alone, and without connection to others may conspire to create a chronic mood of depression and quiet despair, a deep inner feeling that it is never possible to be known or understood. People on the autistic spectrum do often present to psychiatric services with depression, and the autistic traits might not initially be apparent. Tustin (1986) considered depression, linked to a primitive and overwhelming infantile grief over separation and loss, to be often at the core of "psychogenic autism". The normal separation from the original sense of bodily continuity with the mother and the breast has been, for these infants, felt to be a terrifying catastrophe:

> In reality, what happened to the children was in the nature of a sensuous mishap, but in the hypersensitized, illusion-dominated state of early infancy, it had become exaggerated to seem like a catastrophe. But the feelings associated with this illusion had been traumatizing.

As one patient said to me, I know it's an illusion, but the terror is real. (Tustin, 1986, p. 93)

Summary of autistic spectrum characteristics

Here is a list of some of the characteristics of people on the autistic spectrum. It must be emphasised that there is great variability among people on this spectrum and not all characteristics will be present in any one individual.

- High levels of anxiety and confusion:
  - easily overwhelmed by sensory and social stimulation; need to withdraw to recover from states of being overwhelmed;
  - pervasive social anxiety, sometimes hidden by an "apparently normal personality";
- Resort to "autistic defences"—repetitive actions, narrow interests, and a "sensation-dominated" world—particularly when stressed or overwhelmed.
- Visual thinking:
  - people on the autistic spectrum tend not to use verbal strategies for recalling information but primarily use visual images.
- Literal thinking:
  - metaphors and figures of speech may be confusing;
  - words are taken at face value; hidden meanings are not explored;
  - implicit meanings in communications, and subtle hints, are not understood; instructions and questions need to be explicit and clear.
- Deficient self-concept:
  - deficits in the sense of who one is, a person with a history, a family, and cultural lineage, formative experiences, enduring goals and values, etc.
- Deficient theory of mind:
  - lacunae in the understanding of other's emotions, motives, point of view, and thoughts.
- Difficulty in shifting attention:
  - may continue an activity, or topic of conversation, seemingly endlessly.

- Lack of coherent overall perspective:
  - details may be remembered, but with little sense of overall meaning.
- Cognitive inflexibility:
  - impedes transfer of knowledge across situations;
  - unable to engage in "fuzzy logic".
- Organisational deficits:
  - thoughts, tasks, and possessions may be in chaos; or there may be extensive external order, so that the person becomes very upset if anything is moved.
- Source monitoring:
  - problems in knowing the origin of memories, beliefs, knowledge, who said what (e.g., not knowing whether he or she has actually said something or has just thought it in their own mind).
- Deficit in inhibitory functions:
  - might be impulsive and disinhibited, might be unable to refrain from speaking even when this is inappropriate;
  - might speak and behave without regard for how this is experienced by others.
- Systemising *vs.* empathising:
  - a cognitive and hemispheric preference for focusing on an overall system or pattern, rather than understanding the experience of an individual within that system.
- Idiosyncratic logic:
  - strange humour.
- In the moment thinking:
  - unable to take account of past or future contexts.
- Black and white thinking:
  - excessive use of rigid and polarised categories.

Neurobiology of the autistic spectrum

What do we know of the brain functioning of people on the autistic spectrum that might throw light on these various characteristics? There is certainly growing knowledge, but the understanding of the neurobiology of Asperger's and other autistic spectrum conditions is less clear than that of ADHD.

Abnormal brain anatomy

Abnormal early brain development has been noted (Carper & Courchesne, 2005; Courchesne et al., 2004). Kemper and Bauman (2002) have reported on direct brain autopsy studies of nine cases well documented as autistic, finding "a curtailment of maturation in the forebrain limbic system, abnormalities in the cerebellar circuits, and an unusual pattern of change of postnatal brain size" (p. S12). In the forebrain limbic areas, involved in memory and emotionality, there were more neurons than usual, of small size, and packed unusually close together. Complex pathology was found in cerebellar circuits, with a reduction in Purkinje cells at all ages, suggesting some impact on movement and physical coordination. In younger brains, the Purkinje cells were also abnormally large, whereas in older brains they were abnormally small. This study also found the brain weight in the younger autopsy cases was significantly greater than comparable controls, but the authors note the findings of Courchesne and colleagues (2001) that abnormal early brain growth in children with autism is followed by abnormally slow growth.

Abnormal functional connectivity

In recent years, interest has focused on the ways in which autistic phenomena seem to be related to how the brain as a whole functions, and unusual aspects of its internal connectivity. Thus, Schmitz and Rezaie (2008) conclude,

> The neurobiology and neuropathology of the autism spectrum disorders (ASD) remain poorly defined. Brain imaging studies suggest that the deficits in social cognition, language, communication and stereotypical patterns of behaviour that are manifest in individuals with ASD, are related to functional disturbance and 'disconnectivity', affecting multiple brain regions. (p. 4)

There is an emerging impression that disrupted connectivity between different regions of the brain is an important factor (Belmonte et al., 2004; Just et al., 2007; Wass, 2011). Hughes (2007) described *underconnectivity* in autism, including thinning of the corpus collosum, as the "first firm finding". This is not entirely to do with the anatomical aspects of density of neurons, but also concerns how different areas function together. However, the findings in this area are complex and sometimes appear (initially) contradictory, with both *hyper*connectivity and *hypo*connectivity noted. Weng and colleagues (2010) conclude that individuals with ASD have a greater number of short to medium range intra-hemispheric connections and fewer longer range inter-hemispheric connections—too much activity in local regions and insufficient communication between regions, drawing on the work of Herbert and colleagues (2003, 2004)—and that "both structural and functional evidence suggest that there is profound disruption in brain connectivity in ASD" (Weng et al., 2010, p. 2).

Along these line, Courchesne and Pierce (2005) propose,

> It is suggested that connectivity within frontal lobe is excessive, disor-ganized and inadequately selective, whereas connectivity between frontal cortex and other systems is poorly synchronized, weakly responsive and information impoverished. Increased local but reduced long-distance cortical–cortical reciprocal activity and coup-ling would impair the fundamental frontal function of integrating information from widespread and diverse systems and providing complex context-rich feedback, guidance and control to lower-level systems. (p. 225)

This would mean that information would not be processed rapidly or efficiently within the brain. Some areas might be over-active, but not in a way that is helpful for a task, while other areas are not commu-nicating well. The situation would be like a computer with an ineffi-cient processor, causing it to run slowly and sometimes freeze.

Similarly, Takahata and Kato (2008) comment,

> We emphasize the crucial role played by the disruption of global connectivity in a parallel distributed cortical network, which might result in impairment in integrated cognitive processing, such as impairment in executive function and social cognition. On the other hand, the reduced inter-regional collaboration could lead to a disin-hibitory enhancement of neural activity and connectivity in local corti-cal regions. (p. 861)

What is described here is an incoherent brain, where information is not integrated efficiently and smoothly. The necessary balance of excitation and inhibition is disrupted, so that areas whose excitation should subside during a task are too active while other areas that should be active are not.

Some data throw light on the traits of obsession, and the difficulty autistic spectrum people can have with shifting attention. Zikopoulos and Barbas (2013) found that the anterior cingulate cortex, orbito-frontal cortex, and lateral prefrontal cortex are functionally disorgan-ised in autism, showing *local overconnectivity* and *long distance under-connection*. The anterior cingulate cortex, *which is involved in allocating attention*, is over-active, stimulating and inhibiting other neurons to make it difficult for the person to shift attention from one stimulus or thought to another. Reduced long distance connectivity to other brain regions means other information, including from the senses, and between the hemispheres, is insufficiently transmitted.

Default mode network

Weng and colleagues (2010) studied activity within the default mode network (DMN) in adolescents with autistic spectrum conditions, compared with typically developing adolescents. The significance of the DMN is that it is active when the brain is not engaged in any exter-nal task, and so is an indication of "resting" activity. The key parts of the DMN are the posterior cingulate cortex (PCC), retrosplenial, lateral parietal/angular gyrus, medial prefrontal cortex, superior frontal gyrus, regions of the temporal lobe, and the parahippocampal gyrus. Since the activity of this circuitry consumes considerable energy (Laughlin & Sejnowski, 2003), it is presumed that the DMN has some important functions, perhaps to do with processing internally focused thoughts, and with maintaining homeostasis between excitatory and inhibitory neuronal responses. Compared with the control group, the adolescents with autistic traits showed lower connectivity between the PCC and nine of eleven areas of the DMN. Regarding severity of symptoms, they found the following (Weng et al., 2010, p. 6):

- greater social impairment was associated with weaker connectiv-ity between the PCC and the superior frontal gyri, the PCC and the temporal lobes, as well as the PCC and the parahippocampal gyri;
- more severe restricted and repetitive behaviours were associated with weaker connectivity between the PCC and the medial

prefrontal cortex, the PCC and the temporal lobes, as well as the PCC and the superior frontal gyri;

• poorer verbal and non-verbal communicative ability was associated with stronger connectivity between the PCC and the right parahippocampal gyrus as well as the PCC and the temporal lobes.

However, these findings differed somewhat from the same researchers' earlier study of adults with autistic spectrum traits (Monk et al., 2009). In the adult group, more severe restricted and repetitive behaviours were associated with *stronger* connectivity between the PCC and other areas. Since there is some evidence that restricted and repetitive behaviours tend to diminish somewhat as the person moves from adolescence to adulthood (Seltzer et al., 2003), they hypothesise that these stronger connections in adults reflect some compensatory efforts, perhaps resulting from struggles to modify the repetitive behaviours. This point illustrates how brain function and anatomy may be different at different ages, adding to the difficulty in drawing firm conclusions from brain data as to what causes autistic spectrum traits.

Von dem Hagen and colleagues (2013) also found reduced functional connectivity in areas of the DMN in people with autistic traits, particularly the medial prefrontal cortex, but, in addition, reduced connectivity between the mPFC and other areas outside the DMN, the amygdala and insula, and also between the amygdala and insula.

Kennedy and colleagues (2006) found that people on the autistic spectrum, compared with control subjects, failed to show the normal deactivation of the DMN during tasks. Various additional considerations led them to conclude that this reflects an absence of normal activation of this network during rest—i.e. that it did not deactivate during a cognitive task because there was not much activity even during rest. These researchers also found that the autistic spectrum group, compared to controls, did not show the normal bias towards recognition of emotional words (*vs.* neutral words), and did not show the normal activation in the medial orbital frontal region of the resting network when processing emotional words compared with neutral words. Severity of social impairment correlated with the degree of these abnormalities.

Diminished activity and reduced functional connectivity in the DMN might be a crucial neurobiological correlate of autistic spectrum traits, since aspects of this network have been found to be important in tasks and skills, such as self-reflective thought and higher order social and emotional processing, that are difficult for people on this spectrum. Thus, it is involved with processing emotional meaning (Cato et al., 2004; Maddock et al., 2003; Whalen et al., 1998), with "theory of mind" activity involving the understanding of the minds of self and other (Fletcher et al., 1995; Gallagher & Frith, 2003; Vogeley et al., 2001), with the experience of shared "joint attention" with another person (Williams et al., 2005), and with the recognition of familiar faces (Maddock et al., 2001; Pierce et al., 2004)

Attentional abnormalities

You and colleagues (2013) compared a group of neurotypical children with those with autistic spectrum traits on measures of brain function at rest and when engaged in a task requiring attention. The normally developing children showed activation in specific areas concerned with attention, whereas those with autistic traits showed the opposite pattern, of a more diffuse and indiscriminate pattern of cortical activation. These authors also note the findings that activities requiring much attentional resources, such as working memory, face processing, and "theory of mind", show reduced connectivity of task-selective networks comprising distant frontal–posterior regions in children with autistic spectrum traits (Just et al., 2012; Khan et al., 2013). Attentional problems are common among people with autistic spectrum traits, with over 40% of children with ASD also meeting the criteria for ADHD (Leyfer et al., 2006; Sikora et al., 2012; Yerys et al., 2009).

Hyper- and hypo-responsiveness

Some studies report that children with autism show sensory hypo-responsiveness, especially those who are non-verbal (Patten et al., 2013), whilst others describe over-arousal and hyper-reactivity, along with over-focused attention and exceptional memory (Liss et al., 2006). A meta-analysis of fourteen studies showed a significant large difference between those on the autistic spectrum and typical groups in the presence or frequency of sensory symptoms, but these were mixed findings, the greatest proportion showing under-responsivity, and a smaller proportion showing over-responsivity and sensation seeking (Ben-Sasson et al., 2009).

Relatively little is known about the neurobiological basis of sensory over-responsiveness in autistic spectrum conditions. However, Green and colleagues (2013), using an fMRI scan, found that, when presented with mildly aversive visual and auditory stimuli, a sample of adolescents with autistic spectrum traits showed greater activation in primary sensory cortical areas as well as amygdala, hippocampus, and orbital–frontal cortex and the level of activity in these areas was positively correlated with level of severity of sensory over-reactivity. A subsequent study by the same researchers (as yet unpublished but presented at the May 14, 2014 International Meeting for Autism Research, Atlanta) compared the fMRI responses of autistic *vs.* normal adolescents to the sensation of a scratchy sweater and loud traffic noises. The autistic group showed much stronger reactions in the sensory cortex and amygdala, particularly when the two sensations were presented together, and their reactions did not habituate but remained high (unlike the normal group).

Rubenstein and Merzenich (2003) review evidence to support a model of autism based on a disproportionately high level of excitation (and low inhibition) in neural circuits regulating language and social behaviour. They argue that a more excitable cortex is more poorly differentiated in function and is likely to lead to widespread abnormalities in perception, memory and cognition, and motor control and also that such a hyper-excitable and "noisy" cortex is inherently unstable and susceptible to epilepsy.

Orekhova and Stroganova (2014) reviewed behavioural and physiological studies that point to abnormalities in the brain's response to novel stimuli in individuals with autistic spectrum traits. The normal activation of areas involved in processing novel aspects of the sensory world might not take place. The authors argue that brain tasks of responding to novel stimuli are normally strongly lateralised to the right hemisphere and that the autistic subjects react somewhat like certain patients with right hemispheric damage. However, they emphasise the autism should not be regarded as a "right hemisphere disorder", since there is evidence of abnormal functioning of both hemispheres as well as atypical lateralisation.

Abnormal lateralisation: left or right?

The findings in the study just described, of deficits in right hemispheric functioning, is a theme explored more broadly by McGilchrist

(2009), who draws upon a vast amount of neurobiological and socio-cultural data. He points out that many of the capacities in which people on the autistic spectrum are deficient, such as empathy and understanding social language, metaphor, and irony, are all mediated by the right frontal region. The right hemisphere decodes emotional expression in language and is faster than the left hemisphere in discriminating facial expressions. It is the right hemisphere that is primarily involved in "theory of mind" activities. The right hemisphere "has an affinity with whatever is living, but the left hemisphere has an equal affinity for what is mechanical" (p. 55). Whilst the left hemisphere is concerned with getting and making and categorising, the right hemisphere apprehends the novelty of the other and can engage in empathy:

> Because of the right hemisphere's openness to the interconnectedness of things, it is interested in others as individuals, and in how we relate to them. It is the mediator of empathic identification. If I imagine myself in pain I use both hemispheres, but your pain is in my right hemisphere . . . In general the right hemisphere is critical for making attributions of the content, emotional or otherwise, of another's mind, and particularly in respect of the affective state of another individual . . . The right hemisphere has by far the preponderance of emotional understanding. It is the mediator of social behaviour. (McGilchrist, 2009, pp. 57–58)

As I have indicated above, some people on the autistic spectrum do have a capacity for empathy and can sometimes suffer from a state of being overwhelmed by the other person's emotional pain. This can lead to a protective shutting down of the capacity for empathy. I propose a hypothesis that what might sometimes happen in such instances is that a protective, emergency-driven shutting down of aspects of right hemispheric functioning takes place, with the result that no further processing of emotion is possible for a certain period of time. In such a state, the person behaves like a patient with right hemispheric damage (as described above by Orekhova & Stroganova, 2014). This radical shutting off of emotional processing might also result in denuding words of their meaning, and, similarly, of the emotional investment of the inner representations of both self and other. Such a person may then be left in a highly aversive state of depersonalisation and derealisation, trying to communicate with words that are felt to be meaningless. Sometimes, there may be a giving up on words and the emergence of selective mutism.

On the other hand, there has been considerable speculation that autistic spectrum conditions are to do with impaired *left* hemispheric functioning (e.g., Prior & Bradshaw, 1979). Part of the rationale for this hypothesis is that people on the autistic spectrum often show difficulties in areas thought to be normally left hemisphere functions, such as language and communication, while seeming relatively unimpaired in right hemispheric skills such as visuo-spatial tasks. People on the autistic spectrum often think in pictures rather than words. There is some evidence that people on the autistic spectrum attempt to process language with the right hemisphere. Redcay and Courchesne (2008) found that 2–3-year-old autistic children showed greater activity in the right hemisphere when listening to speech, compared to normal children who showed more activity in the left. Similar findings for autistic adults were reported by Koshino and colleagues (2005). Blackstock (1978) found that autistic children preferred listening to music rather than speech, and preferred to listen to both speech and music with the left ear (which is more connected to the right hemisphere); by contrast, normal children showed no preference for music or speech but tended to listen to music with the left ear and speech with the right. Prior and Bradshaw (1979), using a dichotic listening task, found that autistic children tended to show right hemisphere dominance for processing language, in contrast to the left hemisphere dominance shown by non-autistic children. Herbert and colleagues (2002) found that the normal asymmetry of larger frontal language related cortex on the left was reversed into larger on the right in a sample of boys with autism and this was replicated by De Fossé and colleagues (2004). Floris and colleagues (2013) found an atypical rightward shift of connectivity in some parts of the corpus collosum in a sample of male adolescents and the degree of this related to severity of symptoms.

These contradictory observations, with competing hypotheses concerning deficits in both left and right hemispheres (just as with ADHD) do not permit any firm conclusions at this point. What does seem clear is that the anatomy and functioning of the two hemispheres, and the relationship between them, are abnormal in the autistic spectrum (as well as in ADHD). The difficulty in locating the deficit in either the left or right hemisphere perhaps makes the point that the problem lies in the dysfunctional communication and cooperation between the two. Thus, Melillo and Leisman (2009) hypothesise that "the problem of autistic spectrum disorder is primarily one of desynchronization and ineffective interhemispheric communication" (p. 111), although they favour the right hemisphere deficit hypothesis. McGilchrist (2009) has emphasised that more or less all human activity normally involves both hemispheres, and that the corpus collosum between them has inhibitory as well as communicatory functions. Some division of function is apparently necessary, hence the presence of the corpus collosum as (by analogy) a kind of "semi-permeable membrane" between the two, acting to modulate the flow of information for optimum advantage to the overall system. Moreover, it might be that each hemisphere functions to regulate the other. It would appear that this normal partial division of function, and modulation of informational flow, have gone awry in both autistic spectrum conditions and in ADHD, and that *each* hemisphere is used in an "extreme" way.

The amygdala theory

Baron-Cohen and colleagues (2000) have proposed "an amygdala theory of autism", drawing on evidence that the amygdala is part of the "social brain", building on work by Brothers (1990). This proposal was explored further by Hirstein and colleagues (2001), who point to various clues that implicate the amygdala: (1) a strong primate model of autism derives from the work of Bachevalier (1996), who ablated the amygdala and nearby temporal cortices of newborn rhesus monkeys, and found that they later displayed symptoms similar to human autism, including social withdrawal from other monkeys, stereotyped movements, such as spinning or somersaulting, and blank expressionless faces; (2) Bauman and Kemper's (1994) histopathological study of autistic brains found abnormalities in the amygdala as well as other areas of the limbic system; (3) the amygdala has neurons sensitive to gaze direction and it is known that autistic children have difficulty processing gaze information; (4) a high proportion of autistic children suffer seizures and the majority of these seizures are in the temporal lobe, which would affect the amygdala; (5) autism can be caused by a bornavirus that has a predilection for limbic structures, including the amygdala.

The authors (Hirstein et al., 2001) explored the theory further by measuring skin conductance responses, thought to relate to amygdala functioning, when autistic children were looking at a face looking at them, as opposed to looking at inanimate objects. Most of the children (whom they called type A) showed abnormally high electroconductance activity, widely fluctuating, with high base levels. Attempts at interaction with others would raise their electroconductance further, as would any interruption of their activity, and this would be accompanied by agitated behaviour. However, the skin conductance response with these children could be completely shut down by certain activities and experiences, such as eating, sucking on sweets, being wrapped in a heavy blanket, or deep massage. There was a smaller group of autistic children who showed a very different pattern. This "type B" group had a very flat response, sometimes showing skin conductance only in response to extreme activities, such as self-injurious behaviour. Thus, both hyper-reactive and hypo-reactive responses were observed among the autistic children, one group showing both hyper- and hypo-reactivity, depending on the situation and activity, and the other group showing just hypo-reactivity. The authors speculate that each group is trying to manage their sympathetic autonomic nervous system, one by regulating activity to lower arousal, and the other by engaging in self-stimulation, sometimes self-injury, in order to raise arousal. They argue further that part of the amygdala's role is to modulate higher cortical activity by assigning salience to sensory information, telling the brain what to pay attention to and think about. If the autonomic nervous system is constantly on high alert, as if every piece of sensory information is significant (the type A autistic children) then the child may act in such a way as to shut down the whole system. On the other hand, if the system is showing nothing as significant, the type B child may act to create more intense stimulation. The authors suggest that the cortico–limbic system has a function of maintaining a kind of cognitive homeostasis.

The "intense world" theory of autism

Markram and Markram (2010) have presented a most interesting, albeit speculative, unifying theory of autism, based on the idea that people with this condition are suffering a hyper-functioning of local neural circuits, characterised by hyper-reactivity and hyper-plasticity, caused by excitatory neurons dominating their neighbours. This results in these neural circuits achieving an abnormal autonomy, with runaway processing and cycling of excitation—as if the brakes and systems of modulation fail. Some of the consequences are excessive activity along four dimensions: hyper-perception; hyper-memory; hyper-attention (all mediated via the neocortex); hyper-emotionality (mediated via the limbic system). The authors argue that "these four dimensions could potentially explain the full spectrum of symptoms in autism, depending on the severity of the microcircuit pathology in different brain regions".

The theory is inspired by the observation that valproic acid (VPA), a drug widely used to treat epilepsy and bipolar disorder, was found to be associated with autistic spectrum traits when taken during pregnancy. This has also been found to be the case in rats. Thus, the offspring of rats given VPA during pregnancy showed: decreased social interaction; increased repetitive behaviours; enhanced anxiety; locomotor hyperactivity; lower sensitivity to pain; hyper-sensitivity to non-painful sensory stimulation; enhanced eye blink conditioning (an indicator of memory).

The Markrams found that the amygdala in rats exposed to VPA showed greatly amplified responses, with prolonged bursts of neuronal activity, compared to controls. They comment that the slightest stimulation triggers a run-away-like response in the amygdala of rats affected by VPA. Moreover, in the amygdala, the inhibitory currents were greatly reduced. However, in the neocortex the inhibitory currents rose in proportion to the excitation, thus indicating that lowered inhibitory currents could not account for the hyper-reactivity in all brain regions. What did seem to be the cause of the hyper-reactivity was a local increase in connectivity among neighbouring neurons.

They also found that in the VPA-exposed rat offspring there was a great increase in "microcircuit plasticity", which is to do with the rate at which neurons connect and disconnect as a result of stimulation and learning experiences. Consistently with this, the Markrams found that these rats showed great superiority in learning (on a task requiring them to gauge the width of apertures, using their whiskers, to gain a reward). The rats also showed greatly enhanced fear learning, which generalised more to other contexts and was more resistant to extinction:

Enhanced fear memory formation and a progressive generalization of fears could have major consequences on behavior and account for inappropriate reactions to the environment, sudden and apparently inexplicable anxiety attacks, loss of the finesse required in social interactions, and phobias. Over-generalization may also accelerate the progression in autism by more rapidly limiting the repertoire of safe stimuli, environments, and situations. . . . If present, a deficit in extinguishing acquired fear in autism would make it more difficult to relinquish old fears that are no longer relevant or justifiable. This deficit combined with longer-lasting fear memories that are also over-generalized, could lead to a progressive and irreversible reduction in the repertoire of acceptable stimuli and drive a complete lock down and blanketing out of what would rapidly become a painfully intense world. (Markram & Markram, 2010)

The Markrams do not, of course, suggest that most autism is caused by exposure to VTA. The effects of exposure to VTA during foetal development are simply taken as a model of autism and, in fact, they are unable to suggest the precise causal processes that might be involved, other than to hypothesise a "molecular syndrome", possibly involving the glutamatergic system, that drives hyper-reactivity and hyper-plasticity.

The essential idea of the intense world theory is that autonomously acting hyper-functional neural microcircuits create an intensity of sensory and emotional experience, but in fragments that are not processed holistically. It is as if the brain has myriad processing units, each focusing on different elements of experience, creating a cacophony of intense sensation and emotion that is not organised into a coherent pattern. Because of this, the person's progress through ordinary life is inherently traumatic because his or her capacities to cope with sensory and emotional experience are continually overwhelming. In addition, memories are experienced with an amplifying intensity and fear reactions are rapidly generalised. As a result, the person's behavioural repertoire becomes increasingly restricted, limited to a small number of actions compulsively repeated.

As a consequence, the autistic person would remain with a fragmented and amplified perception of bits and pieces of the world. The intense world that the autistic person faces could also easily become aversive if the amygdala and related emotional areas are significantly affected with local hyper-functionality. The lack of social interaction in autism might, therefore, not be because of deficits in the ability to process social and emotional cues, but because a sub-set of cues are overly intense, compulsively attended to, excessively processed, and remembered with frightening clarity and intensity. Typical autistic symptoms, such as averted eye gaze, social withdrawal, and lack of communication, might be explained by an initial over-awareness of sensory and social fragments of the environment, which may be so intense that avoidance is the only refuge. This active avoidance strategy could be triggered at a very early stage in a child's develop-ment and could progress rapidly with each experience manifesting as a regression, which is striking in some cases (Markram & Markram, 2010).

The excessive processing and storage of the autistic brain (accord-ing to this theory) closes the person off from the outside world, which becomes too overwhelming and aversive. In contrast to many pers-pectives that view the autistic brain as displaying *deficits*, the intense world theory postulates a brain that is overactive and oversensitive. Rather than feeling too little emotion, the person on the autistic spec-trum feels too much. Because of the continual threat of being over-whelmed by sensory and emotional stimulation, the person learns ways and preferences that carefully regulate the amount of interaction with others. It is, thus, potentially a much more "psychodynamic" theory than many other views of the autistic spectrum, since it involves the idea that the brain undertakes defensive strategies to protect itself from excessive stimulation (as in Freud's original models). The excessive stimulation is external in origin but is ampli-fied internally, and, thus, the aversive danger is both exogenous and endogenous. Whether or not the intense world theory proves to be supported by further investigation, it presents a picture of autism that seems close to the clinical presentation of people on this spectrum. It also allows a clearer link between autistic spectrum features and those indicated by the concept of "highly sensitive person" (Aron, 1999).

The account of fragmentation of experience, resulting from autonomous hyper-functioning microcircuits, also suggests possible links with psychotic experience and "autism" was, of course, a key feature of Bleuler's (1950) original account of schizophrenia. For many years, I worked with a schizophrenic patient, whom I called Jo and wrote about in a previous book (Mollon, 2001). She described highly fragmented and unintegrated sensory experience, especially when stressed, so that she would be hyper-aware of bits and pieces of her perceptual world, such as the different features of a person's face and sounds as they were talking, without these organising into a coherent perceptual gestalt and narrative. She was hyper-sensitive to intrusive noises: for example, the click of my office clock as the pointers moved each minute would cause her to jump violently, and this did not habituate, so that I was obliged to disconnect the clock. Interaction with others would potentially cause her intense anxiety. She continually feared that her body and mind would disintegrate. Jo did greatly benefit from her psychotherapy sessions. My role was essentially ego-supportive, helping her to make sense of the world and her experiences of it.

Links with psychotic developments are also suggested by psychoanalytic observations on a group of young children with marked autistic features, who showed unusual sensitivities (to light, colour, smell, sound, touch), reported sixty-five years ago by Bergman and Escalona (1949). These children displayed areas of precocious development and "spot-like brilliancy" (p. 348) in their very early development, but this then gave way to regression and psychotic-like presentations, with clear autistic avoidance and attempts to shut out the external world. In some instances, this involved becoming mute. Drawing upon a concept of insufficient barrier against stimulation, the authors explained these developments as follows:

> The hypothesis will be offered that the infant who is not sufficiently protected from stimuli either because of a "thin protective barrier", or because of the failure of maternal protection, may have to resort for such protection to premature formation of an ego. When this premature ego breaks down, possibly as a consequence of a trauma, the psychotic manifestations are thought to set in. (pp. 346–347)

This idea of a precocious formation of the ego seems somewhat similar to the Markrams' hypothesis of premature and unintegrated developments within the brain, except that Bergman and Escalona presume the premature ego development is in response to traumatic intrusion of stimuli, whereas the Markrams propose that it is the premature brain development itself that creates the traumatic hyper-sensitivity. In the Markrams' theory, there is no escape from the sensory bombardment because it is internally amplified by the hyper-connected neural microcircuits.

The Markram's theory was stimulated by Henry Markram's desire to understand and help his son, Kai, who has marked features on the autistic spectrum and was eventually diagnosed with Asperger's. It is of interest that Kai also showed symptoms of ADHD:

> At first, Markram thought Kai had attention deficit/hyperactivity disorder (ADHD): Once Kai could move, he never wanted to be still. "He was running around, very difficult to control," Markram says. As Kai grew, however, he began melting down frequently, often for no apparent reason. "He became more particular, and he started to become less hyperactive but more behaviorally difficult," Markram says. "Situations were very unpredictable. He would have tantrums. He would be very resistant to learning and to any kind of instruction." (online article by Maia Szalavitz: https://medium.com/matter-archive/the-boy-whose-brain-could-unlock-autism-70c3d64ff221)

A clear summary interview with the Markrams is available online at the wrongplanet.net website for people with autism and Asperger's. Here is what the Markrams say about their theory:

> The Intense World Theory states that autism is the consequence of a supercharged brain that makes the world painfully intense and that the symptoms are largely because autistics are forced to develop strategies to actively avoid the intensity and pain. Autistics see, hear, feel, think, and remember too much, too deep, and process information too completely. The theory predicts that the autistic child is retreating into a controllable and predictable bubble to protect themselves from the intensity and pain.

> The brain is supercharged because the elementary functional units of the brain are supercharged. These units are called neural micro-circuits. Neural microcircuits are the smallest ecosystem of neurons that can support each other to carry out functions. The brain is made up of millions of these units. These microcircuits are hyper-reactive and hyper-plastic. That means that they react and process information much faster and more intensely, they can learn much more and remember much longer, and they can remember things with much greater detail. The Intense World Theory proposes that having such powerful units makes orchestration difficult—like trying to play a piano with a million run-a-way keys. The microcircuits that are mostly affected will depend on genetics, toxic insults during pregnancy and the kind of environmental exposure after birth. Each autistic child will therefore be unique because different microcircuits are hyper-

functional and they dominate the idiosyncratic pattern that emerges. (www.wrongplanet.net/article419.html)

In this interview, the Markrams state their view that autism develops through a combination of three factors: a genetic disposition; toxic exposure during pregnancy; environmental exposure after birth. They postulate that these trigger an acceleration of gene expression and brain development that makes "the brain too sensitive, too early". The accelerated development prevents the normal neuronal "pruning" that is essential for optimum brain function, so that "some microcircuits that should wait their turn to develop, develop too early and begin to dominate over the other microcircuits driving hyperpreferences, repetitiveness, idiosyncrasies and eventually making unlearning and rehabilitation very difficult". The Markrams present a very positive view of autism, pointing to the possibilities of harnessing the potential of a highly developed brain:

> The Intense World Theory predicts that all autistic children have exceptional talents that are locked up. The challenge is to free talents and to make it possible for them to integrate in society. We do believe that autism can be turned into a highly beneficial "disorder" if we understand how to help the autistic child harness their genius rather than suffer from it. (www.wrongplanet.net/article419.html)

The Markrams suggest strategies for assisting children with autistic spectrum tendencies, such as protecting them from excessive or aversive stimulation: "a well-structured and filtered environment could allow the sequence of brain development to unfold normally while preserving the hyperfunctional microcircuits". However, there are also clear implications for adults on the autistic spectrum, in terms of assisting the person in coming to terms with the nature of his or her atypical brain, in its positive as well as negative aspects, and helping them to find ways of adapting, such as recognising the need for a protected environment.

Donna Williams: fragmented experience

Support for the Markrams' theory of fragmented experience is provided by the autistic writer Donna Williams's account of her early mode of perception:

Up to the age of four, I sensed according to pattern and shifts in pattern. My ability to interpret what I saw was impaired because I took each fragment in without understanding its meaning in the context of its surroundings. I'd see the nostril but lose the concept of nose, see the nose but lose the face, see the fingernail but lose the finger. My ability to interpret from what I heard was equally impaired. I heard the into-nation but lost the meaning of the words, got a few of the words but lost the sentences. I couldn't consistently process the meaning of my own body messages if I was focusing in on something with my eyes or ears. I didn't know myself in relation to other people because when I focused processing information about "other", I lost "self", and when I focused on "self", I lost other. (Williams, 1998b, p. 33)

Implications

The brains of people on the autistic spectrum appear to be anatomi-cally different from neurotypical people from the beginning. In-evitably, therefore, their neural circuits will process information differently. These affect processes at all levels of the brain and its func-tions. Thus, physical movement may be affected by abnormalities in the cerebellum, resulting in the postural stiffness and awkwardness often (but not always) shown by people on this spectrum. Unusual development is found in the limbic system, involving emotion and anxiety, in the sensory cortex and in the prefrontal areas involving higher attentional, executive, and "theory of mind" functions.

The differences in functional connectivity in the brains of people on the autistic spectrum give some clues as to how the processing of infor-mation may be affected. Their over-connectivity in local areas of the brain, particularly in the anterior cingulate cortex, might lead to exces-sive focus on particular aspects of a situation or task. It might be more difficult to integrate sensory information from the wider context and there might be perseveration, persistence in an activity longer than is adaptive. This perspective is given most emphasis in the intense world theory. Overall processing of complex information, such as that inher-ent in social situations, might be slower than for neurotypical people. When the autistic spectrum person is asked a question, he or she might take longer to respond, and might appear somewhat blank.

The relative lack of activity in the default mode network might play a part in the difficulties some people on the autistic spectrum have with social and emotional intelligence, and with "theory of mind" skills, the capacity to think about one's own mind as well as that of others. The normal states of reverie, the working through and processing of emotional experience, reviewing the interpersonal events of the day, and forming meaningful autobiographical memory, might not take place.

Complex situations—such as more or less any interpersonal context—might consume too many brain resources for the person on the autistic spectrum. Too much of the brain is activated and processing is slow. Not surprisingly, the autistic spectrum person would seek to avoid such situations.

Abnormalities in the anatomy and functioning of left and right hemispheres, and in the modulation of information flowing between them, will mean the person on the autistic spectrum might process information about the world differently and less efficiently. Deficiencies in right brain functioning, as explored at length by McGilchrist (2009), mean that the autistic spectrum person may be deprived of the normal neurobiological substrates for empathy, social comprehension, and "theory of mind" skills in general. They might be trying to accomplish too much with the resources of the left hemisphere that views the world in categories and is biased towards the non-living. At the same time, the relative unavailability of right hemispheric emotional processing might mean that words lose much of their meaning, leaving the person trapped in a world of lists and categories, devoid of emotional significance. On the other hand, the autistic spectrum brain might be trying to process with the right hemisphere tasks that are normally better undertaken by the left. There is a miswiring and mistuning, similar to that in ADHD, which may continually generate tension, frustration, and rage.

Those people on the autistic spectrum who are highly sensitive, "thin skinned", and potentially capable of intense empathy might protectively shut down aspects of their right hemispheric functioning. However, in so doing, they could shift from a state of being flooded with emotion to one in which nothing (including words) has any emotional significance. Both states are aversive. This protective shutting off of aspects of right hemispheric functioning could also occur in response to the person's own emotions. One such woman explained this very clearly when she said, "I am capable of feeling emotions, but if I let myself feel them it would be too much—I would be overwhelmed and could not contain them—it would not be safe—and so I have to be unemotional." In case it might be thought that such a stance seems more "schizoid" than autistic, I must emphasise that in almost every aspect of her functioning this lady displayed marked autistic spectrum traits.

Attentional problems, whereby novel stimuli fail to elicit normal interest, mean the autistic spectrum person might not develop the normal "signal anxiety" (Freud, 1926d) and so is prone to being overwhelmed by anxiety evoked by changing situations and circumstances. There is no prior warning to prepare the person for change, since the cues and clues do not evoke interest.

Some people on the autistic spectrum struggle with chronic high levels of anxiety and physiological arousal. Much of their efforts and energies are focused on trying to manage this arousal, and to find activities and situations that reduce it. Repetitive and obsessive activities might be soothing to the person. This point finds clearest expression in the intense world theory.

Like people with ADHD, the person with autistic spectrum traits might not have been able to use adequately, during infancy and childhood, the responsiveness of carers to help in regulating his or her emotional and physiological state. In some instances, the carers might have been deficient in their capacity to provide soothing. Either way, the normal and necessary selfobject responses described by Kohut (1971, 1977, 1981)—the experience of soothing empathic communications by the other that help regulate the organisation of the self—have not taken place, and have, therefore, not led to the gradual building up of affect regulatory functions within the self. There is much overlap with ADHD. Moreover, the normal means of communication with others, through words, eye contact, and body language, come to be distrusted because the processing of these is flawed for the person on the autistic spectrum.

The continual experience of finding the social and physical world overwhelming, overstimulating, and confusing, can lead the autistic spectrum person to shut down much of their processing more generally, withdrawing from interaction and communication. This might correspond to some extent to Freud's original concept of "decathexis", the withdrawal of emotional investment in the external world and from words, resulting in the outer world seeming unreal and words losing their meaning. Similarly, the emotional sensitivity, alongside the sensory sensitivity, adds to the desire to avoid interacting and relating to others. Repetitive actions and familiar sensations might be substituted in place of a wider engagement with the world, particularly the world of other people (Tustin, 1986). A commonplace example of this among "normal" people is the phenomenon of smoking cigarettes. Because adequate selfobject responses, and subsequent development of psychic structure through "transmuting internalisation" (Kohut 1981), have not occurred to a sufficient extent, the person on the autistic spectrum is inclined to turn to sensory and other forms of non-human stimulation in an endeavour to regulate the experience and structure of the self.

The exceptional sensitivity of people on the autistic spectrum means that ordinary life tends to be traumatising, in so far as "normal" experiences tend to overwhelm the person's capacity to cope. There is too much feeling and seeing and too much fragmentation—a bombardment of intense particles of experience. For such people, the ordinary world is assaultive. Commonplace sensations, of noise or of clothing, create intense discomfort that does not sensitise. Emotional and sensory injuries are amplified and sustained by their brain circuitry. There is nowhere to escape other than through various forms of dissociative defences, sometimes involving the creation of a complex alternative inner world. It is commonly recognised that sustained interpersonal trauma and abuse is one cause of dissociative disorders (Mollon, 1996). The other cause, less commonly recognised, is autistic spectrum sensitivity.

CHAPTER NINE

Psychotherapy with people on the autistic spectrum

A charming young woman, with pronounced autistic features, arrived for her second assessment session at my NHS clinic (accompanied by her mother, as before), smiled, and handed me several sheets of typed notes. Her writing explained with great clarity and coherence that she could not answer questions directly in words, that immediate conversational communication was just too intense and confusing for her. Our first meeting had indeed been difficult for her and most of the talking had taken place between me and her mother. She did indicate that she might be able respond to questions in writing. It was apparent that this autistic lady was highly intelligent. We met a few more times, clarifying the nature of her difficulties, and identifying local sources of support, and she and her mother were then happy to conclude this brief psychotherapeutic exploration. I think both found it helpful.

Another young woman, again accompanied to her sessions always by her mother, would respond to questions only with a nod or a shake of the head. In fact, this allowed quite effective communication between us as I explored various aspects of her experience. The crucial and most helpful point I identified was that she felt extremely anxious much of the time. Her anxiety was constant, but worse in any situation that was unfamiliar, and she felt least anxious at home with her immediate family, where, apparently, she would speak some of the time. Neither she nor her mother had mentioned her high levels of anxiety, and I had asked about it mainly on the basis of intuition. As a result, I asked a psychiatrist colleague to assess her with a view to possible support with anxiolytic medication. This was done and the young woman experienced much benefit. After some further sessions, clarifying her difficulties, identifying some career interests and goals, we were able to conclude the work with a sense of some modest success in alleviating her anxiety and supporting her in ongoing development and finding a place in the world.

I have seen many people with autistic spectrum traits for assessment, ever since the UK government determined that the NHS should provide a service for people with Asperger's. Many people sought such a diagnosis, not only because they wanted to know and understand more about their difficulties, but perhaps also partly because having a diagnosis (a disability) can confer certain benefits and accommodations in the workplace. Most of those who suspected their difficulties were in the realm of Asperger's did indeed show marked autistic spectrum traits. Sometimes, a spouse or parent, or other family member, had come to view the person in these terms. Frequently, a spouse would express an accumulation of emotional wounds and despair at their partner's apparent lack of empathy. Parents would convey mounting anxiety at their offspring's seeming inability or unwillingness to leave the nest and make any kind of autonomous life away from home. Quite a number also had ADHD. All found life away from home very difficult.

There were others who had not sought such a diagnosis, people I had worked with for some time without realising the role that autistic spectrum problems were playing in their struggles. Until I began to understand more about the autistic spectrum, I simply did not recognise these aspects that, in retrospect, were obvious. These were people who felt chronically dis-eased—alienated and puzzled by the motives and strivings of others. They experienced pervasive stress, anxiety, somatic illness, and very low self-esteem. Their usual mood would be deeply morose. Some appeared very disturbed, with periodic and unpredictable acts of serious self-harm or intended suicide. They seemed to value psychotherapy and attended their sessions regularly, but progress was slow. Their difficulties seemed somehow

more profoundly rooted than those conditions of either psychodynamic conflict, acquired anxiety, or traumatic experience that
normally permit resolution through more or less any of the recognised
forms of psychotherapy. Work would be done, but always there would
be more problems, springing up like garden weeds erupting from an
extensive root system that could never be eradicated. Their inner
structures of thought and expectation seemed particularly rigid. They
were wounded by life, inwardly lonely, despairing, and yet grateful
for such elements of understanding and empathy that they experienced during psychotherapy.

Many years ago, Bergman and Escalona (1949) described a group
of children with unusual sensitivities:

> Colors, bright lights, noises, unusual sounds, qualities of material,
> experiences of equilibrium, of taste, of smell, of temperature, seemed
> to have an extraordinarily intensive impact upon these children at a
> very early age. They were "sensitive" in both meanings of the word:
> easily hurt, and easily stimulated to enjoyment. Variations in sensory
> impression that made no difference to the average child made a great
> deal of difference to these children. They were also characterized by a
> certain precocity, though this was very unevenly distributed among
> the diverse functions of their personality. The first impression which
> some of their reactions and abilities gave was that of unusual gifted-
> ness such as might be observed in the budding of a genius. Further
> observation, however, suggested comparison with individuals suffer-
> ing from a traumatic neurosis, or a psychosis, and even with feeble-
> minded children. (p. 333)

These children found the ordinary world overwhelming and traumatising. As a result, they developed ways of screening out or avoiding
intrusive sensation. We might say that such children, and others on
the autistic spectrum, are "too sensitive for the world".

The potentially traumatic impingement of the external world was
discussed by Freud in terms of his concept of the "protective shield",
which he saw as a crucial function of the ego, the precursor of all its
further defensive functions, noting that "*Protection against stimuli* is an
almost more important function for the living organism than *reception*
of stimuli" (1920g, p. 27, my italics). This concept was elaborated by
Khan (1963) and many others to take account of the role of the mother
in protecting the infant against excessive stimuli. However, Freud also
acknowledged that inner stimuli threaten the ego just as do externally

derived impingements: "An excessive strength of instinct can damage the ego in a similar way to an excessive stimulus from the external world" (1940, p. 199). Thus, strong emotions, such as fear, anger, or shame, erupting from within can overwhelm the ego, and are therefore traumatic, just as much as threats from outside. The Markrams' (2010) intense world theory points to possible ways in which external impingements become amplified into fragments of unintegrated intense experience, creating, potentially, a storm of indigestible "beta elements" (Bion, 1962) that do not "make sense" and which assail the person from inside and out.

For the person on the autistic spectrum, the external world can take on qualities of an *assault*. A noisy work environment, a crowd, odours, or stale air, heat and cold, or emotional demands from others, can all be overwhelming and intolerable, leading to a need to withdraw. If external withdrawal is not possible, then dissociative internal withdrawal may result. When such dissociative withdrawals have begun in early childhood, the stage is set for the development of elaborate yet secret alternative inner worlds, sometimes corresponding to a hidden psychotic part of the mind operating with bizarre sensory fragments, hallucination, and concealed delusion (Bion, 1957). For example, Jo, a woman with autistic hypersensitivity and psychotic qualities whom I have described at greater length previously (Mollon, 2001), experienced a group of malign figures around the back of her head, whom she called "the outside people". These entities would provide a running commentary on her behaviour and would control her and give her instructions. We came to see that they were composed of bits and pieces of her fragmented experience of her excitable mother, and their rigid and tyrannical nature provided what she very aptly called her "exoskeleton", without which she felt she would dissolve into a blob on the floor.

Although most autistic spectrum developments do not lead to psychotic outcomes of this kind, life for people with these traits is a continual struggle against impingement and intensity of emotion. Relationships with others are always ambivalent, intimacy desired yet feared, for it always brings the threat of being consumed and overwhelmed with raw need, or of loss of boundaries, *of feeling and needing too much*, and losing the self.

As outlined in the intense world theory, aversive experiences, including anxiety, appear to be amplified and sustained in the autistic spectrum brain, setting the scene for generalised anxiety disorder. Essentially, this extremely distressing condition arises when anxiety becomes the trigger for more anxiety, creating a crescendo of positive feedback. The person is anxious about feeling anxious. However, it is not only anxiety and aversive sensations that are amplified in the autistic spectrum brain. A person on this spectrum will often have felt odd, different, and defective from early in their life, deeply troubled by a sense of something wrong, without being able to identify what this is. Repeated failures in social interaction result in accumulating injuries to self-esteem, sometimes accompanied by desperate attempts to appear "normal" and to present a "false self". The authentic vulnerable self will be a target of rage and *shame*. These feelings, too, become amplified and grow inside in a way that some patients liken to an emotional cancer that seeks to consume and destroy what is left of the more healthy personality. In such instances, self-harm and suicidal acts are frequent dangers.

A teenage autistic boy vividly and poignantly describes the shame and self-hatred he often feels:

> Really you have no idea quite how miserable we are. . . . Whenever we've done something wrong, we get told off or laughed at, without even being able to apologize, and we end up hating ourselves and despairing about our lives, again and again and again. It's impossible not to wonder why we were born into this world as human beings at all. (Higashida, 2013, p. 70)

When these processes of amplified anxiety, shame, and self-directed rage are particularly active, psychotherapy can be very problematic. Any introspection or examination of inner thoughts and feelings can be overwhelming, triggering a further intensity of panic. Because of the relatively autonomous functioning of neural microcircuits (as hypothesised by the Markrams' intense world theory), dissociative and semi-autonomous self-states could easily develop, during which self-harm might take place. For example, one woman functioned as a responsible teacher much of the time, but on more than one occasion would be found in a wooded area where she would be engaged in preparing a noose to hang herself; subsequently, she would have limited recollection of her actions. These events would be triggered by events that evoked unbearably amplified feelings of shame and rage.

There are broadly two components to psychotherapeutic work with people with autistic spectrum traits (and/or ADHD): (1) helping the person identify and understand the nature of their difficulties and sensitivities; (2) helping the person think through strategies for coping and managing these vulnerabilities, as well as making use of their strengths. It is crucial to convey an understanding and empathy with the person's autistic sensitivity, and to evoke the person's own acceptance, empathy, and compassion for their struggles. High levels of anxiety are important to acknowledge. This is a core feature, but the person might not have learnt to give this label to their experience. Since a person with autistic spectrum features might not have had much opportunity to compare their experience of life with that of others, he or she might lack any clear awareness of how and why they find many situations and tasks challenging. Instead, their own emphasis might have been upon trying to appear "normal" and upon berating themselves for being "weak" or "pathetic". Acceptance of the basic autistic temperament is key. It is through acceptance that change is possible. As long as a person is fighting against their own nature, he or she is bound to lose, and most people presenting with these problems have been fighting with themselves for years.

It is not only the clients who might not recognise the nature of their difficulties. Most psychotherapists have little or no appreciation of autistic spectrum traits and might not recognise when these are present in their client, and, thus, their expectations and assumptions about therapeutic progress could be unrealistic. They should be prepared for progress to be slower than with other clients, and for the client's characteristic thoughts, beliefs, and strategies of protection to be more rigid than those found among others.

Although psychotherapy with people on the autistic spectrum can indeed involve slow progress, there are also many instances in which limited clarificatory work over a few sessions is all that is required. Often this is really just a matter of confirming the person's own suspicions about their difficulties, along with discussion of the best ways of managing these. Recognition of the need for protected work environments and avoidance of occupations that involve a lot of direct interaction with others may often be helpful. Work may also usefully be undertaken on understanding other people's minds and motives, and how the client might be viewed by others. Strategies for reducing or managing anxiety, possibilities of behavioural experiments, and examination of self-defeating thoughts can be help-ful. All of this kind of discussion has the bonus of helping to reduce shame and the sense of being "odd and different". A message I like to give people on the autistic spectrum, often quite explicitly, is, "Yes, you are different—your brain and experiences are different from those of most other people—*but there are many people like you*: in fact, you are a member of a sizeable minority". This is usually experienced as helpful.

Anxiety is almost always a significant problem for people on the autistic spectrum, although this is sometimes avoided by the person establishing an extremely restricted lifestyle with minimal contact with others. This is what drives the rigidity of thought and behaviour, and the pervasive avoidance. It is important, therefore, to seek ways of soothing and calming the person, reducing anxiety, and helping him or her to find ways of self-soothing. Some of the simple energy psychology tapping procedures, such as EFT, are often very helpful along these lines, since they are easily learnt by clients.

I always recommend clients on the autistic spectrum to look for helpful books. There are a huge number of excellent ones, as a search for "Asperger's" on any online bookstore will reveal. These include books aimed at relatives or partners of people with autistic spectrum traits. Donna Williams, a writer with high functioning autism, has written a number of valuable books for both the general reader and the professional (e.g., 1996, 1998a,b, 2008). Since autistic traits and Asperger's can be harder to detect in females, who tend to appear less "geeky" and are more socially skilled than males on this spectrum, it is worth mentioning *Asperger's and Girls* (Attwood et al., 2006). Simi-larly, there are many online resources, as well as actual and virtual support groups, which can often provide helpful information, advice, and encouragement.

Psychotherapy with a man with Asperger's: an extended exploration[16]

Peter, a highly intelligent single man in his early thirties, sought consultations to assess whether, as he suspected, he suffered from Asperger's. We met once a month over a period of a couple of years, in an extended exploration of his difficulties. Peter's own evolving insights tell the story of his psychodynamic struggles to deal with his autistic spectrum temperament.

Peter acknowledged feeling depressed and, at times, despairing. His life lacked pleasure or fulfilment. He had a girlfriend but found no satisfaction in this, and feared he was incapable of a relating to others. He spoke of despondency, hopelessness, and a general lack of optimism, and remarked that "Hanging around with me for too long would suck the lifeblood out of anyone."

Peter's moods were changeable, but he considered them to be "evidence-based": "When I am upset I always know why—and when I am unhappy I always know why." He spoke of puzzlement about other people: "Why do normal people not commit suicide? Most people seem unhappy, to varying degrees—walking through town, or seeing people on the tube, most do not seem happy. Is there some factor that allows normal people to drag themselves through despite the evidence?" He felt he did not wish to commit suicide yet "because I have not explored all the options", but if he were to conclude that he had explored all options and there seemed no possibility of improving his life then he would "rationally" decide that it would be appropriate to end his life.

Peter was very aware of his difference from others. He told me that he did not experience sadness, happiness, or other emotions, because he did not see the point in feeling such emotions since to do so did not achieve anything. His girlfriend had apparently pointed out that most people did not have an option about experiencing emotions. His approach to emotional aspects of life had a mathematical, logical, and computer-like systemising quality. For example, on joining a dating agency, he had drawn up a spreadsheet to calculate how many emails on average needed to be sent to result in a date.

He informed me that as a child he had been very sensitive; his mother had told him he had a lot of soft toys, but he would have to take a register of them each day (as if attending school) and line them up by size and colour. He grew up in a large house where he had his own wing, like a separate flat, and he did not eat with his parents, but from an early age always had his computer with the Internet. As an adult, he maintained minimal contact with his parents "because I have nothing in common with those people". He had not seen his mother for some years, but would phone her occasionally to check that she is alive, referring dismissively to how she is "melodramatically emotional".

Peter clearly displayed unusual intellectual and cognitive talents—highly observant and able to elucidate elaborate inferences and scenarios on the basis of tiny details of observation, in a manner similar to that ascribed to the fictional detective, Sherlock Holmes. His discourse was precise, rapid, and concerned with logic and reason, as were his actions: "I do not make mistakes—I am so careful with everything—I cannot remember the last time I made a mistake."

In general, Peter preferred to limit his interactions with other people, and said he wished to be in solitude about 90% of the time. He explained that partly this was in order to protect others from him, since he was aware that he upset people because he had "never learnt to be tactful". If asked a question, in a social or work environment, he would provide a literal and factual answer, without any regard for interpersonal sensitivity, nuance, or implicit meanings. He was quite aware that he lacked empathy. For example, he would find the sight of a woman crying very amusing, but he endeavoured to hide this reaction from his girlfriend because he knew it would upset her more. He said that his girlfriend would very often be crying about something or other that he had said and he felt this was "unfair because it introduces an emotional dimension that I cannot understand". In such ways, Peter revealed himself to be extremely caring and well intentioned, as well as entirely honest and conducting himself with complete integrity. It was the normal *dishonesty* and *lack of integrity* of the wider social world that he had not been able to negotiate. He was a strict vegan, out of both scientific and ethical principles. The idea of animals suffering upset him greatly. He said that ethics and morality were extremely important to him.

Peter said he was rarely sexually intimate with his girlfriend. He found the sensations of sex *too intense*—sensory stimulation often overwhelmed him. Moreover, he did not like feeling dirty. He therefore approached sex "with a degree of apprehension" in case it was overwhelming.

He appeared to experience himself as if from a different species, saying he did not know anyone who was like him. His high intelligence and ability to observe and imitate allowed a superficial social participation: "I will observe people—I never identify with people—but I am adept at fitting in when I need to." He dealt with every situation in terms of a set of rules. Eye contact was difficult for him, although he could manage this in a professional/work context. He told me he was trying to learn recognition of facial emotion—studying each muscle of the face and how the muscles contract—using the Facial Action Coding System (FACS) programme, which provides a taxonomy of human facial expressions, and he was also studying body language. Peter wondered, "Is it because I want to control the universe and know even more about people just by looking at them?" He did not know what people are thinking or feeling, unless they tell him.

We explored his capacity for reciprocity. As a child he would not help others, and would laugh inappropriately if he saw someone hurt or upset; he did not like engaging with others in any way and if children playing sent a ball towards him, he would never return it. Now, as an adult, he would quickly appraise the question of whether helping someone would cause him or them more embarrassment. He would not like to be helped by others. It would depend on his appraisal of "an implicit social rule".

Peter had created a successful business in a niche market for software development. He had designed this with such efficiency that he did not actually have to do very much work. In addition, he sought to minimise his need for material objects so that his living expenses were relatively small. He owned his home, which contained minimal furniture and decoration and was itself relatively isolated on the edge of a town and adjacent to fields. His clothes were few. By using exclusively electronic media, he more or less eliminated paper from his life. He even reduced his electronic devices to the minimum absolutely necessary. In addition, he made his house silent, disabling any device that made a noise.

This left him with a painful need for something to do that would occupy his time and make a useful contribution to society. He studied anatomy textbooks for pleasure, and considered training as a medical doctor. Eventually, he concluded that although he might potentially be a very good doctor in terms of the scientific and technical aspects, he would be completely lacking in any ability to relate sympathetically and tactfully to patients. Neither did he think he could work as part of a team, and he added, "I am too self-aware not to realise the problems I would create for others."

Peter seemed to see life as consisting of a series of experiments, and his overriding concern was for control: "The security system on my computers is overkill—everything boils down to control—everything is an experiment, or an application of a previous experiment." His current hobby was mathematics, particularly geometry.

Despite his preference for being alone, Peter acknowledged that "My depression is caused by my isolation." He wanted to have the option to "dismiss people", to be in a position of control, rather than to be in enforced isolation. His girlfriend would, in fact, be dismissed from his mind as soon as she left the room. However, he came to realise that he felt envious of her ability to relate to family and friends, and this led him to undermine her. He did not like this aspect of himself and wished to protect others from exposure to his negativity and hostility, just as he wished to protect himself from the intrusions and demands of others.

During the course of our work, Peter ended his relationship with this girlfriend, since he considered he could not give her what she wanted in terms of emotional responses and commitment to a future life together, and the situation was clearly causing her great distress. He then began exploring possible relationships with other women via an online dating agency.

As we continued to explore and clarify his difficulties, Peter expressed anger that these had not been picked up and addressed years ago, and anger that so many people had been hurt by him. His distress at causing suffering to others was profound and reminded me of the comments of the thirteen-year-old autistic author, Naoki Higashida (2013):

> The hardest ordeal for us is the idea that we are causing grief for other people. We can put up with our own hardships okay, but the thought that our lives are the source of other people's unhappiness, that's plain unbearable. (p. 71)

However, Peter felt frustrated that his difficulties did not fit neatly into a category and the idea of a *spectrum* of autistic traits struck him as horrifyingly imprecise, and he spoke of "craving classification and definition" of himself and everything else in the world. He could appreciate that many aspects of his experience and behaviour did meet the criteria for Asperger's, but not all. He felt like an alien in a category of aliens. When invited to consider the possibility of a support group for people with Asperger's, he remarked that he did not want to be the odd one out among a group of odd ones out!

Through the process of gradual exploration in the monthly appointments, Peter became more aware and accepting of his human needs and vulnerabilities, with a lessening of a haughty aloofness that seemed more in evidence initially. He remarked, "I would like social interaction—it is just I am hopeless and clueless at it." He became more willing to acknowledge that being alone can be lonely, and that he felt like a person with a disease that could be lethal to others: "I feel I have to protect people from me—so I push them away."

An acquaintance asked Peter to take on the management of a specialist vegan shop and café. He agreed, and set about making it more efficient. Within a week or two, he had sacked all the staff or had, at least, made their position so untenable that they left. Some customers also found him abrupt and rude, and chose not to continue visiting. He was intolerant of people whom he regarded as inept and not trying to improve. The shop and café did become more successful as a business and more profitable.

However, the positive effects of his work at the shop and café came at a cost for Peter. He found the interactions with other people very stressful. As a result, his secret autistic tics increased in frequency, appearing to have a stress-discharge function. These actions, involving shouting certain words, flapping his hands and shaking, and holding his hands against his nose, were always conducted in private. Moreover, the necessity for a social mask in a work setting prompted anxious preoccupations regarding identity and authenticity. His dilemma was that if he functioned as his "true self", this would be unacceptable to others, but if he presented a false mask, then this was a betrayal of his authentic being. He spoke of how he felt "empowered" if he spoke very directly, even if what he said was judged socially unacceptable, but if he made efforts to be accommodating, making socially acceptable remarks, or engaging in small talk, "I die a little inside."

I talked to Peter of the way in which themes to do with the social presentation of self, and the balance between the inner person and the outer persona, are ones which concern most people in one way or another—that we all have to manage this balance as best we can, and that most of us present and express ourselves slightly differently according to the social context. This point seemed to be novel and of interest for Peter.

Peter's position began to change, much to his consternation. He spoke of how the mask he presents to others used to be all he knew, but more recently he had become aware of his "true self" behind this. On the other hand, he was finding that his "forced smile and hello" in the workplace was "not as hateful as I thought". People in the shop and café were making positive and complimentary comments, and he found, to his surprise, that he was enjoying people's approval. He noticed himself feeling "more energised, less depressed, more out-going."

At this point, he reported a dream, which he said had a powerful effect on him. In the dream he had a partner, *whom he cared about a great deal for no reason*. This disturbed him, that he might have been wrong about feelings "on a monumental scale". He said he used to think that because he could not empathise with other's feelings, he did not have feelings himself. "Have I put empathy and feelings in the same category and thought I had neither?" I put to him that the problem might be one of empathy with his own feeling self as well as difficulties in empathising with others, but he may, indeed, have feelings.

His perception of having no feelings led him to ponder whether he might be a psychopath, but, on the other hand, he was aware of a strong ethical sense. He had always assumed that he would not be upset if his parents died, but thought he would be upset to lose someone he saw often because this would involve the loss of that regular "input". His relationship with emotions puzzled him: "I am very scared of emotions and feelings—I think I have experienced emotions, but I am not sure; I experience anger—is that an emotion?—so perhaps I do experience emotion."

Peter went on to speak of how much he valued the sessions: "the only place where I can be myself in the presence of another human being." He added that perhaps he did not have to remain certain that he would never have a meaningful relationship. I said I wondered whether, through his dream, he might be conveying to himself that he would quite like to have a partner whom he cared about a great deal. In response, he spoke gingerly of approaching the idea of warmth and tenderness, exciting and risky, as something he might like, and of a sense of *uncertainty*, contrasting with his sense of certainty in every other area.

The possibility of change evoked great anxiety in Peter. He spoke of his recognition that his Asperger traits underpinned his identity and assumptions about himself in almost every area: "If you told me you could cure me I would be terrified!"

Things became even more alarming for Peter when he formed a new relationship with a woman called Sonya. He found himself experiencing feelings that are normally described as being "in love", and these were novel and shocking for him. He felt that none of his previous assumptions, beliefs, and strategies for living had prepared him for this. He felt he was "out of my comfort zone", finding himself feeling "happy, anxious, frustrated, excited, pessimistic, optimistic." He had told her of his Asperger traits within about half an hour of meeting her: "I have been so honest with her—I've told her everything." Sonya had been interested and not put off. He had allowed himself to be vulnerable and this was "unprecedented". Despite considerable doubts, "I've never maintained a long-term relationship with anyone" and "If I care enough about her I should tell her to run, because the evidence is not in my favour", he spoke of his hope the relationship would work and that they would live together. He found himself caring for Sonya, even while recognising that she was very different from him, and he said he realised and accepted, through our sessions, that "not everyone sees the world the same way I do." Moreover, he noted that he was no longer viewing himself as inherently "toxic".

Over the next few months, Peter complained that "things are getting worse—anxiety and confusion", all triggered by entering a relationship, which meant that "the stable foundation that was there is becoming less and less stable—I am over-analysing—there is no constant." His previous sense of control over every aspect of his life— "every movement—every facet is preordained", with all his body posture and body language intentionally planned, all of this was dissolving. On the other hand, the relationship with Sonya was going well.

He had taken to drinking alcohol too much, because this stopped his excess mental activity. He noted that when he was with Sonya he was happy, but when he was with her and drunk, he felt even happier. Moreover, he observed that alcohol seemed to lessen his Asperger characteristics (suggesting that anxiety played a significant role in these).

However, his happiness with Sonya made him more aware of his unhappiness and feelings of emptiness when he is not with her: "I see the lack of meaning and pointlessness of everything" and he spoke of his "chronic cynicism". He became painfully aware of how he has tended to be "like Scrooge—walled off and isolated", living in his stark and undecorated rooms, and he noted that "I do not like myself in the slightest."

Peter spoke of his awareness that he was trying to push Sonya away, for both self-protection and to protect her: "In my entire life I have pushed everyone away." He realised how he behaved in deliberately hurtful ways towards Sonya, likening his aggressive side to a pack of dogs that he has to lock away and conceal: "this part of me that is arrogant, self-loathing, and inadequate—the person who would make her feel bad—who would take delight in pointing out her foibles and inadequacies." He noted that this created "an incredibly unfulfilling lonely existence" and that "I have not learnt to live with myself."

We saw a conflict between the loving and connecting part of him, and the cruel, anti-life, anti-love, and anti-meaning part—the latter being provoked by the anxiety created by his relationship with Sonya. He related the origin of this grandiose arrogant self to his experiences of being teased, bullied, and rejected as a child, and of his protective strategy of aiming to be "better" than everyone else. Out of his pervasive feeling of inadequacy, "I feel the only thing I have to offer is my mind", and so he felt he must be the most knowledgeable about everything, and must be best at everything. He was fearful of a "gap in my knowledge" because "if it is spotted I am vulnerable again", and this meant "exposing myself to risk". In order to avoid this, he felt he must be "flawless". This extended to his thoughts of studying medicine, where he imagined he must learn everything beforehand, terrified a lecturer might know more than him.

However, he had allowed himself to be ignorant and uncertain in relation to the therapist, although he had, of course, "read every book on Asperger's by now". He was cautiously willing to experiment with incompetence and ignorance, even though he could not "remember the last time I said I don't know". Prior to meeting Sonya, he had commented on his compulsive need to be right: "It is possible that my conversations with you are the only ones where I do not feel superior to the other person." He felt he needed respect as a superior person of knowledge "because that is all I have". However, he added "Perhaps I just need to get over myself" and "I would prefer to be anybody but myself." Thus, a loosening of the stranglehold of his grandiose self might have allowed the relationship with Sonya to develop.

Peter struggled with his deepening attachment to Sonya, and his awareness of potential pain if he lost her. He comforted himself with the thought that if she left him "I think I could get over it in twenty minutes—I would open a spreadsheet or something."

He talked of finding the sessions unsettling, raising more questions rather than providing simple answers. We looked at the way that the psychotherapeutic exploration acted as a sort of "irritant" to his system, provoking psychological growth. As an instance of his changing relationship with emotions, he noted that if Sonya were asleep, he might stroke her hair and this made him feel happy, and he deduced from this that he had an emotional involvement with her. His reading interests had shifted from technical anatomical texts to fiction/literature. He commented also on his increased sense of humour.

He began to reappraise his view of himself as lacking emotions: "I was very sensitive as a child, and at some point I managed to compartmentalise myself to such a degree that I even managed to convince myself that I don't have feelings." He noted that in his relationship with Sonya "I have done 90% of the things people say love means—I can at least care." During a period when they separated for a while, he observed "I miss the mess" (of living with Sonya), and he noted that this marked a significant step.

Following a period when I had been absent from work for a couple of months, he pondered whether it was right to become attached to me, because "then if I am attached to you I will be upset if you are killed in a car crash." This led him to ponder on Buddhism and the idea of attachment as the source of suffering. He tried to reduce his possessions to fifty, discarding everything that was not essential, including digital items such as photos. However, this left him wondering "What is the meaning of life?"

Eventually, he reflected that, at one point, "I removed so much from my life there is nothing left." He felt he had overdone the simplification and minimalisation of his life: "I threw away or sold virtually every possession I had", so that everything became smaller and smaller, on the basis that "The less you have, the less you need." He had applied this same principle to people. However, he concluded that "the people who came up with this idea had other people in their lives—and that without them what is left is just a big hole." He pondered what to do with his time, what to put in "the hole", alone in his house all day with its white desk, white carpet, white walls, and white computer. He found himself somehow liking the mess that Sonya left when she stayed in his house.

Peter reported that Sonya said he makes her feel loved and cared for. He said this must be because he pays careful attention to the task of being with her and he was very much enjoying this. He observed feelings of love in so far as "I like Sonya more than I like anyone else and I want to do nice things for her", and he had not felt this before. They had talked in more detail and practical ways about how to manage their relationship. Regarding children, he had tended to feel he should not reproduce, both because of the danger of passing on Asperger's and also because of the potential effects of his emotional absence. However, he was practising his "people skills" and now considered it more possible to develop the required skills of relating, even if these did not come naturally, and so it seemed possible that he could develop the skills of parenting. He was also working towards being able to visit Sonya's parents and develop a way of being and behaving that would be appropriate in that context.

Moreover, he had begun to wonder whether "faking" his response to others might be preferable to being honest all the time, since being fully himself resulted in people complaining and being upset. He reasoned that "It is going to be like wearing masks—having a repository of masks for different situations—and if I become sufficiently good at it, no one would notice." We talked of the normal degree of deception that is inherent in polite human social intercourse. This was a revelation to him and an important realisation.

Increasingly, Peter became less clear that Buddhism held the answer for him, although he had been watching many lectures by the Dalai Lama. He spoke of a contrast between the "Buddhist approach" and the reality of how he actually felt. He identified his basic wants and needs as: a source of income; people around him; problems to solve; stimulation; opportunities to express himself creatively; using skills to help make people's lives better. He noticed himself becoming warmer and less judgemental, "but it does not come naturally to me", and he had "rediscovered my sense of humour", and was socialising more. He was enjoying playing the piano, as well as writing fiction. His consumption of alcohol had reduced. Crucially, he realised that he cannot "be an island and have needs", noting that "this is stating the obvious, but it was news to me."

A highly significant step he took was to meet Sonya's mother. Prior to this he had been adamant that he would never meet her family. As he thought about this insistence, during an earlier session, he eventually stated clearly that this was because he would feel vulnerable. He would find this vulnerability intolerable, and so he would resort to being dominant and controlling and arrogant; he would feel embarrassed by this behaviour, as well as feeling embarrassed by his vulnerability. This clarity emerged as he spoke. In fact, the meeting with Sonya's mother had been fine, and he had used his practiced social skills.

At our final meeting, Peter spoke with cautious optimism about his progress, his birth into the realm of emotional need, and his evolving relationship with Sonya.

Comment

Most of this process consisted of Peter exploring his own observations, insights, reflections, and questions, through an ongoing conversation with the therapist at monthly intervals. He allowed the protected space of the psychotherapeutic setting to be the arena within which he could experiment with being less certain and more authentic. As he put it, this was initially "the only place where I can be myself in the presence of another human being", but in time he became able to be more fully and vulnerably himself with his girlfriend Sonya. Peter revealed, to himself and the therapist, how he had developed a "grandiose omniscient self", building on his hyper-developed brain, as a protection for his feelings of vulnerability and inadequacy experienced in his early social encounters. His autistic spectrum sensitivity and brain hyper-development had burdened him with a sense of being "different" and potentially ostracised. Against the childhood pain of this, he developed his typical "autistic defences".

Conclusions

People with autistic spectrum traits tend to experience high levels of social anxiety, along with deficits in processing social information. Emotions might be feared as potentially overwhelming, resulting in pervasive psychodynamic defences against experiencing these. Anxiety, and the sense of being "different", give rise to shame. It can be helpful to assist the client in exploring the nature of their autistic spectrum temperament, and the psychodynamics arising from this, thereby reducing shame and facilitating a better adaptation to their circumstances.

CHAPTER TEN

Subtle energetic aspects of ADHD: reversed and scrambled energy fields and yin–yang imbalance

I n writing of "subtle energetic aspects", I am referring both to the energies of meridians and chakras (and related areas of bio-energetic anatomy and function), and also the way the person's energy is experienced by others.[17] The person with ADHD will not only feel "driven mad" by their own energy, but may also have a disturbing and aversive effect on others.

There are several ways in which the more outward "discharging"— or "yang"—forms of ADHD are disturbing to others. First, the person may appear to be "going on and on", in a very repetitive and irritating way, seemingly unable to set an issue aside and move on. Indeed, the person with ADHD might appear to be continually fuelling their own state of agitation, as if "working themselves up" into an ever-increasing frenzy of fury or other negative emotion. He or she might appear like "a dog with a bone", never letting go, once having clamped their emotional teeth into an issue.

The psychotherapist listening to such a person might initially try to follow and explore the nature and origins of the particular state of distress the client is presenting. This will often prove to be a fruitless exercise, although this will not immediately be apparent. On trying to make links back to the emotional state of the previous session, the

221

client might seem to have little persisting memory or awareness of this, having subsequently moved on to another preoccupation. It might take some time before the psychotherapist realises that the consistent theme is that *something* is always bothering and irritating the client, but its content may vary. Exploration of the psychodynamics is rarely, on its own, particularly helpful, although it might initially appear to be. The problem is not essentially one of psychodynamics. It is to do with a brain state and an associated energy state.

An example of the misleading impressions given, if the psychotherapist looks for an explanation rooted in psychodynamics or attachment, is the client's presentation of low self-esteem. The psychotherapist might look for origins of this in early attachment relationships and experiences within the family. The client may provide plenty of indications of this, alluding to a variety of esteem-injuring experiences, such as hurtful, critical, or rejecting responses from carers or peers. For example, one man, Elton, would speak of how his mother would frequently become irritated with him when he asked for her help with his homework—she would exclaim that he was "stupid". It was only after a considerable time of working with Elton in psychotherapy that his own contribution to this became apparent. He would seek the attention from his mother, which she would dutifully give, but he would himself pay no attention to what she was saying. Similar patterns were apparent in his workplace as an adult. Elton would not seem to pay attention to instructions given by managers, who would become annoyed. After a prolonged period of psychotherapy, it became clear that little change was taking place. Work would seem to be done, but no change would result. His discourse became highly repetitive. In short, he was an extremely irritating man! Whenever the psychotherapist tried to address these aspects, Elton would use the comments as further ammunition with which to berate himself and declare what a useless and worthless person he was. It was clear that he gained some masochistic pleasure in his continual discharge of rage at himself. The psychotherapist would offer his thoughts to Elton, but these would be turned into ammunition for masochistic self-attack. In this way, the therapist's thoughts (Bion's alpha elements) would be turned into beta elements, unusable as a basis for thought (Bion, 1962). This can be characteristic of the way in which people with ADHD can give the impression of communicating and thinking, but are, in fact, generating beta elements and discharging tension. One might say that at such times the psychotherapy is being *misused*. Some temporary relief, or masochistic pleasure, is generated, but this does not lead to mental and emotional growth. Whilst Elton tended to discharge rage masochistically, other people with ADHD might direct this towards others, giving the impression of their subjective world being one populated by others who are continually thwarting or wounding them, or letting them down. This can give a highly distorted and misleading impression of the person's childhood, as well as their current family relationships. These patterns tend not to change until the core issue of ADHD is addressed.

Psychoenergetic reversal and homolateral energy flow

There is also commonly a relentless tone of negativity running through the discourse of the person with ADHD. This can have a significantly adverse effect on the psychotherapist. It is as though all of life becomes absorbed and homogenised into a stream of bland yet negative mood and emotion, ground into a dull dust of beta elements (Bion, 1962) that covers everything. This grumbling and whingeing state of being will not be accompanied by any constructive efforts to improve the situation. Moreover, there may be a lack of emotional or spiritual depth to what is presented. The person may also appear not to engage in any activity that is psychologically or spiritually nourishing. This is a highly unpleasant state of mind, both for the person with ADHD and those in that person's field of influence. It lends itself to addictions of various kinds: to smoking, drugs, food, pornography, or other forms of stimulation.

From an energy psychology point of view, the person in this state has a reversed energy field orientated towards self-sabotage and negative emotions in general (Mollon, 2008). In a reversed energetic state, it is difficult for a person to feel positive, or motivated to be constructive, or to function at their best in any realm. Their discourse will be repetitive and monotonous. In colloquial terms, he or she will be "moaning on and on", communicating little other than negativity, and this quality of relentless complaining non-communication is highly characteristic. It is a brain state and an energy state. While giving the impression of communicating, in so far as words are used, it is essentially just an expression of a reversed energy field. To the extent that this is the case, attention to the words and quasi-thoughts that are being generated can be a waste of time. Instead, it is the core of ADHD that must be addressed.

It can be profoundly unpleasant for the psychotherapist, and others, to be in the presence of a person with ADHD whose energy system is in a state of pervasive reversal. This is because one person's energy field can entrain another person's. So, being in the presence of a client's reversed energy field, particularly if giving that person full mental, emotional, and energetic attention, will tend to reverse the therapist's field. This will result in a subtle, yet pervasive mood of depression, frustration, and negativity in the therapist.

Supposing the client with ADHD expresses intense feelings of anger, accompanied by aggressive fantasies, perhaps also including irritation or rage with the psychotherapist. Does this mean that such feelings are an essential part of the problem, perhaps needing further understanding and abreaction, along with learning skills for affect management? Not necessarily: it might mean the person is in a severely reversed energy state, associated with a brain state charac- terised by dysfunctional pleasure pathways and under-functioning frontal lobes. Rage is a product of this state. Of course, the person will speak as if the rage and other strong negative emotions are a response to external events, but this is a case of *emotion looking for a justification*. There can be a search for meaning, but sometimes there is no mean- ing, other than false confabulated ones. It cannot be emphasised enough how frustrating this is for the person with ADHD. He or she is aware of a lack of emotional connection with self, of being trapped in a state of non-communication that is experienced partly as a sense of not being understood by the other. Sometimes, the client might interrupt his or her own discourse with the utterance "you don't understand" or "nobody understands".

When in this state, psychotherapeutic conversation might be point- less. In a state of pervasive energetic reversal, all forms of talking therapy will fail. What is needed is for the client to be helped out of the dysfunctional brain and energy state. Rather than let the client con- tinue sitting and moaning, it can be helpful to invite them to stand up and engage in *cross crawl*, or, indeed, any of the exercises detailed in Donna Eden's energy medicine work (Eden & Feinstein, 2008). The sim- plest version of cross crawl[18] is to have the person sit and tap opposite knees (cross tap), but a more "energetic" form of this is to stand and "march on the spot", slapping hands on opposite knees as the latter are raised. It is the "across the body" stimulation of tapping opposite limbs that is important. Starting by tapping the same side hands and knees *for a few seconds* may be best, thereby mirroring the dysfunctional *homo-lateral* energy flow, before then entraining the system to the correct flow and polarity by cross tapping. This exercise will usually correct reversed energy fields, and also facilitate a good cross flow of energy between the two sides of the body and brain, which is essential for optimum functioning. Moreover, it gets the person out of their stuck mind–brain state and more into their body. Physical exercise is always good for people with ADHD, even though it might be resisted.

Other techniques that encourage cross flow of energy can be helpful in countering ADHD. These include variants of "Cook's hookups", which are calming and enable the person to feel more centred. Collarbone breathing similarly is calming and optimises the energy system. "Brain Gym" exercises are a related collection of methods for inducing greater calm and focus. An article by Jon Peterson on their value with ADHD is provided on the website of the John Hoskins School of Education,[19] and a list of research studies on Brain Gym and Educational Kinesiology is provided on the Brain Gym website.[20]

These energy techniques help the person to feel more awake. Despite the impression of an over-aroused state, the person with ADHD might have a "dozy" brain that is not fully awake. After doing these exercises, the client's discourse will be lighter and more dynamic, flowing with varying emotion and free-associative thought, and thus more like the normal communicative field of a person without ADHD. He or she will be more able to think, to focus, and to feel. Their mood will be more positive, and their actions more constructive. The person might report feeling more awake, colours experienced as brighter, and generally more sensorily aware. Whilst the effect will be temporary, it opens up a window of awareness of different mental and energetic states. If the client practises these techniques regularly, the effect will be more sustained.

Yin–yang imbalance

In terms of traditional Chinese medicine, people with ADHD might suffer from either excess yang (too outgoing and discharging) or excess yin (too withdrawing). By discharging too much energy in yang activity, the body–mind–energy system becomes depleted. There is insufficient energy to sustain good brain function. The depleted yin leads the person (unconsciously) to seek energy from others—to be a kind of psychic vampire. Generating arguments and acrimonious interactions with others can be rewarding for the person with ADHD because it raises their own arousal level and provides stimulation. This, of course, can be most unpleasant for those targeted unconsciously in this way. It is an example of a more general phenomenon, whereby a person who is deficient in a certain psychic or energetic quality will non-consciously seek it in others, and might engage in active efforts to elicit it. Those clients with too much yang need assistance in calming and becoming more centred, containing their energy that is tending to be dissipated in useless brain and physical activity. Those who are too yin need to be encouraged to be more active, perhaps to take up physical exercise or join a gym. Often corrections for excess yang and excess yin are both required.

Joseph was a man with ADD (without hyperactivity) who displayed a deficit in yang and far too much yin. He managed to go to work five days a week, but would spend his weekends mostly in bed, lacking motivation to do anything. His house was in a chronic state of neglect and disrepair. He told me that a pile of broken glass had remained unmoved in his bedroom for several years. His kitchen barely functioned. Whilst acknowledging it would be nice to have a comfortable and pleasingly decorated home, and being well able to afford to have the necessary work done, Joseph seemed unable to motivate himself. He would vaguely think he would do something constructive or enjoyable on his Saturday and Sunday, but almost invariably would, when the time arrived, feel it to be preferable to stay in bed. Although Joseph's mood was chronically morose, he could not be described as clinically depressed. He quite enjoyed his work, liked to help others if he could, and benefited from a strong religious faith. Nevertheless, when left to his own devices, he would stay in bed. His typical state of being could be described as somewhat "dozy". He was seemingly a man with zero initiative. Explorations of the meaning of his passivity—in terms, for example, of his wish to be looked after by his mother, to return to the passivity of the womb, to avoid responsibility, extreme avoidance of oedipal competition (originally with his father and now with other men), secret masochistic pleasure, hidden narcissistic illusions of superiority (of not being concerned with the material trivia that preoccupy and motivate others)—were certainly of interest, but did not lead to any change in Joseph's behaviour. What did bring about change was a focus on his ADD, his understimulated brain state, and a more forceful presentation by the therapist of the need for active measures to counter the default ADD state of doing nothing.

Joseph showed too much yin in his lung meridian (these things can be ascertained through energy muscle testing). He was taught to breathe more deeply, to counter his tendency to under-function in his breathing in and out. This helped him to feel more awake. He was also encouraged to eat with concern for nutrition, an essential aspect of life he had hitherto neglected, seemingly entirely unaware of a link between food and health. The latter illustrated a kind of "stupidity" that was also characteristic, again perhaps reflecting his tendency to journey through life in a "half-asleep" state. Slowly, Joseph began to experience an increase in his appetite for life and its sensory and mate- rial pleasures. He reported showing some greater initiative at work, began to purchase some long-needed items for his house, and made plans for decoration and renovation. He also took up a routine of gentle exercise and cycling to work. All of this was part of becoming more "awake".

By contrast, Petra, a client with ADHD, was noisy and continually discharging her emotional state, complaining about this friend and that neighbour, members of her family, and her dealings with organi- sations, including the health care system—a highly yang state that often left her exhausted. Initially, the therapist would try to follow and understand each emotional state, seeking out its current triggers and its childhood precursors. This would often appear interesting and potentially useful, but it did not seem to lead to any change. Petra would continue to find different events and circumstances to moan about. Gradually, the therapist began to appreciate that these presen- tations of distress were all, in some essential way, misleading. The core problem was Petra's ADHD. Her relationships with others had always been stormy, both within her family and her childhood peer group. Her ADHD affected all her relationships, with her family of origin, her current family and children, neighbours, work colleagues, and health care professionals. She was a continual state of agitation looking for a reason. When ADHD was explained to Petra, she found the concept

228 THE DISINTEGRATING SELF

illuminating and containing. She benefited from energy exercises to calm and centre her brain, mind, and body. Mindfulness practice, involving learning to observe her emotions in a more detached way, also helped her become calmer. By recognising that the core of her difficulties was her neurobiology, rather than her childhood experiences, her current circumstances, her psychodynamics, or her personality, she could more easily accept her own nature, talents, and limitations, and, thereby, feel less of a victim of the external world. She gained a sense of greater authorship of her own life.

People with ADHD find the ordinary world stressful, even without additional traumas. This causes their energy systems to become unbalanced. Some become too yin, and some too yang. Either way, reduction of stress and discharge of tension are necessary for well-being and energetic balance. The stress comes from: (a) being over-sensitive and easily excited and overstimulated (by pleasurable as well as aversive stimuli); (b) intense reactions to being thwarted or frustrated (including having to wait); (c) excess fear reactions to perceived threat (including fears of abandonment); (e) delayed or stunted development of the neocortex, particularly the frontal lobes, and, thus, deficits in the management functions (or the Freudian ego). The latter leaves the brain and energy system in the position of anarchic and overstimulated children in a playground with no teacher in charge. Some of the children tear around manically, getting into fights and screaming at the top of their voices (becoming excessively yang—neurobiologically a state of sympathetic dominance), while others withdraw and try to find quiet and hidden places to sit and dream (the yin reaction—parasympathetic dominance). In terms of the Freudian structural model of the psyche, the ADHD person is at the mercy of the id, the instinctual reactions, and perhaps also oppressed by a severe punishing primitive superego (not based on identification with realistic aspects of the father, but on projected and reintrojected aspects of rage), with insufficient ego to manage the internal and external relations and equilibrium. It follows that what is needed is a combination of calming the id, with stress relief procedures, and assistance to the ego, with help in thinking, planning, and devising strategies for managing emotions and the demands of life in the social world. Trying to support the ego without calming the id is likely to fail and calming the id without assisting the ego will leave the person deficient in resources to manage their involvement in the social world. The person with ADHD is often like a lost child, naïve yet fearful, impulsive, and bewildered, reacting with panic and rage to the inevitable frustrations and humiliations of life, discharging aggression against the self or others. Extreme yang expressions (chaotic discharge, like an uncontrolled fire cracker) or yin (shutting off and shutting down in a dreamy or rigid avoidance of normal social interactions) are two contrasting reactions of the AD(H)D brain when overwhelmed.

The "five energies" metaphor

In his brilliant book, *Fire Child, Water Child*, psychiatrist Stephen Cowan draws upon traditional Chinese medicine to describe different types of ADHD, using the concept of the "five phases", with the metaphors of the seasons and the five energies of nature: wood, fire, earth, metal, water (Cowan, 2012). This draws upon earlier work by Beinfield and Korngold (1991), who applied this perspective to temperament more generally. Not only is this perspective illuminating, but it also helps avoid the pathologising inherent in western-style diagnosis, allowing an appreciation of a person's temperament with both its strengths and vulnerabilities.

The most typical ADHD types, within the five phases system, are those of wood and fire, associated with the seasons of spring and summer. The energies of wood correspond to the power of plant life forcing its way through the ground, bursting forth into the light, and birds building their nests with urgency. The ADHD person with a "wood" temperament is full of curiosity, independent, adventurous, breaking boundaries, constantly moving, and prone to anger. The "wood" temperament has difficulty sleeping.

Summer is the season of the "fire" temperament—a blaze of colour and exuberance. Like bees and butterflies drawn to brightly toned flowers, the "fire" temperament is drawn to novelty and colourful stimulation, prone to excitement, and sometimes charismatic. Absence of novel stimulation and the threat of boredom are highly aversive to the "fire" temperament. On the other hand, he or she can become overwhelmed by novelty and change and so is torn between the dread of too much and too little stimulation. Marked swings of mood might occur. The "fire" person might be particularly impulsive. He or she might be prone to drug or alcohol addiction in an attempt to maintain the "euphoria" of summer. Both fire and wood temperaments have difficulty managing impulses and emotions.

The "earth" temperament, associated with the end of summer, the harvest, places value on connection and attachment. He or she tends to be insecure, clingy, and to worry a great deal. This inner preoccupation interferes with attention and causes indecision. Sleep is disturbed because the "earth" person cannot turn off their hyperactive worry mind. This is more of an ADD presentation than one involving overt hyperactivity.

Metal is the temperament of autumn. In that season, the clearer structures and boundaries of the natural world are revealed, as the foliage dies back. The "metal" temperament shows awareness of patterns and attention to detail and logic and feels secure with consistent schedules and clear categories of thought. It has something in common with the autistic spectrum. Unexpected events and changes of schedule are disturbing for this temperament. When stressed, the "metal" person becomes more rigid. Instead of easily distracted attention, the "metal" tendency is to become hyperfocused and perfectionist, particularly when stressed, sometimes displaying compulsive behaviours, including tics and eating disorders.

Water is the temperament linked to winter—the inward withdrawn state of nature, when life is held underground, bulbs dormant, holding in their potential. The "water" temperament is "deep", tending to withdraw into imagination and pondering the mysteries: the philosopher. Living in accord with external time is particularly difficult for this temperament, and time pressures can cause great stress. As stress mounts, the "water" temperament tends to shut down and lose motivation. Cowan comments,

> For the Water child, it is time itself that is the stressor in their lives. Even the smallest assignment can take forever to complete. These children are often classified by conventional psychiatrists as having "inattentive type ADD". They are not hyperactive or impulsive; on the contrary, they're barely moving. (Cowan, 2012, p. 58)

Like many people whose problems are inherent in their temperament, those within the ADD/ADHD spectrum are continually seeking something that is missing for them—something that is needed to balance, calm, or stimulate their system. Those seeking stimulation might turn to drugs, loud music, gambling, pain, danger, fast driving, and engaging in arguments or physical fights. Those seeking soothing might be clingy and show intolerance of being alone. These two trends may co-exist, so that the person seeking interpersonal stimulation through argument and aggressive provocation could drive others away, thereby evoking the polarised and alternating affects of the borderline personality, captured in the famous book title *I Hate You— Don't Leave Me* (Kreisman & Straus, 1989). The absence of a normal balanced flow of yin–yang energy, combined with reduced dopamine in the ADHD brain, give rise to an inner feeling of deficit in pleasure in being alive, which, all too often, the person with this condition will interpret as an absence of love. It is as if the inner deficit in (Freudian) libido is perceived as an external deficit—that is, in not feeling loved. The person with ADHD is, indeed, continually inclined to feel unloved, neglected, and abandoned.

The child and adult with ADHD frequently live with pervasive inner feelings of disappointment, sadness, and *shame*, as well as anger and irritability. Self-esteem is almost always impaired and vulnerable. The feelings of shame stem from the sense of failing, of being "different", and of evoking rejection, and, in particular, of repeatedly evoking an angry or disapproving maternal face in response to hyperactive childhood behaviour that often drives mothers to the limits of their tolerance. These shame-based yin "energies of withdrawal" may co-exist with the outwardly flowing yang energies of angry protest, which tend to elicit more rejection by others, thus stimulating further shame, in a spiralling negative circle.

Shift the emphasis from emotions to brain state: further use of energy exercises

While exploration of emotion and meaning (including thoughts, fantasies, beliefs, and perceptions), and psychodynamic conflict, can of course be useful, there are often times during work with people with ADHD when the problems of brain state need to take priority. If the brain is not in a calm and organised state, capable of thought and reflection, then exploration of the *content and conflicts* of the mind may be of little use.

The following observations and suggestions are not claimed to be objectively scientific, validated with neurobiological technology, although it would indeed be of interest to explore these with neuro-imaging procedures. Rather, they are procedures that I have found to result in subjective improvements in the "experience of one's brain". People report feeling "clearer", "more centred", "more able to think", "calmer", "more able to focus", "more in the present", or "the world looks brighter". Such reports contrast with prior states described, for example, as "brain fog", "my mind is a jumble", "I can't focus on anything".

In addition to the exercises described by Eden and Feinstein (2008), which are influenced by the *Touch for Health* methods (Thie & Thie, 2005), I find the following procedures helpful.

Modified collarbone breathing

This is one of the simplest and most effective energy psychology procedures. The original collarbone breathing procedure was developed by Dr Roger Callahan (2009), originator of thought field therapy. I have found that this modified version is simple and pleasant to do, and is very effective in calming a person, bringing coherence to the mind and the energy system, correcting energy polarisation, and inducing a good cross flow of energy. If a practitioner knew of only one "energy psychology" procedure, I would recommend this one. Here is what to do.

Cross the palms over the upper chest, with finger tips resting on the ends of the collarbones under the throat.

Carry out the following breathing sequence:

- Breathe in all the way—hold for five seconds
- Breathe out half way—hold for five seconds
- Breathe out all the way—hold for five seconds
- Breathe in half way—hold for five seconds
- Breathe normally.

Then, with your hands still crossed, turn your fingers into knuckles, so that the back of your fingers are against the collar bones.

Then repeat the above breathing sequence.

Internal "table tennis"

This can be very effective in inducing subjective changes in brain state. Here is what to do.

Close your eyes and imagine the brain space inside the skull. Now imagine that a game of ping-pong (table tennis) is being played with a bright ball that is being knocked from side to side across a central net (corpus collosum). The ball will be knocked all over the space, across the midline and also up and down the front–back line, and will also sometimes bounce off the ceiling. For some reason, I find this is even more effective if the imaginary ball is blue.

"Pin ball"

Internal "pin ball" is similar. Imagine that you are launching the ball from the back of your skull. It will bounce off the front and side to side. You can also imagine the ball having the freedom to bounce on a vertical axis as well, so that it sometimes hits the ceiling.

Bouncing to the core of the earth

Picture the ball of light (the ping-pong ball) in the centre of your brain. With a forceful exhalation, send the ball straight down through your brain, down your spine, and down to the very core of the earth, then, with an inhalation, draw it up sharply back to the centre of your brain. With another exhalation, send it straight up out the top of your head into the far distance above; draw it back with another inhalation. These can be repeated if you wish. I like to picture the ball as blue, and as entering a silver ocean of energy at earth's core, but this might simply reflect my personal aesthetic preferences.

Internal eye movements

Eye movement therapy methods are known to be effective, possibly partly to do with their capacity to facilitate inter-hemispheric com-munication (Kinsbourne, 1972; Mollon, 2005). I have found that it is possible to build on this effect with imaginary internal eye move-ments. Here is what to do. Close your eyes. Let your eyes move from side to side comfortably. Now imagine you also have eyes in the back of your head. Scan the field behind you, side to side, with your imaginary eyes. Now imagine you have eyes in the top of your head. Roll these in a circular direction clockwise (if the top of your head were a clock face). Imagine that this movement draws down a stream of fresh cleansing energy, like a pastel rainbow shower. Now imagine that you have eyes in the bottom of your feet. Roll these in a circle counterclockwise (if you were looking down on a clock face). As you breathe in, draw the energy down from above; as you breathe out, direct energy downwards into the earth.

All these exercises require only a minute or so to have their subjective effect.

Those practitioners who are skilled in advanced "energy psychology" procedures might be able to "energy test" different areas of the brain (through the kinesiology technique of "therapy localisation" (Frost, 2002; Mollon, 2008). After using these exercises, the energy test results will be different, suggesting a more optimal brain state.

Further outline of energy methods can be found in Appendix III.

Imagery for energetic balance

I have found the following exercise to be helpful for some clients, as a kind of waking dream functioning to bring greater energetic balance. Endless variations on this theme are possible. This work with imagery can usefully follow any of the exercises described above, all of which induce a calm and slightly altered brain state conducive to the use of dream-like imagery. Here are the instructions.

Place two fingers of one hand just under the collarbones in the centre of your upper chest, and two fingers of the other hand on your heart chakra, a few inches lower in the centre of your chest. Put your attention on a shimmering *blue diamond*, just behind your fingers under the collarbones. Think of this as your access point to your inner resources,[21] and an entry point to a vast *blue ocean*. Using your intention, send your consciousness into the blue diamond. Find yourself floating on a little boat on the blue ocean. The water itself is blue and yet very clear and translucent. You can see down into its depths—it seems to go on for ever. There is a bright yellow sun above. The little boat drifts, eventually coming upon the shore of a little island of trees. You land the boat and get out to explore, walking through the trees until you find a clearing.

At this point, the client is guided to find some element that is needed to bring greater balance to their personality, perhaps guided by the Cowan (2012) outline of ADHD types in terms of the Chinese medicine metaphors of the "five elements" and seasons of earth (harvest), fire (summer), metal (autumn), water (winter), and wood (spring). It is possible to muscle test for which element is most needed for that individual. Thus, the element of "wood" might be provided by an image of a fallen tree trunk on which the person may sit, merging with its "woodenness", the strength and vigour of a life form that has persisted and grown for years, combining the nourishment of the earth with the life-giving energy of the sun. The element "earth" itself may be accessed through the imagery of sitting on the ground, feeling its rich and solid "earthy" qualities, supporting numerous life forms. "Fire" can be represented by the blazing warmth of the sun. "Water" can be expressed in the image of a clear pool or stream in the clearing among the trees, or refreshing rain. "Metal" may be represented by streaks of iron or gold visible in the rocks in the clearing, or in finding a precisely constructed tool, such as a knife. The person is invited to rest for a while, absorbing and enjoying whatever qualities their system needs. Words and phrases can be used to help highlight the relevant required qualities of these elements, guided by what is known of the person and the difficulties that he or she experiences. When it feels as if the process is finished, he or she can make their way back to the little boat, which then drifts on the blue ocean, taking them home.

Why is such an exercise helpful? Conditions such as ADHD and autistic spectrum constellations involve a combination of *too much* of certain qualities, and *too little* of others. For example, there might be *too much* excited pushing through boundaries (wood—spring) and darting here and there towards colourful distractions (fire—summer), and *too little* attention to form and detail (metal—autumn), quiet intro-spection (water—winter), and gathering the fruits of sustained growth and work (earth—harvest). It might seem surprising that the use of imagery can evoke the associated mental or personality qualities, but this seems to be the case and is in line with a fairly common feature of energy psychology modalities (and other approaches, including eye movement therapies), in which desirable resources are "installed". This use of imagery to represent and evoke what is missing is also congruent with the Jungian (1974) emphasis upon the compensatory function of some dream images.

Summary

The agitated emotional state of a person with ADHD is associated with a disturbance at the subtle energetic level. This is experienced as aversive by others. Often the energetic state of a person with ADHD is "reversed", a condition linked with self-sabotage, a mood of negativity, and a failure to function well in any activity. At such times, it is best to engage the client in simple exercises to correct the energetic state and alter their brain state. These tend to help the person become more calm, coherent, and awake. Different forms of ADHD can be formulated in terms of the metaphor of five elements and associated seasons. Exercises using energy and imagery can be used to bring greater balance into the personality.

CHAPTER ELEVEN

Somato–psychic fragility syndromes

Hypermobility and Ehlers–Danlos syndrome as an example

Many patients present with a combination of psychological problems, such as anxiety or depression, and a variety of ill-defined and variable physical problems. Chronic fatigue is frequently part of this picture. Quite often, this combination is dismissed by GPs and psychiatrists as essentially "psychological" and due to "stress", or the person might be treated as suffering from "medically unexplained symptoms" and offered psychotherapy. Such people often receive a poor service from health agencies and psychotherapists because the physical underpinnings of their difficulties are not commonly understood.

The notion of "psychosomatic", or "psychogenic" (that the mind can cause physical symptoms, particularly by means of painful emotions or unwelcome perceptions and thoughts that are somehow warded out of the mind and into the body) has some validity, but is often overused. It is all too easy for medical doctors to assume that if a physical cause of a patient's symptoms cannot be found, then the cause must somehow be "psychological". Since the "psychological" cannot be seen, cannot be detected through any of the senses or through any specialised diagnostic equipment, it becomes a hypothesis that cannot be disproved, except perhaps through eventual discovery of a physical cause, although, even then, there can still be recourse to the notion of "hysterical" or "functional" overlay that exaggerates the real physical problem. If psychotherapists collude with this notion and seek to explore psychodynamic or attachment-based explanations of "medically unexplained symptoms", they will no doubt find these, because that is how it is with psychotherapy. It is always possible to find quite legitimate psychodynamic material in a client's discourse, because *the mind is psychodynamic*, but whether these psychological phenomena are truly a "cause" of the client's physically experienced distress is another matter. On the other hand, there are many psychological *consequences* of physical and neurological problems, and all kinds of intricate interactions between mind and body. I prefer the concept of "somato–psychic" to "psychosomatic", since this emphasises the primacy of physical conditions that affect the mind.

Over the years, I have encountered a number of clients who show the following characteristics.

- Being very sensitive, both emotionally and in the physical senses, corresponding to the concept of "highly sensitive person" (Aron, 1999).
- A tendency to feel generally vulnerable.
- A variety of somatic reactions to stress, or which appear exacerbated by stress.
- Various pains in different parts of the body.
- Chronic fatigue.
- Irritable bowel syndrome.
- Presentation of a social self that might conceal the extent of inner stress.
- Pervasive feelings of shame.
- Unusually soft and relatively wrinkle-free skin, which can give the person the appearance of being younger than their chronological age.
- Unusually flexible joints.
- Vaginismus (sometimes).
- Migraines (sometimes).

I had never heard of the multi-systemic condition known as Ehlers–Danlos syndrome (EDS) until a client drew my attention to it.

She had been Googling for possible reasons for her varied and worsening physical symptoms and was, indeed, subsequently diagnosed with this condition. The various manifestations of EDS result from a core problem of insufficient collagen. This means that the connective tissue of the body, and its various structures, are not adequately held together. Ligaments and joints are loose. Dislocation happens easily. The skin is thin and translucent. The effort of holding the bodily structures together contributes to the chronic tiredness, since the muscles have to compensate for the excessive looseness. A person with this condition lives in a continual struggle with the *threat of falling apart*, of *disintegrating*, both physically and psychologically.

A common feature of EDS is sacroiliac joint dysfunction—a looseness of the joint connecting the sacrum to the pelvis. This can cause extensive pain in the lower back, buttocks, groin, legs, and hips, sometimes exacerbated when bending, climbing, or rising from a seated position, and during sexual intercourse. Various forms of "referred pain" can be experienced in other locations. Insomnia and depression can result from the chronic pain. The condition is often missed because conventional diagnostic testing with X-rays, CT scan, or MRI does not reveal it (although other forms of clinical examination do).

Pain is an inherent feature of EDS, often suffered stoically because it is always there. This may include *muscular pain*, tenderness, and spasms around the joints, *neuropathic pain*, experienced as electrical sensations, tingling, burning or shooting pains around joints, and *osteoarthritic pain* in the joints (Levy, 2013). All of these can be physically and socially disabling.

EDS is a physical condition with many psychological ramifications. It is not "psychosomatic" in the sense of a physical condition expressing psychological conflict or stress, but it is certainly somato–psychic, in so far as it has both mental and bodily expressions, and the underlying physical pathology has psychological effects. The person with EDS may feel *not adequately held together* psychologically as well as physically. Great effort is expended in struggling not to collapse emotionally. The background is often of a prolonged pattern of efforts to conform to the perceived demands of society, frequently displaying a marked degree of perfectionism. Striving to succeed, while denying the inner stress and presenting a positive face to the world, is possible for a finite period, until it is all too much and the person succumbs to emotional and physical depression. Chronic fatigue ensues. The person has striven to appear "normal", engaging in extensive denial of their difficulties.

Because of the stress of struggling with EDS and its integral physical pain, it is associated with a range of psychological and psychiatric conditions (Baeza-Velasco, 2011; Levy, 2013). These can include anxiety states as well as depression, and also presentations similar to ADHD (Pocinki, 2013).

Such people tend to receive an inadequate service from both medical practitioners and psychotherapists, often amounting to neglect or abuse. This is because their problems are not understood, usually being dismissed as "hysterical", "somatoform", "alexithymic", "medically unexplained symptoms", or "functional somatic syndromes". Because modern medicine is so compartmentalised, and because EDS is multi-systemic, causing multiple and diverse symptoms, physicians tend not to join up the dots. Referrals to varied specialists results in inconclusive and dismissive assessments, and mounting frustration for the client. In his review, Levy (2013) states,

> Affected individuals are often diagnosed with chronic fatigue syndrome, fibromyalgia, depression, hypochondriasis, and/or malingering prior to recognition of joint laxity and establishment of the correct underlying diagnosis.

Thus, their experience with doctors and therapists is predominantly of invalidation and of being perceived as an irritation. From crude dismissals as being "all in the mind", through simplistic CBT focused on pacing, distraction, and "behavioural activation", to sophisticated but ultimately unhelpful psychodynamic explorations of attachment patterns, people with these conditions typically will eventually learn that they cannot be helped and their best option is to adapt as best they can to their diminishing capacities.

Invalidation might also have been a marked feature of their childhood experience. Parents and other family members might have tended to dismiss expressions of discomfort, tiredness, and emotional sensitivity, so that the child learns to suppress awareness of these, developing a "false self" persona that conceals the inner psychobiological stress. Lacking validation of their experience through the mirror of family discourse, the inner stress is denied a signifier. As a result, it cannot be thought about or spoken about. It remains an "unthought known" (Bollas, 1987), an invisible "albatross around the neck". The child's struggle to be "normal" and deny his or her inner experience results in ever greater stress and alienation from his/her own body. This suppression of psychobiological reality can be maintained for a certain time, before an ultimate collapse that is expressed both mentally and somatically. The collapse may occur in adolescence or much later.

If such a person comes to the attention of psychiatric or psychological services, his or her problems might be framed as "depression" or "anxiety" and might be treated with antidepressant medication, or CBT, or both. Such interventions might provide modest but temporary relief. Permission to be ill might be a factor in this relief— an explicit component of some approaches, such as interpersonal psychotherapy.

The typical person with this constellation will try their best to comply with therapeutic requests, tasks, and expectations and will feel guilt at reporting an absence of improvement. Sensing that the therapist is interested in matters other than their physical struggles, the client might present material to do with interpersonal relationships, childhood experiences, etc., all of which may be partially relevant yet curiously concealing of the most crucial aspects, these being the underlying somato–psychic condition. Indeed, it is highly unlikely that the client will spontaneously speak of their hypermobility, even if it has been mentioned by a doctor somewhere along the line, because the client is unlikely to understand its implications. Time and again, I have seen patients referred within the NHS who present with anxiety, stress, depression, and pervasive physical pains, and who have been given the impression by GPs and psychiatrists that these are all of an essentially psychological nature. Sometimes, such people are referred for psychotherapy for "medically unexplained symptoms".

Because the person has no concept for their core condition, she or he is likely to look for other (external) causes of their difficulties, perhaps citing various kinds of work or family stress, or somehow blaming the parents. For example, one man explained his decline and depression in terms of discouraging and challenging experiences in his profession as a teacher, following a somewhat sheltered childhood, all of which were no doubt relevant, but his underlying somato–psychic vulnerability was readily apparent. Looking strangely baby-like, despite his mature years, he startled me one day by demonstrating his flexibility by suddenly getting up from the chair and dropping casually into a lotus position. He found psychotherapy very helpful, often remarking that he should have embarked on it years earlier, but clearly having been inhibited from doing so by pervasive shame.

A common pattern in the group of patients I am describing is that of perfectionism and striving excessively prior to the somato–psychic breakdown. It is as if the person sensed, from childhood, that there was something not entirely normal about them, feeling then that the solution would be to try ever harder. One woman attributed the origin of her perfectionism and excessive striving to having failed an important exam at age eleven. She felt this marked the onset of feeling she was not good enough unless she strove for perfection and achieved this. However, there seemed no particular indication of parental pressure to achieve. Rather, it seemed to be her own response to feeling different and vulnerable.

People displaying this pattern turn against their own nature, becoming "at war" with their bodies. Feeling they cannot rely on the physical body for support and adequate functioning, they engage in a continual fight against their own somatic weakness, often pushing themselves beyond their capacity. Hatred and anger toward the body are common, or sometimes a kind of somatic indifference, broken only by intrusions of physical pain or overt collapse of function.

One obvious therapeutic requirement for people with these kinds of somato–psychic fragility is stress relief, whereby the entire mind, brain, and body are calmed down. This is needed to counter the chronic and cumulative stress that has built up over many years. The somato–psychic breakdown has been a long time coming. However, the problem with this solution is that relaxation and stress relief may be directly counter to the person's personality organisation that is orientated to "civil war" with the body. He or she will fight against surrender to the body.

On the other hand, once the somato–psychic collapse has taken place, with ensuing chronic fatigue and depression, the person might be fearful of getting better. Kinesiology muscle signalling will usually indicate a belief that it is *not safe* to recover. Exploration of thoughts and feelings around this will usually reveal an unconscious thought along the lines of "it is not safe for me to get better because then I will exert myself excessively again and exhaust myself further".

The chronic stress to which such people have subjected themselves does real physical damage. The effects are certainly not "all in the mind". Early stress researchers, such as Cannon and Seyle, noted the effects of prolonged and repeated release of excess stress neurotransmitters, such as adrenalin and noradrenaline/cortisol. Prolonged stress, where there is no opportunity to restore the system to optimum functioning and balance between sympathetic and parasympathetic nervous systems, may result in sustained sympathetic dominance, leading eventually to adrenal exhaustion and a *collapse into a default parasympathetic dominance*. In this state, the person feels exhausted and has no motivation, and might feel nauseous, light-headed, and cold.

Pocinki (2013) describes how EDS sufferers experience surges of adrenalin, resulting in states of anxiety, with palpitations, muscle spasms, shortness of breath, trembling, irritability, and sleep difficulties. As their "adrenalin reserve" becomes more and more depleted, they respond more strongly to stress. Sleep becomes disturbed, causing further depletion, resulting in fatigue, difficulties with attention and concentration and taking in information, carelessness and errors, being easily distracted, avoiding tasks requiring sustained effort, and deficiencies of executive functioning such as organisation, planning, and staying on task—that is, *symptoms of ADD*.

A healthy state is one in which the parasympathetic system predominates, shutting off sympathetic activation except when the latter is necessary. In such conditions, the person is calm and able to rest, yet also able to mobilise adrenalin and fight/flight responses when these are required. The collapse into default parasympathetic dominance is not of this kind, since it results from an exhaustion of the sympathetic system. It is a state that Pocinki (2013) described in his conference presentation as like having "a foot on the gas and the brake at the same time".

Despite the exhaustion, the person might feel he or she must be doing more, with a self-condemnation as *lazy*. They might be drawn to sources of stimulation, including arguments with others, or states of anger, or dramas of one kind or another. Such negative emotional states are, in fact, stimulating for the nervous system and may non-consciously be sought out, even though they might be experienced as aversive. On the other hand, the person who feels insufficiently held together by their own physical structure might seek the emotional and physical protection of strong and containing others. The wish, most commonly expressed by women but sometimes less consciously _or a happy, weight tight environment_

present in men, to be held and protected by a strong man (or woman) might exacerbate feelings of shame and self-condemnation.

The mood of a person with this condition can be labile. It is as if the mental container lacks resilience in a manner analogous to the stretchiness of the bodily tissues. Moods and emotional responses might tend to be extreme and highly fluctuating. In psychotherapy, much time might be spent exploring the processes and meanings involved in each particular emotional response, before the therapist eventually realises that the crucial factor is the _lability_ of mood. It can be disconcerting to the therapist when the client presents in such dissimilar mood states, perhaps giving the impression of a defensive "splitting" of incompatible mental states. Sometimes, these characteristics lead psychiatrists to give the fashionable diagnosis of "emotionally unstable personality disorder" (or "borderline"). However, the mood lability may be much more neurobiologically rooted than psychodynamically driven. It is the instability—the "stretchiness" of the psyche—that is important for both therapist and client to understand.

People with hypermobility might have stretchy blood vessels, leading to venous pooling. This can result in "orthostatic intolerance", light-headedness on standing up from a sitting position. To compensate for this, the body could produce extra adrenalin. This is not itself a response to stress, but it does exacerbate stress responses. The increased adrenalin can lead to a seemingly energetic and active mode of being, at least for a time, perhaps a few years. The body is running on adrenalin, but is becoming steadily more exhausted. As the body becomes more tired, it develops an increased sensitivity to adrenalin, responding more to smaller amounts, obscuring the real tiredness as well as disturbing sleep, until eventually chronic fatigue might set it. The stress of having hypermobility, and associated symptoms, may itself raise adrenalin levels, all of which adds to anxiety. Surges of adrenalin can cause states of panic, with palpitations and pounding heart, and might also be a factor in migraine headaches. The body's attempts to deal with excess adrenalin may result in light-headedness, nausea, sweating, and problems in the gut. In general, people with hypermobility seem to display an over-response to physical and emotional stress, but this is a direct physiological reaction and is not essentially psychological. Adrenalin fluctuations may give the impression of a bipolar mood disorder, but this would be an inappropriate diagnosis and mood-stabilising medications are not indicated. If medication is required, Pocinki (2010) recommends beta blockers, since these block adrenalin.

Digestive and gut problems are common in people with hypermobility. The oesophagus might be too stretchy, resulting in acid reflux as the stomach contents leak back upwards. A stretchy stomach might lead to delayed gastric emptying, resulting in prolonged feelings of fullness. Stretchy intestines increase tendencies toward constipation and pain. Irritable bowel syndrome is a common diagnosis with such people, *but the cause is not psychological.* Tears in the abdominal wall might occur, into which small segments of intestine may push through, causing pain, which can be difficult to diagnose since the tears do not show on X-rays, CT scans, or sonagrams.

Sexual intercourse for a woman with hypermobility might be painful because of excessive stretchiness of the vagina, and vaginismus may occur. Stretchiness of the ligaments supporting the uterus and other tissues in the pelvis lead to increased risk of uterine prolapse, pressing on the bladder, and the bladder and rectum may also press on the vagina. Cystitis may be more frequent, possibly due to a stretchy bladder not emptying fully. Endometriosis may also be more common for these women.

Because the body has not been comfortable from early in life, the person could have developed a chronic state of partial dissociation from the body. In subtle energetic terms, this means an excessively yin state: the person is too much "in his head", or even "out of her head", as well as out of the body. Meditation might appeal to such a person because it can enhance the dissociation from the body. On the other hand, some forms of meditation can be helpful, since they can involve mindful awareness of the body.

The vague and pervasive sense of there being something wrong with the body can give rise to various forms of body dysmorphic disorder. In terms of the original Freudian theories of "cathexis" and narcissism, the body of the hypermobile person might not be a source of pleasure or well-being. As a result, it is "decathected"—emotional investment is withdrawn—and there is a regression to the stage of the "fragmented self" (Kohut, 1971). Instead of a coherent and cohesive whole body self, there is a sense of being fragmented into different bits, and any one of these "bits" may become a focus of dysmorphia. The obsessive dissatisfaction might focus on aspects that are a direct expression of the hypermobility and stretchiness, such as the appearance of the skin.

EDS can also be associated with "chiari malformation", where the cerebellum, at the base of the brain, is squashed into the spinal column, giving rise to blockage of blood vessels and the flow and drainage of cerebrospinal fluid (Flanagan, 2010). This can affect not only balance, fine motor movement, and other functions of the cerebellum, but also mood, cognition, and behaviour, and could be a factor in degenerative brain disease.

Composite clinical example: Sally

Sally was in her mid-thirties when she first came to see me, presenting with a history of chronic fatigue, stress, anxiety, and low mood. Because she assumed I was only interested in "psychological" matters, she did not immediately mention her pervasive physical pains in her throat, around her face and head, and in various other parts of her body, or her poor circulation and temperature regulation, or her periodic experiences of tingling and numbness in her limbs. It gradually emerged that she felt continually in pain and no bodily position was comfortable for long. Sally's manner was superficially cheerful and pleasant. She talked readily of stressful situations in her current life and in her childhood. It was easy to discern psychodynamic patterns, such as, for example, a tendency to do too much for others, trying to please and then feeling, partially unconsciously, angry and resentful. We saw that she had developed a pattern of pleasing and looking after others during her childhood with an alcoholic mother and a somewhat passive father.

Previously, Sally had been referred to a specialist psychotherapy service for "unexplained medical symptoms". This work had explored possible links between her physical symptoms and her emotions. Whilst these links seemed meaningful, they did not lead to any improvement in her symptoms. One psychiatrist had diagnosed her with "emotionally unstable personality disorder", while another labelled her as suffering from "generalised anxiety disorder".

Sally gave the impression that she had always felt sensitive and different from others. Her body had always troubled her, with its aches and pains and vulnerability to infections. She had tried to repudiate this reality by striving hard and being somewhat perfectionist. Doing well at school had been very important to her. She was also keen to be accepted and liked socially. Later, she had worked very hard in her career as an accountant, until she eventually succumbed to exhaustion. It gradually became apparent that Sally had viewed her fragile body as her enemy, so that she would override her somatic signals of stress and tiredness, "powering through" in a true 1980s "lunch is for wimps" mode. She also viewed her own emotions as her enemy, endeavouring to avoid experiencing sadness, anger, or shame. However, it became apparent that Sally distrusted not only her own emotions and her body, but also other people and the world in general. Indeed, it was as if she were "allergic" to everything in the world.

Sally told me that, according to her mother, she had been a "floppy baby" who had seemed to lack vigour and resilience. She had been sensitive and did not enjoy the rough and tumble of play with her peers. However, she had tried hard to fit in and be like others, developing a social persona that appeared pleasant, cheerful, and friendly. As she engaged in school sporting activities and dance, she displayed flexibility but would often cause herself slight injuries, resulting in pain, which she would ignore.

Sometimes, during her childhood and adolescent years, Sally would experience periods of exhaustion, but much of the time she would push herself to carry on, and would suffer difficulties sleeping, which we later understood as a result of the excess adrenalin her body was creating in an attempt to keep going. By late adolescence, the first signs of chronic fatigue were appearing. A viral illness, which might have been glandular fever, left her very debilitated. She never really recovered from this. Her extreme fatigue did indeed become chronic, following a fluctuating course.

In her twenties, Sally began chiropractic treatments, which became a recurrent feature of her life. These were prompted by pains in her back. Although the chiropractic adjustments did help alleviate her discomfort, it was noted that they did not last, and needed to be repeated quite frequently. As the years passed, Sally found increasingly that it was hard to maintain any posture for long before pain forced her to shift position. She would try to relax at home by suspending her body between a sofa and a stool, in such a way as to minimise contact.

Sally was constantly irritable, in both her body and her mind (although she tried to conceal this from others). Sounds, lights, temperature, the feel of clothes and furniture, would all tend to evoke irritable discomfort. Similarly, she would often find other people annoying, particularly if they seemed loud or overbearing. She would notice, and often become perturbed by, small changes in the setting of a room or a person's appearance. Her mood could be labile, sometimes shifting from cheerful to depressed over the course of hours or even just minutes, often without any clearly identifiable trigger.

The key part of Sally's psychotherapeutic progress was her acceptance of her somato–psychic fragility. Instead of fighting against her body, she was helped to be more accepting of its needs and vulnerability. She came to accept that she could not sustain full time work— that she needed time to rest and release stress. Regular practice of stress relief methods, based on energetic principles, became an important part of her daily routine. A secondary function of psychotherapy was to understand how her somato–psychic fragility had affected her throughout her life, and her struggles to adapt to, or deny, this.

Summary and conclusion

People presenting with apparently psychological or psychiatric problems are often suffering from an underlying somato–psychic condition, an undiagnosed primary physical syndrome with multiple somatic and psychological symptoms. Ehlers–Danlos syndrome is a good example of this, giving rise to chronic pain, eventual fatigue, depression, anxiety and panic, sleep disturbance, and bi-polar or ADHD-like symptoms.[22] It is probably much more common than is actually diagnosed. Those with this condition struggle with the continual stress of potential physical and mental disintegration. Surges of adrenalin and resulting adrenalin depletion are common features. Typically, the person struggles against the condition for years, taking a hostile stance against his or her own bodily vulnerability, often appearing hyperactive, before the inevitable chronic collapse sets in. Such people usually receive a very poor service from medical, psychiatric, and psychotherapeutic services.

Concluding comments

Many of the observations and perspectives described in this book have taken several decades to coalesce in my own mind. Whether they are of value for others is for the reader to judge, but I have felt a compelling obligation to share my realisation of the importance of the hidden struggle with brain states and body states presented by a significant proportion of our clients and patients. Those with ADHD, autistic spectrum, and somato–psychic conditions are assailed with the continual threat of impairment of self-regulation, of disintegration. For the person with ADHD, impulses and emotions at times cascade through the psyche like convoys of runaway trucks crashing through flimsy road barriers. Those who are "blessed and cursed" with autistic spectrum sensitivity have to find a way of living with the continual sensory and emotional onslaughts of a world too intense to manage. Others have to cope with a body and mind that feel always on the edge of collapse. Once these inherent challenges are perceived, the behaviours and psychodynamics of those afflicted become much less obscure and our therapeutic empathy is enhanced.

The Freudian model of the weakened ego, requiring our therapeutic assistance as it grapples unsuccessfully with overwhelming internal and external stimuli, provides an excellent framework for our endeavours with such clients. However, simple, easy, or formulaic solutions are not to be found, whether we look to psychoanalysis, CBT, energy psychotherapy, or psychopharmacology. The current fashion for manualised therapies and rigid therapeutic protocols are not the answer to these complex problems with varied presentations. By contrast, the benefits to the client of careful and empathic psychotherapeutic enquiry, cumulative clinical observation, and unprejudiced exploration of what might help, should not be underestimated. Each client is an Unknown Other, whose personal story and experience is to be gradually discovered.

Notes on medication for ADHD

Since I am neither a psychiatrist nor a medical doctor, I cannot provide authoritative advice on medication for ADHD and related conditions. I have, however, noticed the effects on adult patients who have been prescribed stimulant and other medication for ADHD. In many instances, the effects of stimulant medication, in normalising brain function and behaviour, are startling. People with marked difficulties with attention, regulation of emotion, and executive functioning, are suddenly able to focus, think before acting and speaking, look ahead towards future goals, and manage emotional expression in ways that are socially appropriate. Such effects last only as long as the drug is active. These observations are supported by meta-analyses of double-blind, placebo-controlled studies with children (Faraone & Buitelaar, 2010) and with adults (Faraone & Glatt, 2010).

There are four types of medication licensed in the UK for treatment of ADHD: the stimulants methylphenidate (or Ritalin), dexamphetamine, lisdexamphetamine, and the selective noradrenaline uptake inhibitor, atomoxetine (or Strattera). Methylphenidate is the most commonly prescribed, and is also available in a slow-release form (Concerta; Equasym).

Volkow and colleagues (2002a,b) have demonstrated with brain imaging studies that the stimulant methylphenidate blocks the uptake of dopamine in the brain, thereby facilitating communication across neurons that utilise dopamine. Similar processes are thought to occur with those medications that affect norepinephrine (atomoxetine).

Glen Elliot, Emeritus Professor of Psychiatry at the University of California, and an investigator in the multimodal treatment study of children with ADHD, comments,

> No medicine available to psychiatrists produces a more rapid and dramatic effect more safely than the proper dose of a stimulant to a patient with ADHD. Again and again, researchers have demonstrated the ability of stimulants to reverse the key symptoms of inattention, hyperactivity, and impulsivity with remarkable precision and relatively minor side effects. I routinely encourage my psychiatry trainees to witness this phenomenon directly by asking a family to bring in their child before he or she receives the usual daily dose. The trainee can experience firsthand the child who tears around the office, impulsively getting into everything but not staying with anything for long because the next unexplored item beckons. After administering the stimulant, the trainee can witness the transformation, which takes no longer than thirty minutes, as that same patient turns into a far more normal child—quieter, more polite, and able to stay on task. (Elliot & Kelly, accessed 17 August 2014)

However, these are powerful drugs, and unwanted side effects are common. The most frequently reported side effects are: insomnia; decreased appetite; slowed growth (in children); anxiety; increased heart rate; headaches; nausea; mood swings; rebound effects when the drug wears off. Atomoxetine has been linked (in rare instances) with more serious side effects. Both stimulants and atomoxetine can be dangerous for people with severe cardiac problems. In adults prescribed stimulant drugs, I have heard (in some instances) of increased aggression and worrying personality behavioural changes. Careful monitoring by the prescribing physician is important (Meijer et al., 2009). A patient should not be left on repeat prescriptions of ADHD medication without periodic review.

Brown (2013a) reviewed the evidence for long-term harmful effects of stimulant medication, including dangers of cardiovascular problems, inhibition of physical growth, and genetic damage. He concluded,

Taken together, these various studies indicate that the risks of serious adverse events from appropriate use of medications currently approved for ADHD are extremely small in both children and adults, so long as the treated individual is in reasonable health. (p. 120)

Nevertheless, the widespread prescribing of stimulant medications, particularly for children, has attracted controversy. Hearn (2004) quotes an official at the US Drug Enforcement Agency expressing concern about over-prescribing of stimulants, their potential long-term effects, their diversion to illicit sale as street drugs, and the possible conflict of interest of certain ADHD researchers and ADHD patient-advocacy charities who might receive funding from pharmaceutical companies.

Keith Conners, Emeritus Professor of Psychology at Duke University, and a long-time authority on ADHD, has described the vastly increased diagnosis of ADHD, with associated prescriptions of medication, as "a national disaster of dangerous proportions" (Conners, 2013), noting that the number of children on such medication in the USA had risen from 600,000 in 1990 to 3.5 million in 2013. In an interview with a *New York Times* journalist, Alan Schwarz (2013), he stated the diagnosis was "a concoction to justify the giving out of medication at unprecedented and unjustifiable levels". This, and a subsequent article also by Schwarz, led Thomas Brown to write two open letters to the editor of the New York Times, complaining of what he saw as their misleading content. Brown (2013b, 2014) argued that: the increase in numbers diagnosed reflects newer understandings of the wider impairment of executive functions in ADHD; the diagnosis of ADHD requires serious impairment in a variety of areas; the adverse side effects of medications were exaggerated in Schwarz's articles; that environmental changes or behavioural therapies do not produce lasting changes.

Concluding comment and caution

ADHD is not one specific thing. Like many psychiatric conditions, it is a spectrum. As a "categorical" diagnosis, it has very fuzzy edges. Many factors may play a part in the development of impairments in executive functioning and the regulation of attention, affect, and impulse. ADHD symptoms are usually combined with states of anxiety, mood dysregulation, and various personality difficulties. The important task is to work towards an understanding of the individual and what might be helpful for him or her. If ADHD symptoms are severe, then medication is certainly worth considering, but it should be carefully monitored. Any worrying new symptoms (physical or mental) or behavioural changes should be reported immediately to the prescribing doctor. As a general point, all psychiatric medications should be regarded with caution, taking heed of Whitaker's (2005, 2010) warnings that medication may have the potential to entrench and worsen mental health problems.[23]

Assessments for ADHD and autistic spectrum (Asperger's) conditions

There are actually no firm and reliable "tests" for ADHD or autistic spectrum conditions, any more than there are for most psychiatric diagnoses. These conditions exist on a spectrum, blending into "normality". Whilst there are questionnaires and checklists, and standardised observational protocols, ultimately the diagnosis rests upon clinical judgement. Some assessment procedures, marketed to the British NHS, seem to me unnecessarily time-consuming and not particularly illuminating.

My own view is that, unless there are research, forensic or other legal or occupation-related circumstances to consider, a precise diagnosis of these conditions is not particularly important. A person might well have tendencies and traits along one of these spectrums, without meeting the full *DSM-V* or *ICD-10* criteria (Ratey & Johnson, 1998). What is more important is to work towards a deepening understanding of the individual. This should be based upon a careful consideration of history, childhood development (perhaps including reports from parents or other relatives), symptoms and their context, the person's experience of daily life, current functioning in work and relationships, as well as ruling out alternative diagnostic possibilities.

In general, diagnoses should be held tentatively, ready to be revised in the light of further emerging information.

Assessment aids in relation to ADHD

In addition to consideration of the criteria listed in the *DSM-V*, the following rating scales are commonly used.

The Brown ADD Assessment Scales[24]

These measure five areas.

- Organising, prioritising, and activating to work.
- Focusing, sustaining, and shifting attention to tasks.
- Regulating alertness, sustaining effort and processing speed.
- Managing frustration and modulating emotions.
- Utilising working memory and accessing recall.

Conners' Adult ADHD Rating Scales (CAARS™)[25]

This combines self-report and observer ratings to provide a number of scales, including:

- Inattention/memory problems.
- Impulsivity/emotional lability.
- Problems with self-concept.
- Hyperactivity and restlessness.
- Total ADHD symptoms.

Assessment aids in relation to autistic spectrum/Asperger's

My preferred assessment aids are the set of questionnaires available from Professor Baron-Cohen's Autism Research Unit of the University of Cambridge.[26] These, including the very useful "Autism spectrum quotient", are available free of charge for research purposes. Although valuable as clinical screening tools, they are not intended to provide a diagnosis.

The *Autism Diagnostic Observation Schedule* (ADOS)[27] is a structured clinical interview providing a series of opportunities for the subject to show social and communication behaviours relevant to the diagnosis of autism. Again, it does not provide a definitive diagnosis, there are no norms, and conclusions rest essentially upon clinical judgement.

Energy psychology methods for ADHD

Whilst energy psychology methods can be subtle and complex, there are many applications that are simple and easy to apply, and which clients can readily learn and use as an aid to self-regulation. Since psychological disturbance is held and expressed within the body's energy system (of acupressure meridians and chakras), we find that engaging with the energy system concurrently with addressing thoughts and emotions can provide a much more rapid and complete resolution of distress (Gallo, 1999; Mollon, 2008, 2014a).[28]

Energy methods are applied essentially in three ways, although there are a variety of techniques and modalities (with various brand names).

- Exercises to correct systemic energy disturbances. These are disturbances in the energy system itself, and are not a *result* of psychological states, but they do have an *effect* on psychological states.
- Stimulation (tapping or holding) acupressure or chakra points (by the client) while thinking of traumatic memories or other emotional distress. The purpose is to clear the distress that is

patterned in the energy system. When the energetic patterning is cleared, the subjective experience is of no distress.

• Stimulating acupressure or chakra points while goals and intentions are held in mind. These help to establish the desired future trajectory, and help to clear emotional blocks to achieving this.

Systemic energy corrections

The energy system has quasi-electrical properties and can, indeed, be measured, to an extent, with an ordinary voltmeter. My reason for describing it as *quasi*-electrical is because it also has many strange qualities that are not normal components of electricity.

An optimally organised energy system has a certain coherence and flows freely. It has a cross flow through the body and brain. In addition, it is polarised, somewhat like a battery. When the palm is placed down over the head, a muscle test should indicate a strong response with correct polarisation, and weak when the back of the hand is placed down over the head—somewhat like the effect of a battery placed the correct or incorrect way against the terminals of a device. Quite often, a person's energy system may be non-polarised (showing no difference between palm down and back of hand down), or may show a reversed polarity. These are common in people with ADHD and autistic spectrum traits. When a person's energy system is not properly polarised and cross flowing, it seems to be difficult for him or her to function well. Certainly, no energy therapy will work until this is corrected.

Sometimes, a drink of water is all that is required. Inadequate hydration will cause malfunction in the energy system.

Without extensive training and practice, practitioners will not be able to use muscle testing competently. However, the following exercises are often of benefit whenever a person appears in an agitated, scrambled, or non-focused state.

Modified collarbone breathing

The following simple procedure (Figure 1) is derived from the collarbone breathing exercise originally developed by Dr Roger Callahan. I discovered that this variant works well one day when I mistakenly

Figure 1.   The collarbone breathing technique.

carried out the Callahan method incorrectly, yet found it had cleared the person's switched energetic state. It is simple, quite rapid, and relaxing as well as effective. In addition to its energetic properties, it can also help to correct tendencies to hyperventilate. If asked to recommend one single energy technique, it would be this. A person who is overwhelmed with emotion, and incoherent in his or her speech will become more calm, fluent, and thoughtful following this simple procedure. It will also help desensitise a person to feared situations and traumatic memories.

Cross the palms over the upper chest, with fingertips resting on the ends of the collarbones under the throat.

Carry out the following breathing sequence:

- breathe in all the way—hold for five seconds;
- breathe out half way—hold for five seconds;
- breathe out all the way—hold for five seconds;
- breathe in half way—hold for five seconds;
- breathe normally.

Then, with your hands still crossed, turn your fingers into knuckles, so that the back of your fingers is against the collarbones.

Then repeat the above breathing sequence.

Cook's hookups

Wayne Cook was an innovative chiropractor who developed a number of techniques to correct energetic disturbances. The following is partly derived from a traditional yoga position (Figure 2). I find that it is particularly beneficial for people with ADHD.

To do this:

- sit with left ankle over right ankle;
- stretch out arms with thumbs facing down;
- place the right hand over the left (so that feet and hands are crossed in opposite directions);
- entwine the fingers;
- bring the entwined hands up and under to rest on the chest;
- the chin may rest on the hands;
- the tongue may rest on the roof of the mouth behind the teeth;
- while sitting calmly in this position, for a minute or two or several minutes, breathe gently.

Cross tap

This modification of "cross crawl" can be very helpful in correcting energetic disturbance, particularly homo-lateral energy flow. For

Figure 2. Wayne Cook's "hookup" technique posture.

those who are proficient in muscle testing, the test for cross flow is for the person to imagine a large letter X (should test strong), *vs.* two vertical parallel lines (should test weak).

- Tap on each knee, alternately, with the same side hand—do this for a few seconds.
- Then switch to cross tapping, so left fingers tap on right knee and right fingers tap on left knee—your arms are crossed.

- Switch back briefly to same side tap.
- Then return to cross tap.
- Always tap longer on cross tap, and always finish with cross tap.

Cross crawl

March on the spot, arms swinging in opposition to the legs, smacking each knee with the opposite hand as the knee is raised (Figure 3).

A range of other helpful exercises can be found in Eden and Feinstein's (2008) book *Energy Medicine*, or by searching "Donna Eden" on websites for internet videos.

Figure 3. The "cross crawl" technique.

*Energy techniques for resolving stress, anxiety,
distress, and traumatic memories*

One of easiest and most well known of the energy psychology methods is emotional freedom techniques (EFT), developed by Gary Craig as a simplified derivative of Roger Callahan's thought field therapy (TFT). Details of how to use this method are readily available by Internet searching.[29] It is also extensively discussed in my two previous books on energy psychology (Mollon, 2005, 2008). The basic idea is to tap on the ends of meridians, as shown in Figure 4, while using

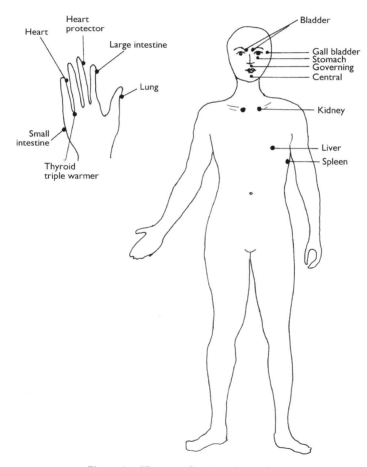

Figure 4.   The meridian tapping points.

a short phrase relating to the target emotional state. It is usually best to start with the side of the hand, small intestine meridian point (see "Psychological reversal" section below).

Self-sabotage correction (psychological reversal)

One of Dr Callahan's greatest discoveries was the phenomenon of "psychological reversal": the conscious mind wishes to resolve a problem or achieve a goal, but the energy system says no. The conscious desire is sabotaged. To some extent (but not entirely) this expresses familiar psychoanalytic ideas of negative therapeutic reaction, masochism through guilt, fears of success, etc. It manifests as a definite reversal in the energy system in relation to the target issue. Two ways that Callahan found to neutralise this were: (1) tapping the "karate chop" side of the hand; (2) making a statement of self-acceptance, along the lines of "Even though I have this problem . . . I completely accept myself". These can be combined by tapping the side of the hand and making the statement of self-acceptance. It should be emphasised that it is not necessary for the person to believe the words of self-acceptance—they have a positive effect on the energy system regardless. Talking and tapping the side of the hand is often beneficial in a variety of ways, and some practitioners of energy psychology have the client do little more than this during a session.

Specific tapping sequences

In contrast with EFT, thought field therapy uses the naturally occurring sequences that pattern distress in the energy system. It is possible (for the skilled practitioner trained in TFT diagnosis) to find these specific sequences for each individual. However, there are some commonly occurring sequences that can be used without specialist skills. Some well-established meridian tapping (or holding and breathing) sequences for different emotional states (originally discovered by Dr Callahan) are as follows.

For anxiety:

- under eye; under arm (bra strap); under end of collarbone.

For claustrophobic anxiety:

- under arm; under eye; under collarbone.

For trauma:

- eyebrow (next to nose); under collarbone.

For trauma with complex emotions, of shock, anger, anxiety, shame, and guilt:

- eyebrow (next to nose); under eye; side of eye; chin; little finger (inside by the nail); under arm; index finger (thumb side, by the nail); collarbone (NB: This is not a standard TFT sequence).

Comprehensive stress relief technique

This begins with the collarbone breathing technique, then moves on to a derivative of Eden and Feinstein's (2008) "crown pull", combined with a meridian sequence for trauma and anxiety. Here is what to do.

- Think of what is troubling with the intention of releasing the stress, to leave all the cells of your body and brain "clear and fresh and free of stress".
- Palms crossed over the heart chakra, fingertips resting under the knobbly ends of the collarbones.
- Rub them around a little—if it helps, you can say or think "I completely accept myself".
- Then breathe in all the way and hold for a few seconds, then breathe out half way, then out all the way, then in half way, then breathe normally.
- Turn the hands into knuckles, still crossed, and repeat the breathing sequence.
- Then place your fingertips in two vertical lines on your forehead, with the little fingers resting on the eyebrows next to your nose— breathe easily and deeply for a few moments.
- Then slowly drag your fingers apart, across your forehead, as if opening a tiny crack in your skull to let out the tension and pressure.
- Drag your fingers around to the sides of the eyes on the bony edge—breathe easily and deeply.
- Then drag them under the eyes—breathe easily and deeply.
- Then wrap your arms around yourself, as if giving yourself a hug—press on the sides of your body (at the bra strap if you are

female, equivalent place if you are male)—breathe easily and deeply.
- Then bring your fingers back resting again under the collarbones, palms crossed—breathing easily and deeply.

Lung meridian breathing

This is very simple and often remarkably effective (Figure 5).

- Cross your hands over your chest and heart centre, with the fingertips resting in the hollows of the shoulder under the collar bone—to find it, move your fingers along from the edge of the shoulder, under the collarbone, there is a "hollow" or indented area, quite large. (A special point relating to the lung meridian is in this area.)

Figure 5.   Lung meridian breathing position.

- As you rest like that, your breathing will become calmer, finding its natural rhythm. It will begin to discharge stress. Since stress is, in many ways, patterned into the breath, such as the way that breathing becomes constricted, shallow, or rapid when a person is anxious, this use of the breath is an excellent way to release stress gently.
- If you bring to mind whatever is troubling you, the calm rhythm of your breath will help to clear the stress.

Energy techniques for goals and intentions

The basic idea here is to use any of the methods above, while holding in mind the intention and goal. Internal objections, and patterns of self-sabotage are likely to be triggered by this, but the exercise inherently releases these, enabling the goal and intention to become more firmly established within a conflict-free body–mind–energy space. This can be helpful for people with ADHD, who often experience difficulty in sustaining work towards goals.

NOTES

1. Some psychoanalytic writers argue that a knowledge of neurobiology has nothing to add to psychoanalytic understanding, and is, in fact, often an unhelpful distraction from the task of exploring meaning and psycho-dynamic conflict (e.g., Blass & Carmeli, 2007; Carmeli & Blass, 2013). Such authors assert that neuropsychoanalysis provides only neurobiological correlates of psychological processes, and actually tells us nothing of a psychological nature that is not already known. Thus, Carmeli and Blass (2013) state that a

> negative consequence of wrongly considering neuroscience to be relevant to psychological change is that it supports the illusion that knowledge of the brain and its plasticity could be therapeutic. Thus we are invited to devote our resources and energy to biolog-ical inquiry, while in fact this cannot help. (p. 408).

What I try to describe here is the effect of brain states on ego functions and psychodynamics, and the need to address these brain states in order to engage in any useful exploration of meaning and conflict. Attempts to explain (to the client) ADHD and autistic spectrum traits purely in terms of psychodynamics and unconscious meanings can indeed be harmful, further undermining self-esteem.

2. When I first began introducing energy psychology techniques to psychotherapists, in the early 2000s, these procedures were, in the UK, mostly confined to practitioners of complementary therapies, although in the USA they were embraced by some leading figures within the clinical psychology mainstream, and particularly by a few "early adopters" and teachers of EMDR. It has been deeply satisfying to observe that by teaching the principles of energy psychology (Mollon, 2005, 2008, 2014a) to psychoanalytic (and other) psychotherapists, as well as to clinical psychologists, a lively and developing field of energy psychotherapy has been established in Britain.

3. I am most grateful to a client for first drawing my attention to Ehlers–Danlos syndrome, which previously was completely unknown to me.

4. See also: www.lymediseaseaction.org.uk/about-lyme/neurology-psychiatry/ and www.mentalhealthandillness.com/Articles/LymeDisease AndCognitiveImpairments.htm.

5. Johansson and Rönnbäck (2014) state that the reason for this fatigue is unknown. However, they hypothesise that it results from "low-grade neuroinflammation with down-regulation of astrocyte glutamate transporters and Na+/K+ ATPase activity" (p. 495), which affects the astroglial cells whose role it is to clear glutamate from extracellular spaces. In such conditions, mental effort with high neuronal activity leads to "metabolic collapse of neuronal circuits". If "low-grade neuroinflammation" is indeed a factor, then this perhaps raises the question of whether conditions such as ADHD, chronic fatigue, and autistic spectrum traits, might, in some instances, be caused or aggravated by a virus, toxin, stress, or autoimmune activity, or mild and overlooked brain injury at birth or in early childhood, all of which are known to cause inflammation. Interestingly, Johansson and Rönnbäck (2014) suggest the use of methyphenidate (the common stimulant medication used for ADHD) to restore this "metabolic collapse" by stimulating Na+/K+ ATPase along the dopaminergic circuits which regulate attention and executive functions.

6. The case of "John: is a fictional composite, based on the author's observations and clinical experiences with many different patients. Any resemblance to an actual person is coincidental.

7. "If the level of cathexis in the ego-nucleus rises, the extent of the ego will be able to expand its range; if it (the level) sinks, the ego will narrow concentrically" (Freud, 1950a, p. 370).

8. To what extent Freud's accounts of the two classes of instincts, libido and aggression, may link to the systems addressed by energy psychotherapists is unclear. However, Freud did write of the flow, blocking, and

diverting of libido, and the quasi bio-electrical charge Q, in ways strikingly similar to those of modern energy psychologists (Mollon, 2008).

9. Freud (1923b) wrote of the way in which "the two classes of instincts are fused, blended, and alloyed with each other" (p. 41) and he saw this as fundamental to the processes of life at every level. He then notes that "Once we have admitted the idea of a fusion of the two classes of instincts with each other, the possibility of a – more or less complete – 'defusion' of them forces itself upon us" (p. 41). He proposed that the more severe states of neurosis and perversion results from defusion of the drives. Although Freud did not greatly elaborate clinically on this theme of fusion and defusion of the drives, it was clear that he saw it as crucially important. It is as if the healthy energetic state is one in which the two drives are fused like a chemical alloy, and in this condition aggression serves life and is not toxic. When the two components are separated, aggression takes a toxic form.

10. An excellent summary of research evidence for energy psychological modalities can be found on the website of the Association for Comprehensive Energy Psychology: www.energypsych.org

11. I am grateful to Asha Clinton and her Advanced Integrative Therapy for this phrasing.

12. The website www.alpha-stim.com provides information about purchase of these devices, and placing the phrase "ADHD" in the site's search engine will retrieve a range of relevant research studies. www.fisherwallace.com offer a similar product.

13. The following website provides a rather extensive list of published research supporting working memory training: www.cogmed.com/published-research.

14. A wide range of perspectives and approaches for ADHD, along with helpful tips and advice, is provided by the following website: www.additudemag.com.

15. This is a fictional account, a composite inspired by experiences with many different patients. "Josephine" does not correspond to any single actual person. Any resemblance to an actual person is purely coincidental.

16. I am most grateful to "Peter" for giving his permission to publish this account based on our work together.

17. The term "subtle energy" was first presented by William Tiller, Emeritus Professor of Materials Science at Stanford University. He has written a number of books describing his research and theorising concerning the nature and behaviour of subtle energy (e.g., Tiller, 2007).

18. Videos of this and other energy corrective exercises can readily be found by searching the Internet: for example, using the search phrases "cross crawl youtube" or "Wayne Cook youtube".
19. http://education.jhu.edu/PD/newhorizons. The article is listed under the section "Exceptional Learners".
20. http://www.braingym.org/brochures/BG_Research.pdf.
21. My intuitive (and entirely subjective) perception is that this position on the body is indeed a subtle energy point of access to higher dimensions of the human bodily system.
22. Lyme Disease is another good example. This is a potentially very severe condition resulting from bites by infected ticks that live on deer and other animals, and which can be found among grass and other vegetation, as well as walls and outdoor benches in areas where deer roam. It causes multiple systemic problems, including cognitive deficits, anxiety and mood disorders, depression and fatigue, sensory sensitivities, and *symptoms resembling ADHD* (Young, 2012). Despite its devastating effects and high incidence, awareness and appropriate treatment are shockingly scarce. The government organisation, Public Health England, estimates 2000–3000 new cases per year in England and Wales: www.gov.uk/government/publications/lyme-borreliosis-epidemiology.
23. Robert Whitaker is a scholarly journalist rather than a mental health professional.
24. www.drthomasebrown.com/assessment-tools/.
25. Available from authorised purveyors of psychological test material.
26. www.autismresearchcentre.com/arc_tests.
27. Available from authorised purveyors of psychological test material.
28. Further information about energy psychology can be found on the author's website www.philmollon.co.uk
29. At the time of writing, the best resource for EFT is the free tutorial available from Gary Craig's own website: www.emofree.com/eft-tutorial/eft-tapping-tutorial.html.

REFERENCES

Adesman, A. R., Altshuler, L. A., Lipkin, P. H., & Walco, G. A. (1990). Otitis media in children with learning disabilities and in children with attention deficit disorder with hyperactivity. *Pediatrics, 85*(3 Pt 2): 442–446.

Adinoff, B., & Devous, M. D. Sr (2010). Response to Amen letter. *American Journal of Psychiatry, 167*: 1125–1126.

Alaghband-Rad, J., McKenna, K., Gordon, C. T., Albus, K. E., Hamburger, S. D., Rumsey, J. M., Frazier, J. A., Lenane, M. L., & Rapoport, J. L. (1995). Childhood-onset schizophrenia: the severity of premorbid course. *Journal of the American Academy of Child and Adolescent Psychiatry, 34*: 1273–1283.

Alpert, A., Neubauer, P. B., & Weil, A. P. (1956). Unusual variations in drive endowment. *Psychoanalytic Study of the Child, 11*: 125–163.

Aman, C. J., Roberts, R. J. Jr, & Pennington, B. F. (1998). A neuropsychological examination of the underlying deficit in attention deficit hyperactivity disorder: frontal lobe versus right parietal lobe theories. *Developmental Psychology, 34*(5): 956–969.

Amen, D. G. (2001a). *Healing ADD. The Breakthrough Program that Allows You to See and Heal the Six Types of Attention Deficit Disorder.* New York: Berkley Books.

Amen, D. G. (2001b). Why don't psychiatrists look at the brain: the case for the greater use of SPECT imaging in neuropsychiatry. *Neuropsychiatry Reviews. 2*(1): 19–21.

Amen, D. G., & Carmichael, B. D. (1997). High-resolution brain SPECT imaging in ADHD. *Annals of Clinical Psychiatry, 9*(2): 81–86.

Amen, D. G., & Willeumier, K. (2011). Brain SPECT imaging: a powerful, evidence-based tool for transforming clinical psychiatric practice. *Minerva Psichiatrica, 52*(3): 109–123.

Amen, D. G., Hanks, C., & Prunella, J. (2008a). Preliminary evidence differentiating AD/HD from healthy controls using brain SPECT imaging in older patients. *Journal of Psychoactive Drugs, 40*(2): 139–146.

Amen, D. G, Hanks, C., & Prunella, J. (2008b). Predicting positive and negative treatment responses to stimulants with brain SPECT imaging. *Journal of Psychoactive Drugs, 40*(2): 131–138.

American Psychiatric Association (2013). *Diagnostic and Statistical Manual of Mental Disorders, Fifth Edition (DSM-V)*. New York: American Psychiatric Press.

Antoine, M. W., Hübner, C. A., Arezzo, J. C., & Hébert, J. M. (2013). A causative link between inner ear defects and long-term striatal dysfunction. *Science, 341*(6150): 1120–1123.

Arias-Carrión, O., & Pöppel, E. (2007). Dopamine, learning and reward-seeking behavior. *Acta Neurobiologiae Experimentalis, 67*(4): 481–488.

Arns, M., de Ridder, S., Strehl, U., Breteler, M., & Coenen, A. (2009). Efficacy of neurofeedback treatment in ADHD: the effects on inattention, impulsivity and hyperactivity: a meta-analysis. *Clinical EEG and Neuroscience, 40*(3): 180–189.

Arns, M., Drinkenburg, W., & Kenemans, J. L. (2012). The effects of QEEG-informed neurofeedback in ADHD: an open-label pilot study. *Applied Psychophysiology and Biofeedback, 37*(3): 171–180.

Aron, E. L. (1999). *The Highly Sensitive Person: How to Thrive When the World Overwhelms You*. London: Thorsons.

Aron, E. L. (2010). *Psychotherapy and the Highly Sensitive Person: Improving Outcomes for that Minority of People Who Are the Majority of Clients*. New York: Routledge.

Asarnow, J. R., & Ben-Meir, S. (1988). Children with schizophrenia spectrum and depressive disorders: a comparative study of onset patterns, premorbid adjustment, and severity of dysfunction. *Journal of Child Psychology and Psychiatry and Allied Disciplines, 29*: 477–488

Asherson, P. (2011). ADHD, bipolar and borderline personality disorder. Presentation to the ADHD Conference, September 22–23, Savoy Place, London.

Ashtari, M., Kumra, S., Bhaskar, S. L., Clarke, T., Thaden, E., Cervellione, K. L., Rhinewine, J., Kane, J. M., Adesman, A., Milanaik, R., Maytal, J., Diamond, A., Szeszko, P., & Ardekani, B. A. (2005). Attention-deficit/

hyperactivity disorder: a preliminary diffusion tensor imaging study. *Biological Psychiatry*, 57(5): 448–455.

Attwood, T. (2006). *The Complete Guide to Asperger's Syndrome*. London: Jessica Kingsley.

Attwood, T., Bolick, T., Faherty, C., Iland, L., Grandin, T., Myers, J. M., Snyder, R., Wagner, S., & Wrobel, M. (2006). *Asperger's and Girls*. Arlington, TX: Future Horizons.

Aylward, E., & Reiss, A. (1996). Basal ganglia volumes in children with attention-deficit hyperactivity disorder. *Journal of Child Neurology, 11*: 112–115.

Bachevalier, J. (1996). Brief report: Medial temporal lobe and autism: a putative animal model in primates. *Journal of Autism and Developmental Disorders*, 26(2): 217–220.

Baeza-Velasco, C., Gély-Nargeot, M. C., Bulbena Vilarrasa, A., Bravo, J. F. (2011). Joint hypermobility syndrome: problems that require psychological intervention. *Rheumatololgy International*, 31(9): 1131–1136.

Baird, B., Smallwood, J., Mrazek, M. D., Kam, J. W., Franklin, M. S., & Schooler, J. W. (2012). Inspired by distraction: mind wandering facilitates creative incubation. *Psychological Science*, 23(10): 1117–1122.

Banich, M. T. (1998). The missing link: the role of interhemispheric interaction in attentional processing. *Brain and Cognition, 36*: 128–157.

Barkley, R. A. (1997). Inhibition, sustained attention, and executive functions: constructing a unified theory of ADHD. *Psychological Bulletin, 121*: 65–94.

Barkley, R. A. (on behalf of 84 experts) (2002). International statement on ADHD. *Clinical Child and Family Psychology Review*, 5(2): 89–111.

Barkley, R. A. (2010). Deficient emotional self-regulation is a core component of attention-deficit/hyperactivity disorder. *Journal of ADHD & Related Disorders*, 1(2): 5–37.

Barkley, R. A. (2012). Distinguishing sluggish cognitive tempo from attention-deficit/hyperactivity disorder in adults. *Journal of Abnormal Psychology*, 121(4): 978–990.

Barkley, R. A., & Fischer, M. (2010). The unique contribution of emotional impulsiveness to impairment in major life activities in hyperactive children as adults. *Journal of the American Academy of Child and Adolescent Psychiatry*, 49(5): 503–513.

Barkley, R. A., Murphy, K. R., & Fischer, M. (2008). *ADHD in Adults. What the Science Says*. New York: Guildford Press.

Barnetta, K., Kirka, I., & Corballis, M. (2005). Right hemispheric dysfunction in schizophrenia. *Laterality: Asymmetries of Body, Brain and Cognition*, 10(1): 29–35.

Baron-Cohen, S. (2003). *The Essential Difference. Men, Women, and the Extreme Male Brain.* London: Allen Lane.

Baron-Cohen, S., Ring, H. A., Bullmore, E. T., Wheelwright, S., Ashwin, C., & Williams, S. C. (2000). The amygdala theory of autism. *Neuroscience Biobehavioral Review, 24*(3): 355–364.

Barr, W. (2001). Schizophrenia and attention deficit disorder two complex disorders of attention. *Annals of the New York Academy of Sciences, 931*: 239–250.

Bateman, B., Warner, J. O., Hutchinson, E., Dean, T., Rowlandson, P., Gant, C., Grundy, J., Fitzgerald, C., & Stevenson. J. (2004). The effects of a double blind, placebo controlled, artificial food colourings and benzoate preservative challenge on hyperactivity in a general population sample of preschool children. *Archives of Disease in Childhood, 89*: 506–511.

Bauman, M., & Kemper, T. (1994). *The Neurobiology of Autism.* Baltimore: John Hopkins.

Beinfield, H., & Korngold, E. (1991). *Between Heaven and Earth. A Guide to Chinese Medicine.* New York: Ballantine.

Bellak, L. (1985). ADD psychosis as a separate entity. *Schizophrenia Bulletin, 11*: 523–527.

Bellak, L. (1994). The schizophrenic syndrome and attention deficit disorder thesis, antithesis, and synthesis? *American Psychologist, 49*: 25–29.

Bellak, L., Hurvich, M., & Gediman, H. K. (1973). *Ego Functions in Schizophrenics, Neurotics, and Normals: A Systematic Study of Diagnostic, Conceptual, and Therapeutic Aspects.* New York: Wiley.

Bellak, L., Kay, S. R., & Opler, L. A. (1987). Attention deficit disorder psychosis as a diagnostic category. *Psychiatric Developments, 5*(3): 239–263.

Belmont, A., Agar, N., & Azouvi, P. (2009). Subjective fatigue, mental effort, and attention deficits after severe traumatic brain injury. *Neurorehabilitation and Neural Repair, 23*(9): 939–944.

Belmonte, M. K., Allen, G., Beckel-Mitchener, A., Boulanger, L. M., Carper, R. A., & Webb, S. J. (2004). Autism and abnormal development of brain connectivity. *Journal of Neuroscience, 24*: 9228–9231.

Benke, T., Delazer, M., Bartha, L., & Auer, A. (2003). Basal ganglia lesions and the theory of fronto–subcortical loops: neuropsychological findings in two patients with left caudate lesions. *Neurocase, 9*: 70–85.

Ben-Sasson, A., Hen, L., Fluss, R., Cermak, S. A., Engel-Yeger, B., & Gal, E. (2009). A meta-analysis of sensory modulation symptoms in individuals with autism spectrum disorders. *Journal of Autism and Developmental Disorders, 39*(1): 1–11.

Benson, D. F. (1991). The role of frontal dysfunction in attention deficit hyperactivity disorder. *Journal of Child Neurology, 6*(suppl.): S9–S12.

Bergman, P., & Escalona, S. K. (1949). Unusual sensitivities in very young children. *Psychoanalytic Study of the Child, 4*: 333–352.

Berridge, K. C., & Robinson, T. E. (1998). What is the role of dopamine in reward: hedonic impact, reward learning, or incentive salience? *Brain Research Reviews, 28*: 309–369.

Bion, W. R. (1957). Differentiation of the psychotic from the non-psychotic personalities. *International Journal of Psychoanalysis, 38*: 266–275.

Bion, W. R. (1962). *Learning from Experience*. London: Tavistock.

Blackstock, E. G. (1978). Cerebral asymmetry and the development of early infantile autism. *Journal of Autism and Child Schizophrenia, 8*(3): 339–353.

Blanck, G. (1966). Some technical implications of ego psychology. *International Journal of Psychoanalysis, 47*: 6–13.

Blanck, G., & Blanck, R. (1974). *Ego Psychology: Theory and Practice*. New York: Columbia University Press.

Blanck, G., & Blanck, R. (1979). *Ego Psychology II*. New York: Columbia University Press.

Blankenship, R., & Laaser, M. (2004). Sexual addiction and ADHD: is there a connection? *Sexual Addiction & Compulsivity, 11*: 7–20.

Blass, R. B., & Carmeli, Z. (2007). The case against neuropsychoanalysis: on fallacies underlying psychoanalysis' latest scientific trend and its negative impact on psychoanalytic discourse. *International Journal of Psychoanalysis, 88*: 19–40.

Bledsoe, J. C., Semrud-Clikeman, M., & Pliszka, S. R. (2013). Anterior cingulate cortex and symptom severity in attention-deficit/hyperactivity disorder. *Journal of Abnormal Psychology, 122*(2): 558–565.

Bleuler, E. (1950). *Dementia Praecox or The Group of Schizophrenias*. New York: International Universities Press.

Blum, K., Lih-Chuan Chen, A., Braverman, E. R., Comings, D. E., Chen, T. J. H., Arcuri, V., Blum, S. H., Downs, B. W., Waite, R. L., Notaro, A., Lubar, J., Williams, L., Prihoda, T. J., Palomo, T., & Oscar-Berman, M. (2008). Attention-deficit-hyperactivity disorder and reward deficiency syndrome. *Neuropsychiatric Disease Treatment, 4*(5): 893–918.

Bollas, C. (1987). *The Shadow of the Object: Psychoanalysis of the Unthought Known*. London: Free Association Books.

Bouchard, M. F., Bellinger, D. C., Wright, R. O., & Weisskopf, M. G. (2010). Attention-deficit/hyperactivity disorder and urinary metabolites of organophosphate pesticides. *Pediatrics*. Published online May 17th 2010 doi: 10.1542/peds: 2009–3058.

Bowirrat, A., & Oscar-Berman, M. (2005). Relationship between dopamin-ergic neurotransmission, alcoholism, and reward deficiency syndrome. *American Journal of Medical Genetics Part B Neuropsychiatric Genetics, 132B*(1): 29–37.

Brothers, L. (1990). The social brain: a project for integrating primate behaviour and neurophysiology in a new domain. *Concepts in Neuroscience, 1*: 27–51.

Brotman, M. A., Rich, B. A., Guyer, A. E., Lunsford, J. R., Horsey, S. E., Reising, M. M., Thomas, L. A., Fromm, S. J., Towbin, K., Pine, D. S., & Leibenluft, E. (2009). Amygdala activation during emotion processing of neutral faces in children with severe mood dysregulation versus ADHD or bipolar disorder. *American Journal of Psychiatry, 167*(1): 61–69.

Brottman, M. (2011). *Phantoms of the Clinic: From Thought-Transference to Projective Identification*. London: Karnac.

Brown, T. E. (2013a). *A New Understanding of ADHD in Children and Adults. Executive Function Impairments*. Hove: Routledge.

Brown, T. E. (2013b). An open letter to the editor of the New York Times from Thomas E. Brown, Ph.D. December 16, 2013. www.drthomase brown.com/an-open-letter-to-the-editor-of-the-new-york-times-from-thomas-e-brown-ph-d/ (accessed 17 August 2014).

Brown, T. E. (2014). Another open letter to the editor of the New York Times. January 2, 2014 www.drthomasebrown.com/another-open-letter-editor-new-york-times/ (accessed 17 August 2014).

Brozoski, T. J., Brown, R., Rosvold, H. E., & Goldman, P. S. (1979). Cognitive deficit caused by regional depletion of dopamine in the prefrontal cortex of rhesus monkeys. *Science, 205*: 929–931.

Buckner, R. L., Andrews-Hanna, J. R., & Schacter, D. L. (2008). The brain's default network: anatomy, function, and relevance to disease. *Annals of the New York Academy of Science, 1124*: 1–38.

Bush, G. (2009). Attention-deficit/hyperactivity disorder and attention networks. *Neuropsychopharmacology, 35*(1): 278–300.

Bush, G., Frazier, J. A., Rauch, S. L., Seidman, L. J., Whalen, P. J., Jenike, M. A., Rosen, B. R., & Biederman, J. (1999). Anterior cingulate cortex dysfunction in attention-deficit/hyperactivity disorder revealed by fMRI and the Counting Stroop. *Biological Psychiatry, 45*(12): 1542–1552.

Callahan, R. J. (2009). Collarbone breathing. http://www.rogercallahan. com/GIN-Gifts/Collarbone-Breathing-Treatment.pdf (accessed 14 September 2014).

Camargo, E. E. (2001). Brain SPECT in neurology and psychiatry. *Journal of Nuclear Medicine, 42*(4): 611–623.

Carmeli, Z., & Blass, R. B. (2013). The case against neuroplastic analysis: a further illustration of the irrelevance of neuroscience to psychoanalysis through a critique of Doige's *The Brain that Changes Itself*. *International Journal of Psychoanalysis, 94*: 391–410.

Carroll, L., & Tober, J. (1999). *The Indigo Children*. Carlsbad, CA: Hay House.

Carroll, L., & Tober, J. (2009). *The Indigo Children 10 Years Later: What's Happening With The Indigo Teenagers!* Carlsbad, CA: Hay House.

Carper, R. A., & Courchesne, E. (2005). Localized enlargement of the frontal cortex in early autism. *Biological Psychiatry, 57*: 126–133.

Carson, S. (2010). Creativity and ADHD may share some common genetic vulnerabilities. www.kevinmd.com/blog/2010/12/creativity-adhd-share-common-genetic-vulnerabilities.html (accessed 31 July 2014).

Castellanos, F. X., Giedd, J. N., Berquin, P. C., Walter, J. M., Sharp, W., Tran, T., Vaituzis, A. C., Blumenthal, J. D., Nelson, J., Bastain, T. M., Zijdenbos, A., Evans, A. C., & Rapoport, J. L. (2001). Quantitative brain magnetic resonance imaging in girls with attention-deficit/hyperactivity disorder. *Archives of General Psychiatry, 58*(3): 289–295.

Castellanos, F. X., Margulies, D. S., Kelly, C., Uddin, L. Q., Ghaffari, M., Kirsch, A., Shaw, D., Shehzad, Z., Di Martino, A., Biswal, B., Sonuga-Barke, E. J., Rotrosen, J., Adler, L. A., & Milham, M. P. (2008). Cingulate-precuneus interactions: a new locus of dysfunction in adult attention-deficit/hyperactivity disorder. *Biological Psychiatry, 63*: 332–337.

Cato, M. A., Crosson, B., Gökçay, D., Soltysik, D., Wierenga, C., Gopinath, K., Himes, N., Belanger, H., Bauer, R. M., Fischler, I. S., Gonzalez-Rothi, L., & Briggs, R. W. (2004). Processing words with emotional connotation: an FMRI study of time course and laterality in rostral frontal and retrosplenial cortices. *Journal of Cognitive Neuroscience, 16*(2): 167–177.

Chabot, R. J., Merkin, H., Wood, L. M., Davenport, T. L., & Serfontein, G. (1995). Sensitivity and specificity of QEEG in children with attention deficit or specific developmental learning disorders. *Clinical Electroencephalography, 27*(1): 26–33.

Chancellor, B., & Chatterjee, A. (2011). Brain branding: when neuroscience and commerce collide. *American Journal of Bioethics Neuroscience, 2*(4): 18–27.

Charach, A., Yeung, E., Climans, T., & Lillie, E. (2011). Childhood attention deficit/hyperactivity disorder and future substance use disorders: comparative metanalyses. *Journal of the American Academy of Child and Adolescent Psychiatry, 50*(1): 9–21.

Christie, P., Duncan, M., Fidler, R., & Healy, Z. (2012). *Understanding Pathological Demand Avoidance Syndrome in Children*. London: Jessica Kingsley.

Clarke, D. D., & Sokoloff, L. (1998). Circulation and energy metabolism of the brain. In: G. Siegel, B. Agranoff, R. Albers, S. Fisher, & M. Uhler (Eds.), *Basic Neurochemistry: Molecular, Cellular, and Medical Aspects* (6th edn) (pp. 637–669). Philadelphia, PA: Lippincott Raven.

Clarke, R. A., Murphy, D. L, & Constantino, J. N. (1999). Serotonin and externalizing behavior in young children. *Psychiatry Research, 86*: 29–40.

Cohen, J., Braver, T., & Brown, J. (2002). Computational perspectives in dopamine function in prefrontal cortex. *Current Opinion in Neurobiology, 12*: 223–229.

Conners, K. (2013). Comment on NY Times article (posted December 17, 2013) & Prevalence of ADHD from APSARD talk Sept. 29, 2013 (posted September 9, 2013), http://adhd-world.blogspot.co.uk/ (accessed 17 August 2014).

Cools, R., & D'Esposito, M. (2011). Inverted-U shaped dopamine actions on human working memory and cognitive control. *Biological Psychiatry, 69*(12): e113–e125.

Cortese, S., Angriman, M., Lecendreux, M., & Konofal, E. (2012). Iron and attention deficit/hyperactivity disorder: what is the empirical evidence so far? A systematic review of the literature. *Expert Review of Neurotherapeutics, 12*(10): 1227–1240.

Costa Diass, T. G., Wilson, V. B., Bathula, D. R., Iyer, S. P., Mills, K. L., Thurlow, B. L., Stevens, C. A., Musser, E. D., Carpenter, S. D., Grayson, D. S., Mitchell, S. H., Nigg, J. T., & Fair, D. A. (2013). Reward circuit connectivity relates to delay discounting in children with attention-deficit/hyperactivity disorder. *European Neuropsychopharmacology, 23*(1): 33–45.

Couch, A. S. (1995). Anna Freud's adult psychoanalytic technique: a defence of classical analysis. *International Journal of Psychoanalysis, 76*: 153–171.

Couch, A. S. (2002). Extra-transference interpretation: a defense of classical technique. *Psychoanalytic Study of the Child, 57*: 63–92.

Courchesne, E., & Pierce K. (2005). Why the frontal cortex in autism might be talking only to itself: local over-connectivity but long-distance disconnection. *Current Opinion in Neurobiology, 15*(2): 225–230.

Courchesne, E., Karns, C. M., Davis, H. R., Ziccardi, R., Carper, R. A., Tigue, Z. D., Chisum, H. J., Moses, P., Pierce, K., Lord, C., Lincoln, A. J., Pizzo, S., Schreibman, L., Haas, R. H., Akshoomoff, N. A., & Courchesne, R. Y. (2001). Unusual brain growth patterns in early life in patients with autistic disorder: an MRI study. *Neurology*, *57*(2): 245–254.

Courchesne, E., Redcay, E., & Kennedy, D. P. (2004). The autistic brain: birth through adulthood. *Current Opinion in Neurology*, *17*(4): 489–496.

Cowan, S. S. (2012). *Fire Child, Water Child: How Understanding the Five Types of ADHD Can Help You Improve Your Child's Self-esteem and Attention*. Oakland, CA: New Harbinger.

Cramond, B. (1994). Attention-deficit hyperactivity disorder and creativity—what is the connection? *Journal of Creative Behavior*, *28*(3): 193–210.

Davenport, N. D., Karatekin, C., White, T., & Lim, K. O. (2010). Differential fractional anisotropy abnormalities in adolescents with ADHD or schizophrenia. *Psychiatry Research*, *181*(3): 193–198.

Davids, E., & Gastpar, M. (2005). Attention deficit hyperactivity disorder and borderline personality disorder. *Progress in Neuropsychopharmacology and Biological Psychiatry*, *29*(6): 865–877.

Davis, G. H., & Stephens, P. H. (2002). ADD/ADHD and fibromyalgia (FMS): where is the connection? Republished at www.reversingchronicdisease.com (accessed 30 July 2014).

De Fossé, L., Hodge, S. M., Makris, N., Kennedy, D. N., Caviness, V. S. Jr, McGrath, L., Steele, S., Ziegler, D. A., Herbert, M. R., Frazier, J. A., Tager-Flusberg, H., & Harris, G. J. (2004). Language-association cortex asymmetry in autism and specific language impairment. *Annals of Neurology*, *56*(6): 757–766.

Decety, J., & Jackson, P. L. (2004). The functional architecture of human empathy. *Behavior and Cognition Neuroscience Review*, *3*(2): 71–100.

del Campo, N., Fryer, T. D., Hong, Y. T., Smith, R., Brichard, L., Acosta-Cabronero, J., Chamberlain, S. R., Tait, R., Izquierdo, D., Regenthal, R., Dowson, J., Suckling, J., Baron, J.-C., Aigbirhio, F. I., Robbins, T. W., Sahakian, B. J., & Muller, U. (2013). A positron emission tomography study of nigro-striatal dopaminergic mechanisms underlying attention: implications for ADHD and its treatment. *Brain*, *136*: 3252–3270.

Dhar, M., Been, P. H., Minderaa, R. B., & Althaus, M. (2010). Reduced interhemispheric coherence in dyslexic adults. *Cortex*, *46*(6): 794–798.

Diehl, D. J., & Gershon, S. (1992). The role of dopamine in mood disorders. *Comprehensive Psychiatry*, *33*(2): 115–120.

Ding, Y.-C., Chi, H.-C., Grady, D. L., Morishima, A., Kidd, J. R., Kidd, K. K., Flodman, P., Spence, M. A., Schuck, S., Swanson, J. M., Zhang, Y.-P., & Moyzis, R. K. (2001). Evidence of positive selection acting at the human dopamine receptor D4 gene locus. *Proceedings of the National Academy of Sciences of the United States of America*, *99*(1): 309–314.

Donev, R., Gantert, D., Alawam, K., Edworthy, A., Hässler, F., Meyer-Lindenberg, A., Dressing, H., & Thome, J. (2011). Comorbidity of schizophrenia and adult attention-deficit hyperactivity disorder. *World Journal of Biological Psychiatry, 12*(Suppl. 1): 52–56.

Dosick, W. (2009). *Empowering Your Indigo Child: A Handbook for Parents of Children of Spirit*. San Francisco, CA: Weiser.

Douglas, V. I. (1999). Cognitive control processes in attention-deficit/hyperactivity disorder. In: H. C. Quay & A. E. Hogan (Eds.), *Handbook of Disruptive Behavior Disorders* (pp. 105–137). New York: Kluwer Academic/Plenum.

Doyle, B. B. (2006). *Understanding and Treating Adults with Attention Deficit Hyperactivity Disorder*. Washington, DC: American Psychiatric Press.

Dunlop, B. W., & Nemeroff, C. B. (2007). The role of dopamine in the pathophysiology of depression. *Archives of General Psychiatry, 64*(3): 327–337.

Eden, D., & Feinstein, D. (2008). *Energy Medicine: How To Use Your Body's Energies for Optimum Health and Vitality*. New York: Penguin.

Ehrenreich, B. (1997). *Blood Rites. The Origins and History of the Passions of War*. London: Granta, 2011.

Eigen, M. (2004). *The Sensitive Self*. Middletown, CT: Wesleyan University Press.

Elliot, G. R. & Kelly, K. *ADHD Medications: An Overview*. http://www.chadd.org/Understanding-ADHD/Parents-Caregivers-of-Children-with-ADHD/Evaluation-and-Treatment/ADHD-Medications-An-Overview.aspx (accessed 10th January 2014).

English, B. A., Hahn, M. K., Gizer, I. R., Mazei-Robison, M., Steele, A., Kurnik, D. M., Stein, M. A., Waldman, I. D., & Blakely, R. D. (2009). Choline transporter gene variation is associated with attention-deficit hyperactivity disorder. *Journal of Neurodevelopmental Disorders, 1*(4): 252–263.

Ensink, K., & Mayes, L. C. (2010). The development of mentalisation in children from a theory of mind perspective. *Psychoanalytic Inquiry, 30*: 301–337.

Eslinger, P. J. (1998). Neurological and neuropsychological bases of empathy. *European Neurology, 39*: 193–199.

Eyestone, L., & Howell, R. J. (1994). An epidemiological study of attention-deficit hyperactivity disorder and major depression in a male prison population. *Journal of the American Academy of Psychiatry Law, 22*(2): 181–193.

Farah, M. J., & Gillihan, S. J. (2012). The puzzle of neuroimaging and psychiatric diagnosis: technology and nosology in an evolving discipline. *American Journal of Bioethics Neuroscience, 3*(4): 31–41.

Faraone, S. V., & Buitelaar, J. (2010). Comparing the efficacy of stimulants for ADHD in children and adolescents using meta-analysis. *European Child and Adolescent Psychiatry, 19*: 353–364.

Faraone, S. V., & Glatt, S. J. (2010). A comparison of the efficacy of medications for adult attention-deficit/hyperactivity disorder using meta-analysis of effect sizes. *Journal of Clinical Psychiatry, 71*(6): 754–763.

Fein, D., Dixon, P., Paul, J., & Levin, H. (2005). Brief report: pervasive developmental disorder can evolve into ADHD: case illustrations. *Journal of Autism and Developmental Disorders, 35*: 525–534.

Feinstein, D. (2012). Acupoint stimulation in treating psychological disorders: evidence of efficacy. *Review of General Psychology, 16*: 364–380.

Ferrer, M., Andión, O., Matalí, J., Valero, S., Navarro, J. A., Ramos-Quiroga, J. A., Torrubia, R., & Casas, M. (2010). Comorbid attention-deficit/hyperactivity disorder in borderline patients defines an impulsive subtype of borderline personality disorder. *Journal of Personality Disorder, 24*(6): 812–822.

Fisher, B. (1998). *Attention Deficit Disorder Misdiagnosis. Approaching ADD from a Brain-Behavior/Neuropsychological Perspective for Assessment and Treatment.* Boca Raton, FL: CRC Press.

Fisher, B. (2013). *What You Think ADD/ADHD Is, It Isn't.* Boca Raton, FL: CRC Press.

Flanagan, M. (2010). *The Downside of Upright Posture.* Minneapolis, MN: Two Harbors Press.

Fletcher, P. C., Happé, F., Frith, U., Baker, S. C., Dolan, R. J., Frackowiak, R. S., & Frith, C. D. (1995). Other minds in the brain: a functional imaging study of "theory of mind" in story comprehension. *Cognition, 57*(2): 109–128.

Floris, D. L., Chura, L. R., Holt, R. J., Suckling, J., Bullmore, E. T., Baron-Cohen, S., & Spencer, M. D. (2013). Psychological correlates of handedness and corpus callosum asymmetry in autism: the left hemisphere dysfunction theory revisited. *Journal of Autism and Developmental Disorders, 43*(8): 1758–1772.

Flory, J. D., Newcorn, J. H., Miller, C., Harty, S., & Halperin, J. M. (2007). Serotonergic function in children with attention-deficit hyperactivity disorder: relationship to later antisocial personality disorder. *British Journal of Psychiatry, 190*: 410–414.

Fotopoulou, A., Solms, M., & Turnbull, O. (2004). Wishful reality distortions in confabulation: a case report. *Neuropsychologia, 42*(6): 727–744.

Freud, A. (1952). The mutual influences in the development of ego and id: introduction to the discussion. *Psychoanalytic Study of the Child, 7*: 42–50.

Freud, A. (1966). *Normality and Pathology in Childhood*. London: Hogarth.

Freud, S. (1911b). Formulation on the two principles of mental functioning. *S. E., 12*: 215–226. London: Hogarth.

Freud, S. (1914c). On narcissism: an introduction. *S. E., 4*: 69–102. London: Hogarth.

Freud. S. (1920g). Beyond the pleasure principle. *S. E., 18*: 1–64. London: Hogarth.

Freud, S. (1923b). *The Ego and the Id. S. E., 19*: 1–66. London: Hogarth.

Freud, S. (1925h). Negation. *S. E., 19*: 233–239. London: Hogarth:

Freud, S. (1925j). Some psychical consequences of the anatomical distinction between the sexes. *S. E., 19*: 243–258. London: Hogarth.

Freud, S. (1926d). *Inhibitions, Symptoms and Anxiety. S. E., 20*: 77–175. London: Hogarth.

Freud, S. (1940a). *An Outline of Psychoanalysis. S. E., 23*: 141–207. London: Hogarth.

Freud, S. (1950a[1895]). *Project for a Scientific Psychology. S. E., 1*: 283–397. London: Hogarth.

Frost, R. (2002). *Applied Kinesiology: A Training Manual and Reference Book of Basic Principles and Practices*. Berkeley, CA: North Atlantic Books.

Gallagher, H. L., & Frith, C. D. (2003). Functional imaging of 'theory of mind'. *Trends in Cognitive Science, 7*(2): 77–83.

Gallo, F. P. (1999). *Energy Psychology. Explorations at the Interface of Energy, Cognition, Behavior and Health*. Boca Raton, FL: CRC Press.

Garrity, A. G., Pearlson, G. D., McKiernan, K., Lloyd, D., Kiehl, K. A., & Calhoun, V. D. (2007). Aberrant "default mode" functional connectivity in schizophrenia. *American Journal of Psychiatry, 164*: 450–457.

George, M. S., Ketter, T. A., Parekh, P. I., Horwitz, B., Herscovitch, P., & Post, R. M. (1995). Brain activity during transient sadness and happiness in healthy women. *American Journal of Psychiatry, 152*(3): 341–351.

Giedd, J. N., Blumenthal, J., Molloy, E., & Castellanos, F. X. (2001). Brain imaging of attention deficit/hyperactivity disorder. *Annals of the New York Academy of Science, 931*: 33–49

Giedd, J. N., Castellanos, F. X., Casey, B. J., Kozuch, P., King, A. C., Hamburger, S. D., & Rapoport, J. L. (1994). Quantitative morphology of the corpus callosum in attention deficit hyperactivity disorder. *American Journal of Psychiatry, 151*(5): 665–669.

Girard, M. (2010). Winnicott's foundation for the basic concepts of Freud's metapsychology? *International Journal of Psychoanalysis, 91*: 305–324.

Glick, S. D., Ross, D. A., & Hough, L. B. (1982). Lateral asymmetry of neurotransmitters in human brain. *Brain Research, 234*(1): 53–63.

Goldberg, E. (2001). *The Executive Brain. Frontal Lobes and the Civilized Mind*. New York: Oxford University Press.

Gomez, R. L., Janowsky, D., Zetin, M., Huey, L., & Clopton, P. L. (1981). Adult psychiatric diagnosis and symptoms compatible with the hyperactive child syndrome: a retrospective study. *Journal of Clinical Psychiatry*, 42: 389–394.

Green, S. A., Rudie, J. D., Colich, N. L., Wood, J. J., Shirinyan, D., Hernandez, L., Tottenham, N., Dapretto, M., & Bookheimer, S. Y. (2013). Overreactive brain responses to sensory stimuli in youth with autism spectrum disorders. *Journal of the American Academy of Child and Adolescent Psychiatry*, 52(11): 1158–1172.

Gropper, R. J., Gotlieb, H., Kronitz, R., & Tannock, R. (2014). Working memory training in college students with ADHD or LD. *Journal of Attention Disorders*, 18(4): 331–345.

Grosswald, S. J. (2013). Is ADHD a stress-related disorder? Why meditation can help. In: S. Banerjee (Ed.), *Attention Deficit Hyperactivity Disorder in Children and Adolescents* (Chapter 4). Published online by InTech www. intechopen.com/books/attention-deficit-hyperactivity-disorder-in-children-and-adolescents/is-adhd-a-stress-related-disorder-why-meditation-can-help (accessed 1 August 2014) (open access).

Hala, S., Rasmussen, C., & Henderson, A. M. (2005). Three types of source monitoring by children with and without autism: the role of executive function. *Journal of Autism and Developmental Disorders*, 35(1): 75–89.

Hale, T. S., Loo, S. K., Zaidel, E., Hanada, G., Macion, J. & Smalley, S. L. (2009). Rethinking a right hemisphere deficit in ADHD. *Journal of Attention Disorder*, 13(1): 3–17.

Hale, T. S., Smalley, S. L., Walshaw, P. D., Hanada, G., Macion, J., McCracken, J. T., McGough, J. J., & Loo, S. K. (2010). Atypical EEG beta asymmetry in adults with ADHD. *Neuropsychologia*, 48(12): 3532–3539.

Hale, T. S., Zaidel, E., McGough, J. J., Phillips, J. M., & McCracken, J. T. (2006). Atypical brain laterality in adults with ADHD during dichotic listening for emotional intonation and words. *Neuropsychologia*, 44(6): 896–904.

Hallowell, E. M., & Ratey, J. J. (1994). *Driven to Distraction*. New York: Simon & Schuster.

Halmøy, A., Johansson, S., Winge, I., McKinney, J. A., Knappskog, P. M., & Haavik, J. (2010). Attention-deficit/hyperactivity disorder symptoms in offspring of mothers with impaired serotonin production. *Archive of General Psychiatry*, 67(10): 1033–1043.

Halperin, J. M., Sharma, V., Siever, L. J., Schwartz, S. T., Matier, K., Wornell, G., & Newcorn, J. H. (1994). Serotonergic function in aggressive and nonaggressive boys with attention-deficit hyperactivity disorder. *American Journal of Psychiatry, 151*: 243–248.

Hartmann, H. (1939). *Ego Psychology and the Problem of Adaptation*. New York: International Universities Press.

Hartmann, H. (1952). The mutual influences in the development of the ego and the id. In: *Essays in Ego Psychology* (pp. 155–181). London: Hogarth, 1964.

Hartmann, H. (1956). Notes on the reality principle. In: *Essays in Ego Psychology* (pp. 241–267). London: Hogarth, 1964.

Hartmann, H., Kris, E., & Loewenstein, R. M. (1946). Comments on the formation of psychic structure. *Psychoanalytic Study of the Child, 2*: 11–38.

Hartmann, H., Kris, E., & Loewenstein, R. M. (1949). Notes on the theory of aggression. *Psychoanalytic Study of the Child, 3*(4): 9–36.

Hartmann, T. (1993). *Attention Deficit Disorder. A Different Perspective*. Grass Valley, CA: Underwood Books.

Hartmann, T. (2003). *The Edison Gene. ADHD and the Gift of the Hunter Child*. Rochester, NY: Park Street Press.

Hayden, D. (2006). The vicious cycle of adult ADD, shame and compulsive sexuality. Psych Central. Available at: http://psychcentral.com/lib/the-vicious-cycle-of-adult-add-shame-and-compulsive-sexuality/000520 (accessed on 18 June 2014).

Healy, M. D. (2013). *Energetic Keys To Indigo Kids: Your Guide to Raising and Resonating with the New Children*. Pompton Plains, NJ: Career Press.

Hearn, K. (2004). USA: drug companies pushing ADHD drugs for children. CorpWatch. www.corpwatch.org/article.php?id=11717 (accessed 17 August 2014).

Heilman, K. M., Bowers, D., Valenstein, E., & Watson, R. T. (1986). The right hemisphere: neuropsychological functions. *Journal of Neurosurgery, 64*(5): 693–704.

Herbert, M. R., Harris, G. J., Adrien, K. T., Ziegler, D. A., Makris, N., Kennedy, D. N., Lange, N. T., Chabris, C. F., Bakardjiev, A., Hodgson, J., Takeoka, M., Tager-Flusberg, H., & Caviness, V. S. Jr (2002). Abnormal asymmetry in language association cortex in autism. *Annals of Neurology, 52*(5): 588–596.

Herbert, M. R., Ziegler, D. A., Deutsch, C. K., O'Brien, L. M., Lange, N., Bakardjiev, A., Hodgson, J., Adrien, K. T., Steele, S., Makris, N., Kennedy, D., Harris, G. J., & Caviness, V. S. Jr (2003). Dissociations of cerebral cortex, subcortical and cerebral white matter volumes in autistic boys. *Brain, 126*: 1182–1192.

Herbert, M. R., Ziegler, D. A., Makris, N., Filipek, P. A., Kemper, T. L., Normandin, J. J., Sanders, H. A., Kennedy, D. N., Caviness, V. S. Jr (2004). Localization of white matter volume increase in autism and developmental language disorder. *Annals of Neurology, 55*: 530–540.

Hesslinger, B., Tebartz van Elst, L., Nyberg, E., Dykierek, P., Richter, H., Berner, M., & Ebert, D. (2002). Psychotherapy of attention deficit hyperactivity disorder in adults—a pilot study using a structured skills training program. *European Archives of Psychiatry & Clinical Neuroscience, 252*(4): 177–184.

Higashida, N. (2013). *The Reason I Jump*. London: Sceptre.

Hinshaw, S. P., & Scheffler, R. M. (2014). *The ADHD Explosion: Myths, Medication, and Money, and Today's Push for Performance*. New York: Oxford University Press.

Hinshaw, S. P., Owens, E. B., Zalecki, C., Huggins, S. P., Montenegro-Nevado, A. J., Schrodek, E., & Swanson, E. N. (2012). Prospective follow-up of girls with attention-deficit/hyperactivity disorder into early adulthood: continuing impairment includes elevated risk for suicide attempts and self-injury. *Journal of Consulting and Clinical Psychology, 80*(6): 1041–1051.

Hirstein, W., Iversen, P., & Ramachandran, V. S. (2001). Autonomic responses of autistic children to people and objects. *Proceedings of the Royal Society London. Biological Science, 268*: 1883–1888.

Hirvikoski, T., Waaler, E., & Alfredsson, J. (2011). Reduced ADHD symptoms in adults with ADHD after structured skills training group: results from a randomized controlled trial. *Behavior Research and Therapy, 49*(3): 175–185

Hirvikoski, T., Waaler, E., Lindstrom, T., Bolte, S., & Jokinen, J. (2014). Cognitive behavior therapy-based psychoeducational groups for adults with ADHD and their significant others (PEGASUS): an open clinical feasibility trial. *ADHD Attention Deficit and Hyperactivity Disorders*. doi 10.1007/s12402–014–0141–2 (open access).

Holman, B. L., & Devous, M. D. Sr (1992). Functional brain SPECT: the emergence of a powerful clinical method. *Journal of Nuclear Medicine, 33*(10): 1888–1904.

Howell, B. R., McCormack, K. M., Grand, A. P., Sawyer, N. T., Zhang, X., Maestripieri, D., Hu, X., & Sanchez, M. M. (2013). Brain white matter microstructure alterations in adolescent rhesus monkeys exposed to early life stress: associations with high cortisol during infancy. *Biology of Mood & Anxiety Disorders, 3*: 21. Electronic journal www.biolmood anxietydisord.com/content/3/1/21 (accessed 10 June 2014) (open access).

Hughes, J. R. (2007). Autism: the first firm finding = underconnectivity? *Epilepsy and Behavior, 11*(1): 20–24.

Hurry, A. (1998). *Psychoanalysis and Developmental Therapy.* London: Karnac.

Hynd, G. W., Semrud-Clikeman, M., Lorys, A. R., Novey, E. S., Eliopulos, D., & Lyytinen, H. (1991). Corpus callosum morphology in attention deficit-hyperactivity disorder: morphometric analysis of MRI. *Journal of Learning Disability, 24*(3): 141–146.

Impey, M., & Heun, R. (2012). Completed suicide, ideation and attempt in attention deficit hyperactivity disorder. *Acta Psychiatrica Scandinavica, 125*(2): 93–102.

Jackson, P. L., Brunet, E., Meltzoff, A. N., & Decety, J. (2006). Empathy examined through the neural mechanisms involved in imagining how I feel versus how you feel pain. *Neuropsychologia, 44*(5): 752–761.

Jacobson, E. (1965). *The Self and the Object World.* London: Hogarth.

Jang, J. H., Jung, W. H., Kang, D.-H., Byun, M. S., Kwon, S. J., Choi, C.-H., & Kwon, J. S. (2011). Increased default mode network connectivity associated with meditation. *Neuroscience Letters, 487*(3): 358–362.

Johansson, B., & Rönnbäck, L. (2014). Long-lasting mental fatigue after traumatic brain injury—a major problem most often neglected. Diagnostic criteria, assessment, relation to emotional and cognitive problems, cellular background, and aspects on treatment. Open Access published online by InTech: http://dx.doi.org/10.5772/57311 (accessed 31 July 2014).

Johansson, B., Bjuhr, H., & Rönnbäck, L. (2012). Mindfulness-based stress reduction (MBSR) improves long-term mental fatigue after stroke or traumatic brain injury. *Brain Injury, 26*(13–14): 1621–1628.

Jones, B., & Alison, E. (2010). An integrated theory for attention-deficit hyperactivity disorder (ADHD). *Psychoanalytic Psychotherapy. 24*(3): 279–295.

Jung, C. G. (1974). *Dreams.* Princeton, NJ: Princeton University Press.

Just, M. A., Kellera, T. A., Malavea, V. L., Kanab, R. K., & Varmac, S. (2012). Autism as a neural systems disorder: a theory of frontal–posterior underconnectivity. *Neuroscience & Biobehavioral Reviews, 36*(4): 1292–1313.

Kaplan, S. L. (2011). *Your Child Does Not Have Bipolar Disorder: How Bad Science and Good Public Relations Created the Diagnosis.* Santa Barbara, CA: Praeger.

Kapur, N., & Coughlan, A. K. (1980). Confabulation and frontal lobe dysfunction. *Journal of Neurology, Neurosurgery, and Psychiatry, 43*: 461–463.

Kean, S. (2014). *The Tale of the Dueling Neurosurgeons: The History of the Human Brain as Revealed by True Stories of Trauma, Madness, and Recovery.* New York: Little Brown.

Kemper, T. L., & Bauman, M. L. (2002). Neuropathology of infantile autism. *Molecular Psychiatry, 7*: S12–S13. doi:10.1038/sj.mp.4001165.

Kennedy, D. P., Redcay, E., & Courchesne, E. (2006). Failing to deactivate: resting functional abnormalities in autism. *Proceedings of the National Academy of Science U.S.A., 103*: 8275–8280.

Keown, D. (2014). *The Spark in the Machine. How the Science of Acupuncture Explains the Mysteries of Western Medicine.* London: Jessica Kingsley.

Kessler, R. C., Adler, L., Barkley, R., Biederman, J., Conners, C. K., Demler, O., Faraone, S. V., Greenhill, L. L., Howes, M. J., Secnik, K., Spencer, T., Ustun, T. B., Walters, E. E., & Zaslavsky, A. M. (2006). The prevalence and correlates of adult ADHD in the United States: results from the National Comorbidity Survey Replication. *American Journal of Psychiatry, 163*(4): 716–723.

Kessler, R. C., Green, J. G., Adler, L. A., Barkley, R. A., Chatterji, S., & Faraone, S. V. (2010). Structure and diagnosis of adult attention-deficit/hyperactivity: analysis of expanded symptom criteria from the adult ADHD clinical diagnostic scale. *Archives of General Psychiatry, 67*(11): 1168–1178.

Khan, M. R. (1963). The concept of cumulative trauma. *Psychoanalytic Study of the Child, 18*: 286–306.

Khan, M. R. (1972). Dread of surrender to resourceless dependence in the analytic situation. *International Journal of Psychoanalysis, 53*: 225–230.

Khan, S., Gramfort, A., Shetty, N. R., Kitzbichler, M. G., Ganesan, S., Moran, J. M., Lee, S. M., Gabrieli, J. D. E., Tager-Flusberg, H. B., Joseph, R. M., Herbert, M. R., Hamalainen, M. S., & Kenet, T. (2013). Local and long-range functional connectivity is reduced in concert in autism spectrum disorders. *Proceedings of the National Academy of Science U.S.A, 110*: 3107–3112. doi: 10.1073/pnas.1214533110.

Kim, S., Arora, M., Fernandez, C., Landero, J., Caruso, J., & Chen, A. (2013). Lead, mercury, and cadmium exposure and attention deficit hyperactivity disorder in children. *Environmental Research, 126*: 105–110.

Kinsbourne, M. (1972). Eye and head turning indicates cerebral lateralisation. *Science, 176*: 539–541.

Klein, M. (1935). A contribution to the psychogenesis of manic-depressive states. *International Journal of Psychoanalysis, 16*: 145–174.

Klein, M. (1946). Notes on some schizoid mechanisms. *International Journal of Psychoanalysis, 27*: 99–110.

Klein, M. (1957). Envy and gratitude. In: *Envy and Gratitude and Other Works 1946–1963* (pp. 176–235). London: Hogarth Press, 1975.

Klein, M. (1975). *Envy and Gratitude and Other Works 1946–1963*. London: Hogarth Press.

Kohut, H. (1971). *The Analysis of the Self*. New York: International Universities Press.

Kohut, H. (1972). Thoughts on narcissism and narcissistic rage. *Psychoanalytic Study of the Child, 27*: 360–400.

Kohut, H. (1977). *The Restoration of the Self*. New York: International Universities Press.

Kohut, H. (1981). *How Does Analysis Cure?* Chicago, IL: Chicago University Press.

Konrad, K., & Eickhoff, S. B. (2010). Is the ADHD brain wired differently? A review on structural and functional connectivity in attention deficit hyperactivity disorder. *Human Brain Mapping, 31*: 904–916.

Konrad, K., Dielentheis, T. F., & El Masri, D. (2010). Disturbed structural connectivity is related to inattention and impulsivity in adult attention deficit hyperactivity disorder. *European Journal of Neuroscience, 31*: 912–919.

Kooij, S. (2011). Presentation to the ADHD Conference, 22–23 September, Savoy Place, London.

Koshino, H., Carpenter, P. A., Minshew, N. J., Cherkassky, V. L., Keller, T. A., & Just, M. A. (2005). Functional connectivity in an fMRI working memory task in high-functioning autism. *NeuroImage, 24*(3): 810–821.

Krause, K. H., Krause, J., & Magyarosy, I. (1998). Fibromyalgia syndrome and attention deficit hyperactivity disorder: is there a comorbidity and are there consequences for the therapy of fibromyalgia syndrome? *Journal of Muscoloskeletal Pain, 6*: 111–116.

Kreisman, J. J., & Straus, H. (1989). *I Hate You—Don't Leave Me: Understanding the Borderline Personality*. New York: Avon Books

Kruesi, M. J., Rapoport, J. L., Hamburger, S., Hibbs, E., Potter, W. Z., Lenane, M., & Brown, G. L. (1990). Cerebrospinal fluid monamine metabolites, aggression, and impulsivity in disruptive behavior disorders of children and adolescents. *Archives of General Psychiatry, 47*: 419–426.

Lacan, J. (1948). Aggressivity in psychoanalysis. In: *Ecrits: A Selection* (pp. 8–29). London: Tavistock, 1977.

Lacan, J. (1949). The mirror stage as formative of the function of the I as revealed in psychoanalytic experience. In: *Ecrits: A Selection* (pp. 1–7). London: Tavistock, 1977.

Lacan, J. (1957). On a question preliminary to any possible treatment of psychosis. In: *Ecrits: A Selection* (pp. 179–225). London: Tavistock, 1977.

Lacan, J. (2013). *On the Names-of-the-Father*. Cambridge: Polity Press.

Langleben, D. D., Austin, G., Krikorian, G., Ridlehuber, H. W., Goris, M. L., & Strauss, H. W. (2001). Interhemispheric asymmetry of regional cerebral blood flow in prepubescent boys with attention deficit hyperactivity disorder. *Nuclear Medicine Communications*, 22(12): 1333–1334.

Laughlin, S. B., & Sejnowski, T. J. (2003). Communication in neuronal networks. *Science*, 301(5641): 1870–1874.

Leuchter, A. F. (2009). Review of 'Healing the Hardware of the Soul: Enhance Your Brain to Improve Your Work, Love, and Spiritual Life' by Daniel Amen. *American Journal of Psychiatry*, 166(5): 625.

Levy, H. P. (2013). Ehlers–Danlos syndrome, hypermobility type. *GeneReviews®* *(Internet)* www.ncbi.nlm.nih.gov/books/NBK1279/ (accessed 28 August 2014).

Leyfer, O. T., Folstein, S. E., Bacalman, S., Davis, N. O., Dinh, E., Morgan, J., Tager-Flusberg, H., & Lainhartet, J. E. (2006). Comorbid psychiatric disorders in children with autism: interview development and rates of disorders. *Journal of Autism & Developmental Disorders*, 36: 849–861, doi: 10.1007/s10803–006–0123–0.

Linehan, M. M. (1993). *Skills Training Manual for Treating Borderline Personality Disorder*. New York: Guilford Press.

Liss, M., Saulnier, C., Fein, D., & Kinsbourne, M. (2006). Sensory and attention abnormalities in autistic spectrum disorders. *Autism*, 10(2): 155–172.

Lofthouse, N., Arnold, L. E., Hersch, S., Hurt, E., & DeBeus, R. (2012). A review of neurofeedback treatment for pediatric ADHD. *Journal of Attention Disorders*, 16(5): 351–372.

Lubar, J. F. (1991). Discourse on the development of EEG diagnostics and biofeedback for attention-deficit/hyperactivity disorders. *Biofeedback and Self Regulation*, 16(3): 201–225.

Lubar, J. F., Swartwood, M. O., Swartwood, J. N., & Timmermann, D. L. (1995). Quantitative EEG and auditory event-related potentials in the evaluation of attention-deficit/hyperactivity disorder: effects of methylphenidate and implications for neurofeedback training. *Journal of Psychoeducational Assessment*, 34: 143–160.

Luman, M., Tripp, G., & Scheres, A. (2010). Identifying the neurobiology of altered reinforcement sensitivity in ADHD: a review and research agenda. *Neuroscience and Biobehavioral Reviews*, 34: 744–754.

Lustman, S. L. (1966). Impulse control, structure, and the synthetic function. In: R. M. Loewenstein, L. M. Newman, M. Schur, & A. J. Solnit

(Eds.), *Psychoanalysis—A General Psychology. Essays in Honor of Heinz Hartmann* (pp. 190–221). New York: International Universities Press.

Mackie, S., Shaw, P., Lenroot, R., Pierson, R., Greenstein, D. K, Nugent, T. F., Sharp, W. S., Giedd, J. N., & Rapoport, J. L. (2007). Cerebellar development and clinical outcome in attention deficit hyperactivity disorder. *American Journal of Psychiatry, 164*(4): 647–655.

Maddock, R. J., Garrett, A. S., & Buonocore, M. H. (2001). Remembering familiar people: the posterior cingulate cortex and autobiographical memory retrieval. *Neuroscience, 104*(3): 667–676.

Maddock, R. J., Garrett, A. S., Buonocore, M. H. (2003). Posterior cingulate cortex activation by emotional words: fMRI evidence from a valence decision task. *Human Brain Mapping, 18*(1): 30–41.

Mann, C., Lubar, J., Zimmerman, A., Miller, C., & Muenchen, R. (1991). Quantitative analysis of EEG in boys with attention-deficit-hyperactivity disorder: controlled study with clinical implications. *Pediatric Neurology, 8:* 30–36.

Marchetti, I., Koster, E. H. W., Sonuga-Barke, E. J., & Raedt, R. D. (2012). The default mode network and recurrent depression: a neurobiological model of cognitive risk factors. *Neuropsychology Review, 22*(3): 229–251.

Markram, K., & Markram, H. (2010). The intense world theory—a unifying theory of the neurobiology of autism. *Frontiers of Human Neuroscience,* 21 December 2010: doi: 10.3389/fnhum.2010.00224 (open access).

Marsh, P. J., & Williams, L. M. (2006). ADHD and schizophrenia phenomenology: visual scanpaths to emotional faces as a potential psychophysiological marker? *Neuroscience and Biobehavioral Reviews, 30*: 651–665.

Martel, M. M. (2009). Research review: a new perspective on attention-deficit/hyperactivity disorder: emotion dysregulation and trait models. *Journal of Child Psychology and Psychiatry, 50*(9): 1042–1051.

Marzillier, S. L. (2009). What psychologists need to know about Lyme Disease. *Clinical Psychology Forum, 194*: 37–41.

Maté, G. (1999). *Scattered Minds. A New Look at the Origins and Healing of Attention Deficit Disorder*. Toronto: Vintage Canada.

Matthies, S. D., & Philipsen, A. (2014). Common ground in attention deficit hyperactivity disorder (ADHD) and borderline personality disorder (BPD)—review of recent findings. *Borderline Personality Disorder and Emotion Dysregulation, 1*(3). doi:10.1186/2051–6673–1–3 (open access).

Mazaheri, A., Fassbender, C., Coffey-Corina, S., Hartanto, T. A., Schweitzer, J. B., & Mangun, G. R. (2013). Differential oscillatory electroencephalogram between attention-deficit/hyperactivity disorder subtypes and typically developing adolescents. *Biological Psychiatry*, Oct 1. pii: S0006–3223(13)00776–2. doi:10.1016/j.biopsych.2013.08.023.

Mazoyer, B., Zago, L., Mellet, E., Bricogne, S., Etard, O., Houdé, O., Crivello, F., Joliot, M., Petit, L., & Tzourio-Mazoyer, N. (2001). Cortical networks for working memory and executive functions sustain the conscious resting state in man. *Brain Research Bulletin, 54*(3): 287–298.

McCann, D., Barrett, A., & Cooper, A. (2007). Food additives and hyperactive behaviour in 3-year-old and 8/9-year-old children in the community: a randomized, double-blinded, placebo-controlled trial. *Lancet, 370*(9598): 1560–1567.

McDaid, A. M., Easton, T., Higgins, C. J., Kidane, L., Calvin, C. M., & Corrie, A. C. (1999). Schizotypal traits and attention deficit/hyperactivity. *Schizophrenia Bulletin, 36*: 25.

McGilchrist, I. (2009). *The Master and His Emissary: The Divided Brain and the Making of the Western World*. London: Yale University Press.

Meijer, W. M., Faber, A., van den Ban, E., & Tobi, H. (2009). Current issues around the pharmacotherapy of ADHD in children and adults. *Pharmacy World and Science, 31*: 509–516.

Melillo, R., & Leisman, G. (2009). Autistic spectrum disorders as functional disconnection syndrome. *Review of Neuroscience, 20*(2): 111–131.

Meltzer, D. (1975). The psychology of autistic states and post-autistic mentality. In: D. Meltzer, J. Bremner, S. Hoxter, D. Weddell & I. Wittenberg (Eds.), *Explorations in Autism. A Psychoanalytic Study* (Chapter II). Strathtay, Perthshire: Clunie Press.

Menkes, M. M., Rowe, J. S., & Menkes, J. H. (1967). A twenty-five year follow-up study on the hyperkinetic child with minimal brain dysfunction. *Pediatrics, 39*: 393–399.

Merikangas, K. R., He, J. P., & Burstein, M. (2010). Lifetime prevalence of mental disorders in U.S. adolescents: results from the National Comorbidity Survey Replication—Adolescent Supplement (NCS-A). *Journal of the American Academy of Child and Adolescent Psychiatry, 49*(10): 980–989.

Merwood, A., Chen, W., Rijsdijk, F., Skirrow, C., Larsson, H., Thapar, A., Kuntsi, J., & Asherson, P. (2014). Genetic associations between the symptoms of attention-deficit/hyperactivity disorder and emotional lability in child and adolescent twins. *Journal of the American Academy of Child & Adolescent Psychiatry, 53*(2): 209–220.

Mollon, P. (1979). Developmental diagnosis and the assessment of ego functions. Unpublished manuscript, available from the author.

Mollon, P. (1985). The non-mirroring mother and the missing paternal dimension in a case of narcissistic disturbance. *Psychoanalytic Psychotherapy, 1*(2): 35–47.

Mollon, P. (1993). *The Fragile Self: The Structure of Narcissistic Disturbance.* London: Whurr.

Mollon, P. (1996). *Multiple Voices, Multiple Selves: Working with Trauma, Violation, and Dissociation.* Chichester: Wiley.

Mollon, P. (2001). *Releasing the Self: The Healing Legacy of Heinz Kohut.* London: Whurr.

Mollon, P. (2002a). *Remembering Trauma. A Psychotherapist's Guide to Memory and Illusion* (2nd edn). London: Whurr.

Mollon, P. (2002b). *Shame and Jealousy: The Hidden Turmoils.* London: Karnac.

Mollon, P. (2005). *EMDR and the Energy Therapies: Psychoanalytic Perspectives.* London: Karnac.

Mollon, P. (2008). *Psychoanalytic Energy Psychotherapy.* London: Karnac.

Mollon, P. (2011). A Kohutian perspective on the foreclosure of the Freudian transference in modern British technique. *Psychoanalytic Inquiry, 31*(1): 28–41.

Mollon, P. (2014a). Attachment and energy psychology: explorations at the interface of bodily, mental, relational, and transpersonal aspects of human behaviour and experience. In: K. White (Ed.), *Talking Bodies: How Do We Integrate Working with the Body in Psychotherapy from an Attachment and Relational Perspective?* (pp. 65–88). London: Karnac.

Mollon, P. (2014b). Revisiting 'Analysis Terminable and Interminable': expressions of death instinct by patients and analyst. *Psychoanalytic Inquiry, 24*(1): 28–38.

Monk, C. S., Peltier, S. J., Wiggins, J. L., Weng, S. J., Carrasco, M., Risi, S., & Lord, C. (2009). Abnormalities of intrinsic functional connectivity in autism spectrum disorders. *Neuroimage, 47*(2): 764–772.

Murias, M., Swanson, J. M., & Srinivasan, R. (2007). Functional connectivity of frontal cortex in healthy and ADHD children reflected in EEG coherence. *Cerebral Cortex, 7*: 1788–1799.

Nagano-Saitoa, A., Liua, J., Doyona, J., & Daghera, A. (2009). Dopamine modulates default mode network deactivation in elderly individuals during the Tower of London task. *Neuroscience Letters, 458*(1): 1–5.

Nagel, B. J., Bathula, D., & Herting, M. (2011). Altered white matter microstructure in children with attention-deficit/hyperactivity disorder. *Journal of the American Academy of Child and Adolescent Psychiatry, 50*(3): 283–292.

Nakao, T., Radua, J., & Rubia, K. (2011). Gray matter volume abnormalities in ADHD: voxel-based meta-analysis exploring the effects of age and stimulant medication. *American Journal of Psychiatry, 168*(11): 1154–1163.

Negishia, T., Kawasakib, K., Sekiguchia, S., Ishiia, Y., Kyuwaa, S., Kurodac, Y., & Yoshikawaa, Y. (2005). Attention-deficit and hyperactive neurobehavioural characteristics induced by perinatal hypothyroidism in rats. *Behavioural Brain Research*, 159(2): 323–331.

NICE Guideline (2008). *Attention Deficit Hyperactivity Disorder: Diagnosis and Management of ADHD in Children, Young People and Adults*. www.nice.org.uk/guidance/cg72.

Nieoullon, A. (2002). Dopamine and the regulation of cognition and attention. *Progress in Neurobiology*, 67(1): 53–83.

Nigg, J. T. (2006). *What Causes ADD? Understanding What Goes Wrong and Why*. New York: Guilford Press.

Nigg, J. T., & Casey, B. J. (2005). An integrative theory of attention-deficit/hyperactivity disorder based on the cognitive and affective neurosciences. *Developmental Psychopathology*, 17: 785–806.

Nikolas, M., Friderici, K., Waldman, I., Jernigan, K., & Nigg, J. T. (2010). Gene x environment interactions for ADHD: synergistic effect of 5HTTLPR genotype and youth appraisals of inter-parental conflict. *Behavioral and Brain Functions*, 6: 23. doi:10.1186/1744–9081-6-23 (open access).

Nilsen, E. S., Buist, T. A. M., Gillis, R., & Fugelsang, J. (2013). Communicative perspective-taking performance of adults with ADHD symptoms. *Journal of Attention Disorders*, 17(7): 589–597.

Noble, E. B. (2000). Addiction and its reward process through polymorphisms of the D2 dopamine receptor gene: a review. *European Psychiatry*, 15(2): 79–89.

Nunberg, H. (1931). The synthetic function of the ego. *International Journal of Psychoanalysis*, 12: 123–140.

Nutt, D. J. (2006). The role of dopamine and norepinephrine in depression and antidepressant treatment. *Journal of Clinical Psychiatry*, 67(Suppl 6): 3–8.

Ogden, T. H. (1989). *The Primitive Edge of Experience*. New York: Jason Aronson.

Ohlmeier, M., Peters, K., Te Wildt, B. T., Zedler, M., & Ziegenbein, M. (2008). Comorbidity of alcohol and substance dependence with attention-deficit/hyperactivity disorder (ADHD). *Alcohol and Alcoholism*, 43(3): 300–304.

Orekhova, E. V., & Stroganova, T. A. (2014). Arousal and attention re-orienting in autism spectrum disorders: evidence from auditory event-related potentials. *Frontiers of Human Neuroscience*, 8: 34. Published online Feb 6. doi: 10.3389/fnhum.2014.00034.

Overmeyer, S., Simmons, A., Santosh, J., Andrew, C., Williams, S. C. R., Taylor, A., Chen, W., & Taylor, E. (2000). Corpus callosum may be similar in children with ADHD and siblings of children with ADHD. *Developmental Medicine & Child Neurology, 42*: 8–13.

Ozonoff, S., Pennington, B., & Rogers, S. J. (1991). Executive function deficits in high-functioning autistic individuals: relationship to theory of mind. *Journal of Child Psychology and Psychiatry, 32*: 1081–1105.

Panksepp, J. (1998). *Affective Neuroscience: The Foundations of Human and Animal Emotions.* New York: Oxford University Press.

Panksepp, J. (2007). Can PLAY diminish ADHD and facilitate the construction of the social brain? *Journal of the Canadian Academy of Child and Adolescent Psychiatry, 16*(2): 57–66.

Patten, E., Ausderau, K. A., Watson, L. R., & Baranek, G. T. (2013). Sensory response patterns in nonverbal children with ASD. *Autism Research and Treatment, 2013*: Article ID 436286, 9 pages http://dx.doi.org/10.1155/2013/436286.

Philipsen, A. (2006). Differential diagnosis and comorbidity of attention-deficit/hyperactivity disorder (ADHD) and borderline personality disorder (BPD) in adults. *European Archives of Psychiatry and Clinical Neuroscience, 256*(1 Suppl.): i42–i46.

Philipsen, A. (2012). Psychotherapy in adult attention deficit hyperactivity disorder implications for treatment and research. *Expert Review of Neurotherapeutics, 12*(10): 1217–1225.

Philipsen, A., Feige, B., Hesslinger, B., Scheel, C., Ebert, D., Matthies, S., Limberger, M. F., Kleindienst, N., Bohus, M., & Lieb, K. (2009). Borderline typical symptoms in adult patients with attention deficit/hyperactivity disorder. *Attention Deficit and Hyperactivity Disorders, 1*(1): 11–18.

Philipsen, A., Limberger, M. F., Lieb, K., Feige, B., Kleindienst, N., Ebner-Priemer, U., Barth, J., Schmahl, C., & Bohus, M. (2008). Attention-deficit hyperactivity disorder as a potentially aggravating factor in borderline personality disorder. *British Journal of Psychiatry, 192*(2): 118–123.

Philipsen, A., Richter, H., Peters, J., Alm, B., Sobanski, E., Colla, M., Münzebrock, M., Scheel, C., Jacob, C., Perlov, E., Tebartz van Elst, L., & Hesslinger, B. (2007). Structured group psychotherapy in adults with attention deficit hyperactivity disorder: results of an open multicentre study. *Journal of Nervous and Mental Disorders, 195*(12): 1013–1019.

Pierce, K., Haist, F. Sedaghat, F., & Courchesne, E. (2004). The brain response to personally familiar faces in autism: findings of fusiform activity and beyond. *Brain, 127*(12): 2703–2716.

Pine, D. S., Klien, R. G., Lindy, D. C., & Marshall, R. D. (1993). Attention-deficit hyperactivity disorder and comorbid psychosis: a review and two clinical presentations. *Journal of Clinical Psychiatry, 54*: 140–144.

Pliszka, S. R. (2005). The neuropyschopharmacology of attention-deficit/hyperactivity disorder. *Biological Psychiatry, 57*: 1385–1390.

Pocinki, A. G. (2010). Joint hypermobility and joint hypermobility syndrome. Available from: www.dynakids.org/Documents/hyper mobility.pdf (and other websites) (accessed 28 August 2014).

Pocinki, A. G. (2013). Pseudo-psychiatric symptoms in Ehlers–Danlos syndrome. Presentation to the Ehlers–Danlos National Foundation Learning Conference, Providence, RI, 1–3 August 2013.

Polanczyk, G., Silva de Lima, M., & Horta, B. L. (2007). The worldwide prevalence of ADHD: a systematic review and meta-regression analysis. *American Journal of Psychiatry, 164*: 942–948.

Posner, J., Nagel, B. J., Maia, T. V., Mechling, A., Oh, M., Wang, Z., & Peterson, B. S. (2011). Abnormal amygdalar activation and connectivity in adolescents with attention-deficit/hyperactivity disorder. *Journal of the American Academy of Child & Adolescent Psychiatry, 50*(8): 828–837.

Prediger, R. D. (2005). Caffeine improves spatial learning deficits in an animal model of attention deficit hyperactivity disorder (ADHD)—the spontaneously hypertensive rat (SHR). *International Journal of Neuropsychopharmacology, 8*: 583–594.

Previc, F. H. (2009). *The Dopaminergic Mind in Human Evolution and History.* New York: Cambridge University Press.

Prince, J. (2008). Catecholamine dysfunction in attention-deficit/hyperactivity disorder: an update. *Journal of Clinical Psychopharmacology, 28*(3, Suppl. 2): S39–S45.

Prior, M. R., & Bradshaw, J. L. (1979). Hemisphere functioning in autistic children. *Cortex, 15*(1): 73–81.

Proal, E., Reiss, P. T., & Klein, R. G. (2011). Brain gray matter deficits at 33-year follow-up in adults with attention-deficit/hyperactivity disorder established in childhood. *Archives of General Psychiatry, 68*(11): 1122–1134.

Qiu, A., Crocetti, D., Adler, M., Mahone, M., Denckla, M. B., Miller, M. I., & Mostofsky, S. H. (2009). Basal ganglia volume and shape in children with attention deficit hyperactivity disorder. *American Journal of Psychiatry, 166*: 74–82.

Ratey, J. J., & Johnson, C. (1998). *Shadow Syndromes. The Mild Forms of Major Mental Illness that Sabotage Us.* New York: Bantam.

Redcay, E., & Courchesne, E. (2008). Deviant functional magnetic resonance imaging patterns of brain activity to speech in 2–3-year-old children with autism spectrum disorder. *Biological Psychiatry, 64*(7): 589–598.

Reiersen, A., Constantino, J. N., & Volk, H. E. (2007). Autistic traits in a population-based ADHD twin sample. *Journal of Child Psychology and Psychiatry and Allied Disciplines, 48*(5): 464–472.

Reimherr, F. W., Wender, P. H., & Ebert, M. H. (1984). Cerebrospinal fluid homovanillic acid and 5-hydroxy-indoeacit acid in adults with attention deficit disorder, residual type. *Psychiatry Research, 11*: 71–78.

Reyero, F., Ponce, G., Rodriguez-Jimenez, R., Fernandez-Dapica, P., Taboada, D., Martin, V., Navio, M., & Jimenez-Arriero, M. A. (2011). High frequency of childhood ADHD history in women with fibromyalgia. *European Psychiatry, 26*(8): 482–483.

Richter, A., Richter, S., Barman, A., Soch, J., Klein, M., Assmann, A., Libeau, C., Behnisch, G., Wüstenberg, T., Seidenbecher, C. I., & Schott, B. H. (2013). Motivational salience and genetic variability of dopamine D2 receptor expression interact in the modulation of interference processing. *Frontiers in Human Neuroscience*, www.frontiersin.org (June 2013, Volume 7, Article 250).

Robinson, D. S. (2007). The role of dopamine and norepinephrine in depression. *Primary Psychiatry, 14*(5): 21–23.

Roessner, V., Banaschewski, T., Uebel, H., Becker, A., & Rothenberger, A. (2004). Neuronal network models of ADHD—lateralization with respect to interhemispheric connectivity reconsidered. *European Child & Adolescent Psychiatry, 13*(Supplement 1): I71–179.

Rommelse, N., Franke, B., & Geurts, H. (2010). Shared heritability of attention deficit/hyperactivity disorder and autism spectrum disorder. *European Child and Adolescent Psychiatry, 19*(3): 281–295.

Rosenfeld, H. (1987). *Impasse and Interpretation: Therapeutic and Antitherapeutic Factors in the Psychoanalytic Treatment of Psychotic, Borderline, Neurotic Patients.* London: Tavistock.

Roy, M., Ohlmeier, M. D., Osterhagen, L., Prox-Vagedes, V., & Dillo, W. (2013). Asperger syndrome: a frequent comorbidity in first diagnosed adult ADHD patients. *Psychiatria Danubina, 25*(2): 133–141.

Rubenstein, J. L. R., & Merzenich, M. M. (2003). Model of autism: increased ratio of excitation/inhibition in key neural systems. *Genes, Brain and Behavior, 2*(5): 255–267.

Rubia, K., Overmeyer, S., Taylor, E., Brammer, M., Williams, S. C. R., Simmons, A., & Bullmore, T. (1999). Hypofrontality in attention deficit hyperactivity disorder during higher-order motor control: a study with functional MRI. *American Journal of Psychiatry, 156*: 891–896.

Rubia, K., Smith, A. B., Brammer, M. J., Toone, B., & Taylor, E. (2005). Abnormal brain activation during inhibition and error detection in medication-naive adolescents with ADHD. *American Journal of Psychiatry, 162*(6): 1067–1075.

Rüsch, N., Luders, E., Lieb, K., Zahn, R., Ebert, D., Thompson, P. M., Toga, A. W., & van Elst, L. T. (2007). Corpus callosum abnormalities in women with borderline personality disorder and comorbid attention-deficit hyperactivity disorder. *Journal of Psychiatry and Neuroscience, 32*(6): 417–422.

Sagiv, S. K., Thurston, S. W., Bellinger, D. C., Amarasiriwardena, C., & Korrick, S. A. (2012). Prenatal exposure to mercury and fish consumption during pregnancy and attention-deficit/hyperactivity disorder-related behavior in children. *Archives of Pediatrics and Adolescent Medicine, 166*(12): 1123–1131.

Sambhi, R. S., & Lepping, P. (2009). Adult ADHD and psychosis: a review of the literature and two cases. *Clinical Neuropsychiatry, 6*(4): 174–178.

Saul, R. (2014). *ADHD Does Not Exist.* New York: HarperCollins.

Schaeffer, J. L., & Ross, R. G. (2002). Childhood-onset schizophrenia: premorbid and prodromal diagnostic and treatment histories. *Journal of the American Academy of Child and Adolescent Psychiatry, 41*: 538–545.

Schmitz, C., & Rezaie, P. (2008). The neuropathology of autism: where do we stand? *Neuropathology and Applied Neurobiology, 34*(1): 4–11.

Schneider, M., Retz, W., Coogan, A., Thome, J., & Rösler, M. (2006). Anatomical and functional brain imaging in adult attention-deficit/ hyperactivity disorder (ADHD)—a neurological view. *European Archives of Psychiatry and Clinical Neuroscience, 256*(Suppl. 1): i32–i41.

Schore, A. N. (1994). *Affect Regulation and the Origin of the Self.* Hillsdale, NJ: Lawrence Erlbaum.

Schore, A. N. (2003). *Affect Regulation and the Repair of the Self.* New York: Norton.

Schore, A. N. (2011). *The Science of the Art of Psychotherapy.* New York: Norton.

Schredl, M., & Sartorius, H. (2010). Dream recall and dream content in children with attention deficit/hyperactivity disorder. *Child Psychiatry & Human Development, 41*(2): 230–238.

Schrimsher, G. W., Billingsley, R. L., Jackson, E. F., & Moore, B. D. (2002). Caudate nucleus volume asymmetry predicts attention-deficit hyperactivity disorder (ADHD) symptomatology in children. *Journal of Child Neurology, 17*(12): 877–884.

Schwarz, A. (2013). The selling of attention deficit disorder. *New York Times*, December 14th. www.nytimes.com/2013/12/15/health/the-selling-of-attention-deficit-disorder.html?_r=0 (accessed 17 August 2014).

Schweitzer, L. (1982). Evidence of right cerebral hemisphere dysfunction in schizophrenic patients with left hemisphere overactivation. *Biological Psychiatry*, *17*(6): 655–673.

Seltzer, M. M., Krauss, M. W., Shattuck, P. T., Orsmond, G., Swe, A., & Lord, C. (2003). The symptoms of autism spectrum disorders in adolescence and adulthood. *Journal of Autism & Developmental Disorders*, *33*: 565–581.

Shaffer, R. J., Jacokes, L. E., Cassily, J. F., Greenspan, S. I., Tuchman, R. F., & Stemmer, P. J. Jr (2001). Effect of interactive metronome training on children with ADHD. *American Journal of Occupational Therapy*, *55*(2): 155–156.

Shaw, P., Eckstrand, K., & Sharp, W. (2007). Attention-deficit/hyperactivity disorder is characterised by a delay in cortical maturation. *Proceedings of the National Academy of Sciences*, *104*(49): 19649–19654.

Shaw, P., Lalonde, F., Lepage, C., Rabin, C., Eckstrand, K., Sharp, W., Greenstein, D., Evans, A., Giedd, J. N., & Rapoport, J. (2009). Development of cortical asymmetry in typically developing children and its disruption in attention-deficit/hyperactivity disorder. *Archives of General Psychiatry*, *66*(8): 888–896.

Shaw, P., Malek, M., & Watson, B. (2012). Development of cortical surface area and gyrification in attention-deficit/hyperactivity disorder. *Biological Psychiatry*, *72*(3): 191–197.

Shaw, P., Stringaris, A., Nigg, J., & Leibenluft, E. (2014). Emotion dysregulation in attention deficit hyperactivity disorder. *American Journal of Psychiatry*, *171*: 276–293.

Shaywitz, B. A., Cohen, B. J., & Bowers, M. B. Jr (1977). CSF metabolites in children with minimal brain dysfunction: evidence for alteration of brain dopamine. *Journal of Paediatrics*, *90*: 67–71.

Sikora, D. M., Vora, P., Coury, D. L., & Rosenberg, D. (2012). Attention-deficit/hyperactivity disorder symptoms, adaptive functioning, and quality of life in children with autism spectrum disorder. *Pediatrics*, *130*(Suppl. 2): S91–S97, doi: 10.1542/peds.2012–0900G.

Sobanski, E., Banaschewski, T., & Asherson, P. (2010). Emotional lability in children and adolescents with attention deficit/hyperactivity disorder (ADHD). Clinical correlates and familial prevalence. *Journal of Child Psychology and Psychiatry*, *51*(8): 915–923.

Solms, M., & Turnbull, O. (2002). *The Brain and the Inner World. An Introduction to the Neuroscience of Subjective Experience*. London: Karnac.

Solnit, A. J. (1966). Some adaptive functions of aggressive behaviour. In: R. M. Loewenstein, L. M. Newman, M. Schur, & A. J. Solnit (Eds.), *Psychoanalysis—A General Psychology. Essays in Honor of Heinz Hartmann* (pp. 169–189). New York: International Universities Press.

Sonuga-Barke, E. J., & Castellanos, F. X. (2007). Spontaneous attentional fluctuations in impaired states and pathological conditions: a neurobiological hypothesis. *Neuroscience and Biobehavioral Reviews*, 31(7): 977–986.

Spencer, E. K., & Campbell, M. (1994). Children with schizophrenia: diagnosis, phenomenology, and pharmacotherapy. *Schizophrenia Bulletin*, 20: 713–725.

Spencer, T. (2006). Norepinephrine: understanding its role in ADHD. In: *The Current and Emerging Role of Alpha-2 Agonists in the Treatment of ADHD, Volume 1: ADHD Etiology and Neurobiology* (pp. 12–16). Hasbrouck Heights, NJ: Veritas Institute for Medical Education.

Sroufe, L. A. (1996). *Emotional Development: The Organization of Emotional Life in the Early Years*. New York: Cambridge University Press.

St Pourcain, B. S., Mandy, W. P., & Heron, J. (2011). Links between co-occurring social-communication and hyperactive-inattentive trait trajectories. *Journal of the American Academy of Child and Adolescent Psychiatry*, 50(9): 892–902.

Starka, F., Bauera, E., Merza, C. J., Zimmermanna, M., Reuterd, M., Plichtae, M. M., Kirsch, P., Lesche, K. P., Fallgatterg, A. D., Vaitla, D., & Herrmanne, M. J. (2011). ADHD related behaviors are associated with brain activation in the reward system. *Neuropsychologia*, 49: 426–434.

Stefanatos, G. A., & Wasserstein, J. (2001). Attention deficit/hyperactivity disorder as a right hemisphere syndrome. Selective literature review and detailed neuropsychological case studies. *Annals of the New York Academy of Science*, 931: 172–195.

Stevens, F. L., Taber, K. H., Hurley, R. J., & Hayman, L. A. (2011). Anterior cingulate cortex: unique role in cognition and emotion. *Journal of Neuropsychiatry and Clinical Neurosciences*, 23: 121–125.

Stuss, D. T. (1991). Self, awareness, and the frontal lobes: a neuropsychological perspective. In: J. Strauss & G. R. Goethals (Eds.), *The Self: Interdisciplinary Approaches* (pp. 255–278). New York: Springer.

Stuss, D. T., Gallup, G. G. Jr, & Alexander, M. P. (2001). The frontal lobes are necessary for 'theory of mind'. *Brain*, 124: 279–286.

Swanson, C. (2010). *Life Force. The Scientific Basis*. Tucson, AZ: Poseidia Press.

Swanson, J. M., & Castellanos, F. X. (2002). Biological bases of ADHD; neuroanatomy, genetics, and pathophysiology. In: P. S. Jensen & J. R. Cooper (Eds.), *Attention-deficit Hyperactivity Disorder: State of the Science, Best Practices* (Chapter 7, pp. 1–12). Kingston, NJ. Civic Research Institute.

Szasz, T. S. (2001). *Pharmacracy: Medicine and Politics in America*. Westport, CT: Praeger.

Takahata, K., & Kato, M. (2008). Neural mechanism underlying autistic savant and acquired savant syndrome. *Brain and Nerve, 60*(7): 861–869.

Tani, P., Joukamaa, M., Lindberg, N., Nieminen-von Wendt, T., von Wendt, L., & Porkka-Heiskanen, T. (2006). Childhood inattention and hyperactivity symptoms self-reported by adults with Asperger syndrome. *Psychopathology, 39*: 49–54.

Tartakovsky, M. (2014). Cutting down on chronic lateness for adults with ADHD. Psych Central. http://psychcentral.com/blog/archives/2014/04/01/cutting-down-on-chronic-lateness-for-adults-with-adhd/ (accessed 19 June 2014).

Teicher, M. H., Anderson, C. M., Polcari, A., Glod, C. A., Maas, L. C., & Renshaw, P. F. (2000). Functional deficits in basal ganglia of children with attention-deficit/hyperactivity disorder shown with functional magnetic resonance imaging relaxometry. *Nature Medicine, 6*: 470–473.

Thapar, A., Harrington, R., & McGuffin, P. (2001). Examining the co-morbidity of ADHD-related behaviours and conduct problems using a twin study design. *British Journal of Psychiatry, 179*: 224–229.

Thie, J., & Thie, M. (2005). *Touch for Health. A Practical Guide to Natural Health with Acupressure Touch*. Camarillo, CA: DeVorss.

Tian, L., Jiang, T., Liang, M., Zang, Y., He, Y., Sui, M., & Wang, Y. (2008). Enhanced resting-state brain activities in ADHD patients: an fMRI study. *Brain Development, 30*: 342–348.

Tiller, W. A. (2007). *Psychoenergetic Science. A Second Copernican Scale Evolution*. Walnut Creek, CA: Pavior.

Timimi, S. (2004). A critique of the International Consensus Statement on ADHD. *Clinical Child and Family Psychology Review, 7*(1): 59–63.

Tomasi, D., & Volkow, N. D. (2012). Abnormal functional connectivity in children with attention-deficit/hyperactivity disorder. *Biological Psychiatry, 71*(5): 443–450.

Treadway, M. T., Buckholtz, J. W., Cowan, R. L., Woodward, N. D., Li, R., Sib Ansari, M., Baldwin, R. M., Schwartzman, A. N., Kessler, R. M., & Zald, D. H. (2012). Dopaminergic mechanisms of individual differences in human effort-based decision-making. *Journal of Neuroscience, 32*(18): 6170–6176.

Tripp, G., & Wickens, J. R. (2008). Research review: dopamine transfer deficit: a neurobiological theory of altered reinforcement mechanisms in ADHD. *Journal of Child Psychology and Psychiatry and Allied Disciplines*, 49: 691–704.

Tripp, G., & Wickens, J. R. (2009). Neurobiology of ADHD. *Neuropharmacology*, 57: 579–589.

Tucker, D. M., & Williamson, P. A. (1984). Asymmetric neural control systems in human self-regulation. *Psychological Review*, *91*(2): 185–215.

Tustin, F. (1986). *Autistic Barriers in Neurotic Patients*. London: Karnac.

Tweedy, R. (2013). *The God of the Left Hemisphere: Blake, Bolte Taylor and the Myth of Creation*. London: Karnac.

Van den Berg, C. J. (1986). On the relation between energy transformation in the brain and mental activities. In: R. Hockey, A. Gaillard, & M. Coles (Eds.), *Energetics and Human Information Processing* (pp. 131–135). Dordrecht: Martinus Nijhoff.

Van der Glind, G. (2011). Presentation to the ADHD Conference, September 22–23, Savoy Place, London.

Van der Meer, J. M. J., Oerlemans, A. M., & van Steijn, D. J. (2012). Are autism spectrum disorder and attention deficit/hyperactivity disorder different manifestations of one overarching disorder? Cognitive and symptom evidence from a clinical and population-based sample. *Journal of the American Academy of Child and Adolescent Psychiatry*, *51*(11): 160–172.

Van Dijk, F., Lappenschaar, M., Kan, C., Verkes, R. J., & Buitelaar, J. (2011). Lifespan attention deficit/hyperactivity disorder and borderline personality disorder symptoms in female patients: a latent class approach. *Psychiatry Research*, *190*(2–3): 327–334.

Van Dijk, F. E., Lappenschaar, M., Kan, C. C., Verkes, R. J., & Buitelaar, J. K. (2012). Symptomatic overlap between attention-deficit/hyperactivity disorder and borderline personality disorder in women: the role of temperament and character traits. *Comprehensive Psychiatry*, *53*(1): 39–47.

Van Emmerik-van Oortmerssen, K., van de Glind, G., van den Brink, W., Smit, F., Crunelle, C. L., Swets, M., & Schoevers, R. A. (2012). Prevalence of attention deficit/hyperactivity disorder in substance abuse disorder patients: a meta-analysis and meta-regression analysis. *Drug and Alcohol Dependence*, *122*(1–2): 11–19.

Van Ewijk, H., Heslenfeld, D. J., & Zwiers, M. P. (2012). Diffusion tensor imaging in attention-deficit/hyperactivity disorder: a systematic review and meta-analysis. *Neuroscience and Biobehavioral Reviews*, *36*(4): 1093–1106.

Vance, A., Silk, T. J., Casey, M., Rinehart, N. J., Bradshaw, J. L., Bellgrove, M. A., & Cunnington, R. (2007). Right parietal dysfunction in children with attention deficit hyperactivity disorder, combined type: a functional MRI study. *Molecular Psychiatry*, 12(9): 826–832.

Viggiano, D., Vallone, D., Ruocco, L. A., & Sadile, A. G. (2003). Behavioural, pharmacological, morpho-functional molecular studies reveal a hyperfunctioning mesocortical dopamine system in an animal model of attention deficit and hyperactivity disorder. *Neuroscience and Biobehavioral Reviews*, 27: 683–689.

Voeller, K. K. S. (2004). Attention deficit hyperactivity disorder. *Journal of Child Neurology*, 19(10): 798–814.

Vogeley, K., Bussfeld, P., Newen, A., Herrmann, S., Happé, F., Falkai, P., Maier, W., Shah, N. J., Fink, G. R., & Zilles, K. (2001). Mind reading: neural mechanisms of theory of mind and self-perspective. *Neuroimage*, 14(1 Pt 1): 170–181.

Volkow, N. D., Fowler, J. S., Wang, G., Ding, Y., & Gatley, S. J. (2002a). Mechanism of action of methylphenidate: insights from PET imaging studies. *Journal of Attention Disorders*, 6(Suppl. 1): S31–S43.

Volkow, N. D., Fowler, J. S., Wang, G. J., Ding, Y. S., & Gatley, S. J. (2002b). Role of dopamine in the therapeutic and reinforcing effects of methylphenidate in humans: results from imaging studies. *European Neuropsychopharmacology*, 12(6): 557–566.

Volkow, N. D., Wang, G. J., & Newcorn, J. H. (2011). Motivation deficit in ADHD is associated with dysfunction of the dopamine reward pathway. *Molecular Psychiatry*, 16(11): 1147–1154.

Volkow, N. D., Wang, G. J., Kollins, S. H., Wigal, T. L., Newcorn, J. H., & Telang, F. (2009). Evaluating dopamine reward pathway in ADHD: clinical implications. *Journal of the American Medical Association*, 302: 1084–1091.

Volkow, N. D., Wang, G. J., Newcorn, J., Telang, F., Solanto, M. V., Fowler, J. S., Logan, J., Ma, Y., Schulz, K., Pradhan, K., Wong, C., & Swanson, J. M. (2007). Depressed dopamine activity in caudate and preliminary evidence of limbic involvement in adults with attention-deficit/hyperactivity disorder. *Archives of General Psychiatry*, 64(8): 932–940.

Von dem Hagen, E. A. H., Stoyanova, R. S., Baron-Cohen, S., & Calder, A. J. (2013). Reduced functional connectivity within and between social resting state networks in autism spectrum conditions. *Social Cognitive and Affective Neuroscience*, 8: 694–701. doi:10.1093/scan/nss053.

Wagner, H. N. Jnr, Burns, H. D., Dannals, R. F., Wong, D. F., Langstrom, B., Duelfer, T., Frost, J. J., Ravert, H. T., Links, J. M., Rosenbloom, S. B., Lukas, S. E., Kramer, A. V., & Kuhar, M. J. (1983). Imaging dopamine receptors in the human brain by positron emission tomography. *Science, 221*(4617): 1264–1266.

Wang, L., Zhu, C., He, Y., Zang, Y., Cao, Q., Zhang, H., Zhong, Q., & Wang, Y. (2009). Altered small-world brain functional networks in children with attention-deficit/hyperactivity disorder. *Human Brain Mapping, 30*: 638–649.

Wass, S. (2011). Distortions and disconnections: disrupted brain connectivity in autism. *Brain and Cognition, 75*(1): 18–28.

Weinberger, D. R., Aloia, M. S., Goldberg, T. E., & Berman, K. F. (1994). The frontal lobes and schizophrenia. *Journal of Neuropsychiatry and Clinical Neurosciences, 6*(4): 419–427.

Weissman, D. H., Roberts, K. C., Visscher, K. M., & Woldorff, M. G. (2006). The neural bases of momentary lapses in attention. *Nature Neuroscience, 9*: 971–978.

Weng, S. J., Wiggins, J. L., Peltier, S. J., Carrasco, M., Risi, S., Lord, C., & Monk, C. S. (2010). Alterations of resting state functional connectivity in the default network in adolescents with autism spectrum disorders. *Brain Research, 1313*: 202–214.

Whalen, P. J., Bush, G., McNally, R. J., Wilhelm, S., McInerney, S. C., Jenike, M. A., & Rauch, S. L. (1998). The emotional counting Stroop paradigm: a functional magnetic resonance imaging probe of the anterior cingulate affective division. *Biological Psychiatry, 44*(12): 1219–1228.

Whitaker, R. (2005). Anatomy of an epidemic: psychiatric drugs and the astonishing rise of mental illness in America. *Ethical Human Psychology and Psychiatry, 7*(1): 23–35. Also available online: www.cchr.org/sites/default/files/Anatomy_of_an_Epidemic_Psychiatric_Drugs_Rise_of_Mental_Illness.pdf (accessed 16 September 2014).

Whitaker, R. (2010). *Anatomy of an Epidemic: Magic Bullets, Psychiatric Drugs, and the Astonishing Rise of Mental Illness in America*. New York: Random House.

Wilens, T. E., McDermott, S. P., Biederman, J., Abrantes, A., Hahasy, A., & Spencer, T. J. (1999). Cognitive therapy in the treatment of adults with ADHD: a systematic chart review of 26 cases. *Journal of Cognitive Psychotherapy: An International Quarterly, 13*: 215–226.

Williams, D. (1996). *Autism. An Inside-Out Approach*. London: Jessica Kingsley.

Williams, D. (1998a). *Nobody Nowhere: The Remarkable Autobiography of an Autistic Girl*. London: Jessica Kingsley.

Williams, D. (1998b). *Autism and Sensing: The Unlost Instinct*. London: Jessica Kingsley.

Williams, D. (2008). *Exposure Anxiety – The Invisible Cage: An Exploration of Self-Protection Responses in the Autism Spectrum and Beyond.* London: Jessica Kingsley.

Williams, J. H., Waiter, G. D., Perra, O., Perrett, D. I., & Whiten, A. (2005). An fMRI study of joint attention experience. *Neuroimage, 25*(1): 133–140.

Winnicott, D. W. (1945). Primitive emotional development. *International Journal of Psychoanalysis, 26*: 137–143.

Winnicott, D. W. (1949). Hate in the counter-transference. *International Journal of Psychoanalysis, 30*: 69–74.

Winnicott, D. W. (1955). Metapsychological and clinical aspects of regression within the psychoanalytical set-up. In: *Through Paediatrics to Psychoanalysis: Collected Papers* (pp. 278–294). London: Karnac, 1992.

Winnicott, D. W. (1956). The antisocial tendency. In: *Through Paediatrics to Psychoanalysis* (pp. 305–314). London: Hogarth Press, 1975.

Winnicott, D. W. (1960a). The theory of the parent—infant relationship. In: *The Maturational Processes and the Facilitating Environment: Studies in the Theory of Emotional Development* (pp. 37–55). London: Karnac, 1990.

Winnicott, D. W. (1960b). Ego distortion in terms of true and false self. In: *The Maturational Processes and the Facilitating Environment* (pp. 140–152). London: Karnac, 1990.

Winnicott, D. W. (1962). Further remarks on the theory of the parent–infant relationship. In: C. Winnicott, R. Shepherd, & M. Davis (Eds.), *Psycho-analytic Explorations* (pp. 73–75). London: Karnac, 1989.

Winnicott, D. W. (1965). Ego integration in child development (1962). In: *The Maturational Processes and the Facilitating Environment: Studies in the Theory of Emotional Development* (pp. 56–63). London: Karnac, 1990.

Wymbs, B. T., Pelham Jr, W. E., Molina, B. S. G., Gnagy, E. M., Wilson, T. K., & Greenhouse, J. B. (2008). Rate and predictors of divorce among parents of youths with ADHD. *Journal of Consulting and Clinical Psychology, 76*(5): 735–744.

Yang, B., Chan, R. C., Zou, X., Jing, J., Mai, J., & Li, J. (2007). Time perception deficit in children with ADHD. *Brain Research, 1170*: 90–96. Epub 2007, July 17.

Yen, J. Y., Ko, C. H., Yen, C. F., Wu, H. Y., & Yang, M. J. (2007). The co-morbid psychiatric symptoms of Internet addiction: attention deficit and hyperactivity disorder (ADHD), depression, social phobia, and hostility. *Journal of Adolescent Health, 41*(1): 93–98.

Yerys, B. E., Wallace, G. L., Sokoloff, J. L., Shook, D. A., James, J. D., & Kenworthy, L. (2009). Attention deficit/hyperactivity disorder symptoms moderate cognition and behavior in children with autism spectrum disorders. *Autism Research, 2*: 322–333.

You, X., Norr, M., Murphy, E., Kuschner, E. S., Bal, E., Gaillard, W. D., Kenworthy, L., & Vaidya, C. J. (2013). Atypical modulation of distant functional connectivity by cognitive state in children with autism spectrum disorders. *Frontiers in Human Neuroscience, 27*: Article 482, 1–13. doi: 10.3389/fnhum.2013.00482.

Young, J. (2012). ADHD is a notable characteristic of patients suffering from chronic Lyme disease: a survey of adults at the Michigan Lyme Disease Association Conference. Presentation at the American Psychiatric Association Annual Conference, 8 May, Philadelphia.

Young, J. L. (2013). Chronic fatigue syndrome: 3 cases and a discussion of the natural history of attention-deficit/hyperactivity disorder. *Postgraduate Medicine, 125*(1): 162–168.

Young, J. L., & Redmond, J. C. (2007). Fibromylagia, chronic fatigue, and adult attention deficit hyperactivity disorder in the adult: a case study. *Psychopharmacology Bulletin, 40*(1): 118–126.

Young, S. N., & Leyton, M. (2002). The role of serotonin in human mood and social interaction. Insight from altered tryptophan levels. *Pharmacology Biochemistry and Behavior, 71*(4): 857–865.

Yu, S., & Kim, B. (2009). The correlation among maternal object relation, personality and symptoms of children with attention deficit hyperactivity disorder. *Journal of the Korean Neuropsychiatric Association, 48*(6): 474–480.

Zikopoulos, B., & Barbas, H. (2013). Altered neural connectivity in excitatory and inhibitory cortical circuits in autism. *Frontiers of Human Neuroscience, 7*: 1–27.

Zylowska, L., Ackerman, D. L., Yang, M. H., Futrell, J. L., Horton, N. L., Hale, T. S., Pataki, C., & Smalley, S. L. (2008). Mindfulness meditation training in adults and adolescents with ADHD: a feasibility study. *Journal of Attentional Disorders, 11*(6): 737–746.

INDEX

Abrantes, A., 144
abuse, 178, 201, 240
  alcohol, 95, 103, 109
  drug, 95
  internal, 158
  self-, 158
    directed, 157
  severe, 168
  sexual(ity), 153
  substance, 32, 78, 90, 97, 103
  violence, 123
Ackerman, D. L., 145
Acosta-Cabronero, J., 88–89
Adesman, A. R., 34, 83
Adinoff, B., 96
Adler, L. A., 21, 29, 83, 86
Adrien, K. T., 183, 189
affect(ive), 27, 41, 55, 63, 68, 75, 80, 92, 114,
    118, 127, 129, 161, 193, 196, 200, 248,
    253
  alternating, 231
  dysregulation, 10
  frightening, 128
  impaired, 61
  management of, 45, 145, 174, 224
  regulation, 12, 48, 75, 174
  state, 188
  storms of, 63
  uncontained, 62
  unregulated, 62
Agar, N., 40
aggression, 9, 16, 22, 29–30, 49, 77, 91,
    102–104, 109–113, 120–121, 124, 128,
    130, 133, 140, 150, 158, 217, 229,
    272–273
  act, 63
  actual, 112
  behaviour, 114
  controlled, 130
  counter-, 49, 52, 114, 129–130
  defused, 129
  destructive, 112, 114, 128, 133
  disintegrative, 109
  drives, 109–110, 112, 115, 118
  encounters, 48, 140
  energies, 133
  exploration, 41
  explosive, 113
  expression of, 120

  fantasy, 224
  fear of, 112
  increased, 252
  infant, 112–113
  interactions, 32, 61
  mutual, 114
  narcissistic assault, 135
  neutralisation of, 117
  potential for, 114
  projected, 112, 130
  provocation, 231
  self-directed, 158–159
  severe, 122
Aigbirhio, F. I., 88–89
Akshoomoff, N. A., 182
Alaghband-Rad, J., 19
Alawam, K., 13
Albus, K. E., 19
Alexander, M. P., 82
Alfredsson, J., 145
Alison, E., 116
Allen, G., 182
Alm, B., 145
Aloia, M. S., 13
Alpert, A., 125
Althaus, M., 92
Altshuler, L. A., 34
Aman, C. J., 84
Amarasiriwardena, C., 34
Amen, D. G., 28–29, 79, 82–84, 94–98, 101
Amen, D. J., 94
American Psychiatric Association, 13
Anderson, C. M., 83
Andión, O., 18
Andrew, C., 83
Andrews-Hanna, J. R., 86
anger, 16–17, 26, 33, 40, 48–49, 52–53,
    60–61, 63–64, 66, 77, 94, 98–100, 114,
    116, 124, 131–132, 147, 159, 206, 213,
    215, 224, 229, 231, 242–243, 246–247,
    267
Angriman, M., 34
Antoine, M. W., 34
anxiety (*passim*) *see also*: disorder
  amplified, 207
  associated, 22
  background, 66
  -based, 6
  catastrophic, 99, 118